THE SECOND SHOPPER'S GUIDE TO MUSEUM STORES

Compiled by Shelley Hodupp

Universe Books

New York

Acknowledgments

I would like to thank the many managers
of museum stores across the North
American continent who responded to
my request for product information and
photographs. Without their cooperation,
this guide would not have been possible.
A special thanks to Brian Rushton and to
Miriam Friedman. I would also like to
extend my appreciation to the publisher for
recognizing the timeliness of this project.

To
Museum Store Association, Inc.
and
B.R.

Published in the United States of America in 1978
by Universe Books
381 Park Avenue South, New York, N.Y. 10016

Library of Congress Catalog Card Number: 78-052191
ISBN 0-87663-983-X

Design by Harry Chester Associates

Printed in the United States of America

Contents

Introduction

THE SECOND SHOPPER'S GUIDE TO MUSEUM STORES has been compiled because of the favorable response by the readers to the first edition. It provides a concise, illustrated, and informative review of the ever-expanding range of museum products, many of which have been produced since the first edition. It creates a single-volume reference to merchandise from more than one hundred museums in the United States and Canada whose subject matter ranges from art, archaeology, crafts, music, and photography to natural history, air and space, and science and technology. The guide is not limited to the larger institutions or to those in major cities; it also includes art centers, libraries, historical societies, and restoration villages, many of which may be, until now, unknown to the reader. The second edition includes many museums that appeared in the first edition as well as more than forty additional museums.

Those readers who have used the first edition of THE SHOPPER'S GUIDE TO MUSEUM STORES will find that this introduction resembles the last very closely, since the basic facts and history of the museum shop are still relevant.

Although America's first public museum (1773) predates the nation's founding, there is no record of the advent of the first museum store, primarily because almost every one began as a humble, unwanted, partially hidden "information desk" that dispensed a flier outlining the museum's *raison d'être* and an occasional post card reproduction of a work in the museum's collection. Despite the need to accommodate the steadily increasing amount of material published in association with the growth of museum activity, the sales desk—forerunner of the museum store—remained an afterthought or "necessary nuisance" to museum planners and administrators. Indeed, they were reluctant to relinquish space to this "commercial" enterprise despite its value as an inherently educational link between the institution and its public, nor were they greatly moved by the revenue that such an undertaking might generate.

In contrast, the museum of the 1970s takes great care to position the store to its best advantage in the mainstream of the museum's traffic pattern and to evaluate the physical requirements of the museum retailing. Architects, with the aid of highly detailed briefs, are now designing stores, not sales desks. The museum store has become a vital entity, fully integrated with the more established traditional facilities of a museum. This concern with visibility relates to the museum as a whole and to its store, and has led to an increasing number of mail-order operations designed to broaden exposure of the museum's collections as well as its products, which are, in turn, a source of additional financial support.

As the museum store grew, so did the need for professional management. In 1956, twenty-four representatives of museums in thirteen states met in New York City to discuss their mutual problems, and the Museum Store Association, Inc., was founded. In the past twenty-one years, membership in the MSA has grown to more than 350 and includes museum store managers from every state, Australia, Canada, and the United Kingdom. An annual convention held in a different state each year is now supplemented by an increasing number of regional meetings throughout the United States. The Association exists to channel information to its membership that will help each museum store in its responsibility to its museum and to the public it serves.

The museum store has responded to its favored position by continually striving to involve itself with merchandise of the highest quality only. The post cards, greeting and note cards, and books that have been the staple wares of the museum store since its inception are still among the best available anywhere. The posters and 2- and 3-dimensional reproductions of museum pieces—the major response to the explosion in museum attendance in the 1960s reflect the same concern with quality. The sixties were a decade when every sector of the community became aware of the museum store; this led to the recognition of museum merchandise as more than a token of an enjoyable visit.

A museum's association with a product has become an important attribute at a time when consumers are often skeptical about quality and workmanship. Coincidentally, the museum-going public has reached a point at which its appetite and enthusiasm for aesthetics, history, and science extends beyond the ownership of nonutilitarian replicas—not to mention the space in which to house them—to useful adaptations. Recognition of these two marketing factors was not simultaneously or quickly comprehended by museum store management or by those manufacturers, distributors, and department stores party to the development of museum-related products. Nonetheless, although the catalyst varies, more and more companies with little or no prior commercial contact with museums are becoming involved in the development of useful adaptations of works in museum collections.

For centuries, the almost unlimited variety, richness, and quality of museum collections has been a source of inspiration to artists and craftsmen alike. Now, the museum—inherently concerned with quality, relevance, and educational context—is becoming directly involved with manufacturing adaptations of objects in its collections. This guide includes many examples of adaptations: a 14th- to 15th-century French iron door grill becomes a piece of jewelry; the architectural structure of a building creates an overall design for an umbrella; a Chinese T'ang dynasty ceramic tray becomes a needlepoint kit; an accurate representation of a fish fossil decorates a tie. In every case, the transposition increases one's awareness of the imagery, and a product's usefulness can lead to a degree of familiarity with the image's detail that might otherwise be missed.

In addition to the royalties it derives from sales of merchandise produced under contract, the museum benefits indirectly from the exposure that results from national, and sometimes international, distribution of a product bearing its name. The base support for most museums lies in individual membership; one of the main privileges of this membership is usually a discount on purchases from the museum store, made both on the premises and through mail order. A glance at the Museum Index at the back of this guide, which shows the annual dues for each museum operating a membership program and the discount allowed, will quickly illustrate the value to both museum and member of the availability of nationally distributed merchandise.

In conclusion, some notes on the compilation of THE SECOND SHOPPER'S GUIDE TO MUSEUM STORES: The merchandise included had to be produced by or for a museum and had to be based on a work in the museum's collection. When a product was not based on a work in the collection, it had to have been made expressly for a museum (an "original" product). It was also necessary for each museum represented to be a non-profit organization operating a museum store with mail-order facilities. In all cases, the museum stores submitted detailed product information and a photograph of each item they wished considered for inclusion in the guide. As in the first edition, the selection of material was based on an item's general appeal as well as a desire for a balanced and varied assortment of products. In order to accommodate the myriad new products, many of the items in the previous edition have of necessity been eliminated. Many of them are, however, still available. The integrity of the museums has been relied upon where quality, safety, and availability of products is concerned. No independent testing has been undertaken; thus, inclusion of a product in this volume cannot be taken as an endorsement.

The response to the call for information was outstanding and included some museums whose product development was at too early a stage for inclusion, or whose merchandise fell outside of the main scope of this guide. Others were not in a position to offer mail-order facilities. Unfortunately, a few inquiries fell on deaf ears, and undoubtedly, in the search to present a cross-section of institutions, some museums were unintentionally overlooked. Both circumstances are matters for regret.

S. H.

How To Use This Guide

THE SHOPPER'S GUIDE TO MUSEUM STORES is planned to provide enough information so that the reader need not acquire a catalogue from each museum. To this end, it is made as explicit as possible. The reader need only become familiar with the following pattern to use the guide effectively.

Product name appears at the beginning of each entry and is printed in **boldface.** The product name *must* be used when ordering.

Description includes details of any option available in design title, color, material, or size. Where applicable, your choice must be specified when ordering, including clothbound or paperbound in the case of cookbooks and other publications, and "with greeting" or "without greeting" in the case of cards.

Dimensions given in the guide show height followed by width, with the exception of cookbooks and other publications, where width precedes height. Where applicable, a third figure indicates depth. The dimensions given for posters indicate sheet size, but in the case of reproductions on paper, the dimensions refer to the image area.

Price is printed throughout in **boldface** following the description. Every effort has been made to show current prices but they remain subject to change without notice.

Sales tax at the applicable rate must be added to the purchase price if the merchandise is ordered from a museum in your state and delivered to an address in the same state.

Handling and shipping charges are shown in parentheses following the price. These charges *must* be included in the prepayment, and are not subject to member's discount privilege.

Order numbers are not generally employed by museums in the guide. However, in the very few cases where the museum involved will not supply without the appropriate product order number, it is shown either immediately following the handling and shipping charge or, where there are several items with one description, after the name of the item.

Member's discount is indicated in parentheses following the museum's name. The percentage discount shown may be deducted from the purchase price by current members *of that museum only* and may not be applied to sales tax or handling and shipping charges. The cost of annual membership to each museum is noted in the Museum Index.

Where to order is shown in **boldface** following the price. *Orders must be placed directly with the museum shown* and cannot be accepted or forwarded by Universe Books. Full addresses are provided in the Museum Index.

Payment *must* accompany all orders. Checks and money orders are to be made payable as detailed in the Museum Index.

Delivery varies in method and time from museum to museum. In general, however, a period of four weeks should be allowed for processing and delivery.

General notes on ordering

Museums differ from other mail-order sources only in the scale of their operations and the nature of the merchandise available. In every way, they require the same approach as their commercial counterparts; the customer must provide a legible name, address, and complete product information.

Make a copy of your order, the date you send it, and the number of any check or money order you enclose. If you have any problems, this information is vital to both the museum store and you. Without it, the problems only multiply.

Most museum stores do not operate a giftwrap service, but they will ship your gift to a friend if you instruct them and enclose your own gift card.

The Museum Publications Index provides an opportunity to review the number of products included in the guide from any one of the more than one hundred museums represented. In addition to providing the page references on which the entries appear, it also indicates if (and how often) the museum issues a mail-order catalogue, and whether lists of greeting and note cards, post cards, and other publications are available on request.

Pembroke Gaming Table

Thomas Jefferson Library Ladder

Furniture

Pembroke Gaming Table

Mahogany and mahogany veneer with rosewood banding and boxwood inlay. Front and back identical in appearance: lower drawer opens from one side; others are for effect only. Center top slides forward to invert; reverse side has inlaid maple and walnut veneer chess or checker board. With center top removed (can slide under apron for storage), compartment bottom has red and black leather backgammon board with gold tooling. 28¼″ x 41½″ x 28″ open; 28¼″ x 23″ x 28″ closed.
1,955.00 (handling and shipping charges included) CW84
The Colonial Williamsburg Foundation (does not operate a membership program)

Thomas Jefferson Library Ladder

An ingenious idea! A faithful reproduction of a library ladder designed by Thomas Jefferson in the late 18th-early 19th century for George Mason of Gunston Hall. Closed, it resembles a thick solid cherrywood pole. With a flick of a wrist, it opens into a sturdy ladder. It measures 7′ x 2½″ closed; 6′1″ x 11½″ extended.
125.00 (10.00)
Alexandria Bicentennial Museum Shop (does not operate a membership program)

Furniture

Coffee Table

An antique butler's tray was copied for the top of this table. It is fitted to a specially designed base shaped to the contour of the tray. The original is in the Moody House. English, late 18th century, Chippendale (George III). Mahogany. 21½" x 27¾" x 21¾".
370.00 (handling and shipping charges included)
WA 1042

Cellarette

This handsome cellarette is an exact copy of the American antique now in the Williamsburg collection. The top compartment provides ample storage space for bottles and the lower section has a convenient drawer for necessary bar equipment and a handy sliding shelf for service. Both sections may be locked. The original is in the Coke-Garrett House. American, c. 1790, Hepplewhite. Mahogany. 40¾" x 25¼" x 15½". Inside cellarette compartment: 11¾" x 22" x 12⅞".
1,185.00 (handling and shipping charges included)
CW 162

Fire Screen

An approved Williamsburg reproduction of an antique English fire screen. The stand, frame, and finial are of mahogany. The original of this piece is in the George Wythe House. English, c. 1760, Chippendale (George III). Height 47½", panel 17¾" square. Muslin.
485.00 (handling and shipping charges included)
CW 92

All items on this page are from
The Colonial Williamsburg Foundation
(does not operate a membership program)

Coffee Table

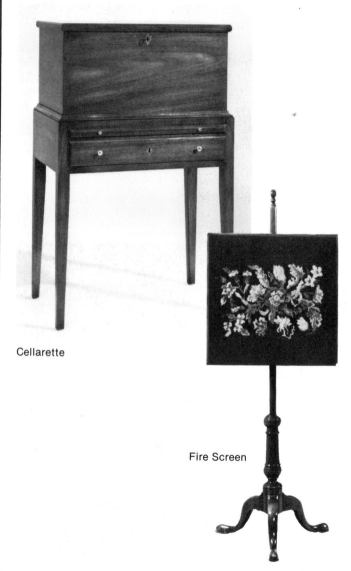
Cellarette

Fire Screen

Pineapple Sconce

Ship's Gimbaled
Candlestick

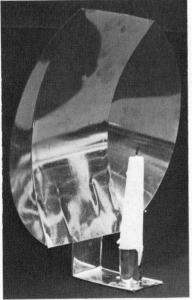

Concave Reflector
Sconce

Reflector Sconce

Furniture

Pineapple Sconce

Because the pineapple is a symbol of hospitality, it would be appropriate to enhance your home with this sconce, which has been reproduced for Sleepy Hollow Restorations. The original is a rare Hudson Valley double candle sconce (dated 1704) in the collection at Philipsburg Manor, Upper Mills. Antiqued tin. 15¼" x 8⅞".
38.00 (3.00)
Sleepy Hollow Restorations, Inc., Tarrytown, New York (member's discount 10%)

Ship's Gimbaled Candlestick

An ingenious candlestick which with the help of lyre-shaped brackets will remain upright on board a ship despite the heavy seas. The 19th-century original from which this has been reproduced, found in the collection of Mystic Seaport, has an added swivel that allows the candlestick to swing 360°. This reproduction will not only serve on board but at home on the wall or on the table. Solid brass. 7" x 5".
42.50 (1.00)
Mystic Seaport (member's discount 10%)

Concave Reflector Sconce

This reproduction, from the 18th-century home of George Mason, is made from hot-dipped tinplate and is made by employing the methods and tools of the 18th- and 19th-century craftsman. Sure to enhance the walls of any dining area. The flicker of candlelight will add romance. Tin. 9" x 10".
25.00 (2.00)
Gunston Hall, Lorton, Virginia (member's discount 10%)

Reflector Sconce

A pointed oval reflective wall sconce with crimped edges and an indented design of a heart and three diamonds has been reproduced from an original in Gunston Hall, the 18th-century home of George Mason. The glow of the candle will shine against the high polish of the tin. 10" x 6½".
25.00 (2.00)
Gunston Hall, Lorton, Virginia (member's discount 10%)

Miniatures

Sterling Silver Miniatures

The Metropolitan Museum of Art has reproduced in miniature several pieces from its collection of American and English silver. Some of the originals were miniatures; others were not. Each piece is executed in sterling silver.
Chamberstick (G9028) is based on a design of Henry Hopper, New York, c. 1845. 1″ high.
16.50
Plate (G9031) was part of a miniature table setting made by David Clayton, a London silversmith in the 17th century. The set was a faithful imitation of silver used at the time. 1¼″ diameter.
7.50
Spoon (G9012) was part of the same setting mentioned above. 1½″ long.
5.00
Cup (G9004) was originally made by Andrew Tyler of Boston, c. 1720. ¾″ high.
12.50 (2.00)
The Metropolitan Museum of Art, New York (member's discount 25%)

Cradle

The original from which this miniature was reproduced is on display in the Crowninshield-Bentley House of the Essex Institute. It was made in the 18th century with one hood. The second hood was added about 1825, perhaps for the arrival of twins. Basswood with maple finish.
8.00 (1.00)
Essex Institute, Salem, Massachusetts (member's discount not available)

Sewing Table

A miniature reproduction of a sewing table in the parlor of the Gardner-Pingree House of the Essex Institute. The original was made in New England c. 1810. Mahogany with oil finish.
16.00 (1.00)
Essex Institute, Salem, Massachusetts (member's discount not available)

Sterling Silver Miniatures

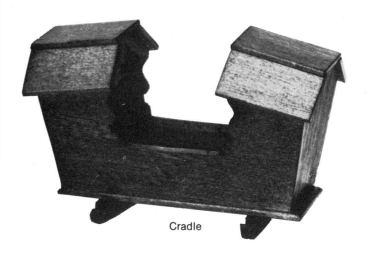

Cradle

Sewing Table

Miniatures

Shaker Miniatures

Shaker Miniatures

The Shaker Museum, located in Old Chatham, New York, is dedicated to promoting the interest in, and the understanding of, the Shaker cultural heritage. It is near Mt. Lebanon where in 1787 the Shakers set up what was to become their largest and most significant community, and the Mother House of the Order. The sect was founded by Mother Ann Lee (1736–84) in Manchester, England. Their basic principles were purity of life, confession of sin, and consecration of strength, time, and talent. Shaker furniture is known for its functional simplicity of design. The miniatures are all exact reproductions of pieces in the Shaker Museum. Miscellaneous hardwoods. Medium stain.

Two drawer candle stand. 2¼" high	**25.00**
Lidded blanket chest, 1820	**40.00**
Rocking chair with arms	**14.50**
Tin cupboard. 7" high	**45.00**
Rocking chair without arms	**13.00**
Stove with super heater	**6.00**
Woodbox with dustpan and brush	**10.50**

(1.00 for each item)
Shaker Museum, Old Chatham, New York (member's discount 10%)

Mammy Rocking Bench

Mammy Rocking Bench

An unusual piece for the collector. The busy mother would place the baby behind the bar so that she could continue with the chores. It is a reproduction of an early Texas piece. Light brown wood. Scale: 1" to the foot. 3½" x 3" x 2½".
10.00 (1.50)
McCall's at Old City Park, Dallas (member's discount not available on purchases)

Miniatures

Trundle Bed

For the spare bedroom in a doll house, this is an exceptionally well-crafted rope-strung pine trundle bed with cotton mattress (colors vary). Steps, panda bear, and teddy bear are included. Made expressly for McCall's at Old City Park. Scale: 1″ to the foot. 3½″ x 6″ x 4″.
15.00 (2.00)

Fireplace

This early Texas fireplace with all of the pictured accessories, handcrafted in wood for McCall's at Old City Park, is authentic in every detail. The candles have been hand-dipped. Even the scene and the face of the clock are hand-painted. Measurements may vary slightly. Scale: 1″ to the foot. 4¾″ x 6⅜″ x 2″.
20.00 (2.50)

Rocker, Stool, and Pincushion

An inviting addition to any collection of miniatures. An early Texas rocker and milk stool, complete with its own pincushion with pins, has been handcrafted in great detail for McCall's at Old City Park. Light brown wood. Red cloth pincushion. Scale: 1″ to the foot. 3½″ x 1½″ x 2½″.
10.00 (1.50)

All items on this page are from **McCall's at Old City Park, Dallas** (member's discount not available)

Trundle Bed

Fireplace

Rocker, Stool, and Pincushion

Meissen Dinnerware

Potpourri Dinner Service

Eastern Palm Dinner Service

Tableware

Meissen Dinnerware

The delicate flower and butterfly pattern is adapted from an 18th-century Meissen plate in the Metropolitan's collection. It is produced by Robert Haviland and G. Parlon of Limoges, France, in fine porcelain with dishwasher-proof colors.

10″ diameter dinner plate (F0601)	**19.00**
7½″ salad plate (F0602)	**14.25**
6½″ bread and butter plate (F0603)	**12.50**
Tea cup and saucer (F0604)	**21.50**
5-piece place setting (F0605)	**67.25**

(2.00 per order)
The Metropolitan Museum of Art, New York
(member's discount 25%)

Potpourri Dinner Service

In 1759, Josiah Wedgwood, a skilled and successful potter, founded a firm of potters in Burlsem, England. The firm is still in existence and continues in the family tradition of producing fine ceramic ware. Named for Queen Charlotte, Wedgwood's Queen's Shape dinnerware has been made since 1765. This delightful commemorative is imaginatively decorated in a rich fruit and flower pattern of red and blue taken from an antique block-printed cotton made in England.
Dinner plate **12.00** (0.95)
5-piece place setting (dinner plate, salad plate, bread and butter plate, cup and saucer) **40.00** (1.75)
The Colonial Williamsburg Foundation
(does not operate a membership program)

Eastern Palm Dinner Service

Part of The Brooklyn Museum Collection of fine hand-painted porcelain by Block China. This pattern was inspired by a motif on a Mesopotamian bowl of the 9th century A.D. Terra cotta on china-gray porcelain.

10½″ dinner plate (illustrated)	**12.00**
7¾″ dessert plate	**6.00**
6⅜″ bread and butter plate	**4.50**
Tea cup (illustrated)	**8.00**
Tea saucer (illustrated)	**4.50**
8¼″ coupe soup	**10.00**

(2.00 for first item plus 0.50 for each additional item)
The Brooklyn Museum (member's discount 15%)

Tableware

"Edo Pattern" Dinner Service

A fine hand-painted porcelain dinner service made by Vista Alegre in Portugal for the Block China Corporation, expressly for the Philadelphia Museum of Art. The early 17th century was the beginning of porcelain manufacture on the southernmost island of the Japanese archipelago, Kyūshū. Kilns were established in the vicinity of the town of Arita, near the main port of Imari, from which the Japanese shipped their so-called Imari ware to Nagasaki for export by foreign traders. In 1603, the Emperor granted the title of Shōgun to Tokugawa Ieyasu and he established his military government at Edo (ancient Tokyo), hence the name of the period during which he and his descendants remained in power (1603-1868). The design on this dinner service combines two family crests: That of the Matsudaira family (collateral descendants of the Tokugawa) is known as *nanatsuboshi* (seven stars) and the crest of the Tokugawa is reflected in the comma design on the border. The simplicity and asymmetry of the design reflects an aesthetic sense that is uniquely Japanese. The original was manufactured c. 1725. Blue on porcelain body.

10½" dinner plate (illustrated)	**12.00**
8" dessert plate	**8.50**
6¼" bread and butter plate	**6.50**
Cup (illustrated)	**6.50**
Saucer (illustrated)	**6.50**
5-piece dinner service	**40.00**
8¼" coupe soup	**10.00**

(1.50 for first item plus 0.50 for each additional item)
Philadelphia Museum of Art
(member's discount 10%)

Tobacco Leaf Dinnerware

China Trade and Chinese Export are the terms used to describe porcelain made in China for the European and American markets. The Portuguese were engaged in trade with China as early as the 16th century. This design, which features a flowering Nicotina plant, is commonly known as "Tobacco Leaf." The origin of the pattern is unknown and exists in several variations, but from the vivid combination of colors and the shapes of some of the individual pieces, it appears to have been developed about 1780, possibly for the Portuguese market.

The museum's dinnerware has been produced by the porcelain factory of Vista Alegre in Portugal. 27 colors, two glazings, and 24 karat gold decoration are used on each piece.

10¾" dinner plate (F0470)	**55.00**
8½" salad plate (F0471) (not illustrated)	**45.00**
6¾" bread and butter plate (F0472)	**35.00**
Cup and saucer (F0473)	**55.00**
5-piece place setting (F0474)	**190.00**

(2.00 per order)
The Metropolitan Museum of Art, New York
(member's discount 25%)

"Edo Pattern" Dinner Service

Tobacco Leaf Dinnerware

Tableware

Ovenware

Ship Plate

Wedgwood Plate

Soup Tureen

Ovenware

This contemporary ovenware is decorated with designs from *The Ladies' Amusement,* a rare pattern book engraved by Robert Hancock and published in London in about 1760. 18th-century women trimmed out with "scisars" the hand-colored designs from these books, and applied them to various objects. Produced in France for the museum in ovenproof porcelain with dishwasher-proof colors. Shades of brown, red, blue, and yellow on white background.
Covered casserole (F0497): 2 quarts **32.50**
Baking dish (F0495): 9″ x 13″ **26.00**
Soufflé dish (F0496): 2³/₄ quarts **14.95**
(2.00 per order)
The Metropolitan Museum of Art, New York
(member's discount 25%)

Ship Plate

Friendship, Salem is a reproduction in celadon porcelain of a plate in the Peabody Museum's collection. Manufactured in Limoges, the edition is limited to 1,000 plates. Border background is blue; with four vignettes and vessel depicted in full color, and cartouches and rim in gold. 10″ diameter.
125.00 (member's price 100.00) (5.00)
Peabody Museum of Salem

Wedgwood Plate

For the collector! A Wedgwood plate with a drawing of Gunston Hall, Lorton, Virginia. Black on white or brown on white. (Please specify color choice when ordering.) 10¹/₂″ diameter.
16.50 (2.00)
Gunston Hall, Lorton, Virginia (member's discount 10%)

Soup Tureen

Unique and bizarre—a Stegosaurus soup tureen with bowls. Designed especially for the Carnegie Institute, Museum of Natural History, by Barbara Ford. The set has been hand thrown and the scales, ladle, tail, and feet have been hand built. It is made so that the scales serve as the handle and the ladle is the head of the dinosaur. Six bowls (not illustrated) accompany the tureen. They are in the shape of the lower portion of the tureen and they have the dinosaur foot print on the interior of the bowl. Pottery. Burnt umber with moss green overtones. Oven proof. Glaze is lead free. Tureen: 14″ x 13″. Bowls: 4¹/₂″ diameter.
150.00 Tureen and 6 bowls (8.00)
Carnegie Institute, Pittsburgh (member's discount 10%)

Tableware

Dinosaur Plates

Produced in Langenthal, Switzerland, by the Block China Corporation, expressly for the Carnegie Institute, Museum of Natural History. Four different dinosaurs are depicted in each set. Gray and black design on white porcelain. Available in two sizes. (Please specify when ordering.)
20.00 set of 4 plates, 6¾" diameter (2.00)
25.00 set of 4 plates, 7¾" diameter (2.00)
Carnegie Institute, Pittsburgh (member's discount 10%)

Dinosaur
Plates

Fern Plates

The delicacy of the maidenhair fern, lady fern, Christmas fern, and sensitive fern is evident in these designs created specifically for The New York Botanical Garden which are certain to enhance the serving of a salad or dessert. The name of the fern, both in English and Latin, is printed on the back of each plate. Green on white porcelain body. 7⅝" x 7⅝".
35.00 set of 4 (3.00)
The New York Botanical Garden (member's discount 10%)

Maidenhair Fern

Lady Fern

Christmas Fern

Sensitive Fern

Children's Dinner Set

The delightful pattern is from an early 17th-century Arita ware porcelain plate in the Metropolitan's collection. Any child will be happy to clean his plate. It may also be used as a breakfast or luncheon set for parents. Blue and white porcelain. 3-piece set includes plate (8½" diameter), mug (6-oz. capacity), and bowl (6½" diameter).
38.00 the set (2.00) F0510
The Metropolitan Museum of Art, New York (member's discount 25%)

Children's Dinner Set

Pie Plate

The Alliance Museum Shop of the Indianapolis Museum of Art commissioned Peggy Ahlgren to create this utilitarian pie plate. As each is handcrafted, they will vary slightly in size and color of glaze. Glazed stoneware. Variations of gray/brown or blue/blue. (Please specify when ordering.) Lead-free. May be placed in oven and dishwasher. 8" diameter.
8.00 (1.00)
Indianapolis Museum of Art (member's discount not available on this item)

Pie Plate, Indianapolis Museum of Art

Pie Plates, Old Sturbridge Village

Cup Plate

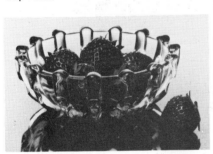

Broken Column Pattern

Pepper Shaker and Open Salt

Tableware

Pie Plates

Your favorite pie will bake to perfection in these ovenproof slipware pie plates from Old Sturbridge Village. Glazed: yellow on brown. Available in two sizes. (Please specify when ordering.)
9.00 small (9" diameter)
12.00 large (12" diameter)
(1.50 east of the Mississippi; 2.25 west of the Mississippi)
Old Sturbridge Village (member's discount 10%)

Cup Plate

The Follett House, a splendid example of Greek Revival architecture, was built by Oran Follett, editor and publisher. This cup plate, depicting the house, was made exclusively for the Museum. Clear pressed glass.
4.00 (1.00)
Follett House Museum, Sandusky, Ohio (does not operate a membership program)

Broken Column Pattern

Begin your collection of Smithsonian glass reproductions with these three pieces. The Broken Column pattern was first made in the 1880s by the Columbia Glass Company in Findlay, Ohio. The pattern was reissued by the U.S. Glass Company after 1891.
Nappy. Perfect for serving sweets and desserts. 4¹/₂" diameter.
9.50 set of two (1.00) #333260
Spooner. This was originally used for showing and storing spoons. Today, it is perfect for serving vegetables or displaying flowers. 4¹/₂" high.
9.00 (1.00) #333w45
Server. 8" diameter.
8.00 (1.00) #333252
Smithsonian Institution, Washington, D.C. (member's discount 10%)

Pepper Shaker and Open Salt

An elegant and utilitarian addition to any table are these Delft pepper shaker and open salt, reproduced from pieces in the collection of Old Sturbridge Village. Glazed pottery: opaque white with Delft blue rim and design. Pepper shaker: 4¹/₂" high. Open salt: 1³/₄" high, 2³/₄" diameter.
7.50 pepper shaker (0.75) SV-4
4.25 open salt (0.75) SV-5
Old Sturbridge Village (member's discount 10%)

Tableware

American Pewter Reproductions

The Brooklyn Museum's collection of decorative arts includes many outstanding examples of early American pewter. This group of five reproductions has been accurately handcrafted in pewter, and hand-polished to a bright finish.

Teapot. The original was made by William Will in Philadelphia between 1765 and 1798. This pear-shaped teapot with S-curve lines popular in the Queen Anne period has cabriole legs and claw and ball feet. 8″ high.
125.00 (2.00)

Chalice Cup. The original was made by Peter Young in New York City or Albany between 1775 and 1795. Most chalices from this period were made for the celebration of communion and were often donated to a church by one of its more affluent members. 8³/₈″ high, 3¹⁵/₁₆″ maximum diameter.
75.00 (2.00)

Stemmed Baptismal Basin. The original was made by Lorenzo L. Williams in Philadelphia between 1838 and 1842. 4³/₄″ high, 6⁵/₈″ diameter.
70.00 (2.00)

Porringer. Porringers were used for both drinking and eating. This piece has a "crown handle," a style based on an old English design. The original was made by Joseph Leddell, Sr. or Jr., in New York City between 1712 and 1754. 1⁷/₈″ high, 5″ diameter. Length including handle 7³/₈″.
48.00 (2.00)

Inkstand. Originally a container for pens, sand, and wafers used in letter writing, the interior dividers to the two compartments have been repositioned to allow its use as a cigarette box. The original, made by Henry Will in New York or Albany between 1761 and 1793, is the only known example of an incised American inkstand of this type. 2¹/₈″ high, 4⁵/₈″ wide, 7⁷/₈″ long.
125.00 (2.00)
The Brooklyn Museum (member's discount 15%)

Cake Stand

The crisp glass sculpture of the "Three Face" design, with its fine frosted satin finish, is both a *tour de force* in contemporary mold cutting and a charming example of American Victorian neoclassicism. The original was made in 1875 by John Ernest Miller. The goddess-like head is a portrait of his wife. According to legend, her beauty had to be viewed from three angles—full face, three quarters, and profile—to be fully appreciated. Crystal. 7¹/₄″ high, 9¹/₂″ diameter.
38.00 (2.00) F1500
The Metropolitan Museum of Art, New York (member's discount 25%)

Sauce Boat

Reproduced from one of a pair in The Metropolitan Museum of Art's collection, this gravy or sauce boat was probably made by an American pewterer working in the early 19th century. Pewter. 3³/₄″ high.
48.00 (2.00) G8095
The Metropolitan Museum of Art, New York (member's discount 25%)

American Pewter Reproductions

Cake Stand

Sauce Boat

Flatware

Fish Slice

Puritan Spoon

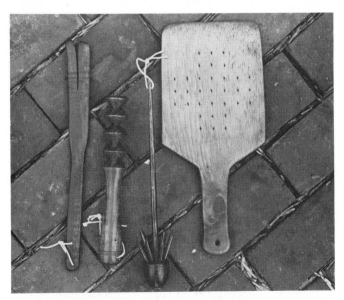
Kitchen Utensils

Tableware

Flatware

Smithsonian, as newly interpreted by one of America's leading silversmiths, Ronald Hayes Pearson. The elegant simplicity was inspired by a silver pattern bought in France by John Quincy Adams and his bride Louisa early in the 19th century. The original pattern was used in the White House during his presidency. The pattern is available as a 4-piece place setting which includes a dinner knife, dinner fork, salad fork, and teaspoon. The following serving pieces are also available: ice-tea spoon, sugar spoon, gravy ladle, cold meat fork, and serving spoon.
Prices available upon request.
Smithsonian Institution, Washington, D.C. (member's discount 10%)

Fish Slice

Though the fish slice was a common silver implement in England by the end of the 18th century, it was rarely used elsewhere. Therefore, the Dutch origin of this piece, with its comparatively small oval-shaped blade, makes it of particular interest. The original was made in Leyden, c. 1763, probably by Hendrik Fortman. Available in either sterling silver or silver plate. (Please specify when ordering.) 15″ long.
265.00 sterling silver (2.00) G8099
52.00 silver plate (2.00) G8098
The Metropolitan Museum of Art, New York (member's discount 25%)

Puritan Spoon

This spoon is of the earliest form known to have been made in America. Its form, with its shallow, flat bowl, derives from the late Middle Ages. The original, crafted by America's first native-born goldsmith, Jeremiah Dummer (1645–1718), was discovered in the foundation of a ruined building in Salem, Massachusetts, in the late 19th century. 5⅛″ long.
23.00 sterling silver (2.50)
8.50 silver plate (1.95)
Museum of Fine Arts, Boston (member's discount 10%)

Kitchen Utensils

Any cook will be delighted to prepare meals with these handcrafted kitchen utensils made exclusively for The Bucks County Historical Society by Eric Miller. They have been inspired by Early American utensils in The Mercer Museum. Each piece has a water-impervious finish.
Stirring Fork. Hardwood. Light or dark. (Please specify when ordering.) 14″ long.
6.50 (1.75)
Tenderizer. Hardwood. Light or dark. (Please specify when ordering.) 10″ long.
6.00 (1.75)
Whisk. Hardwood. Light or dark. (Please specify when ordering.) 12½″ long.
8.00 (1.75)
Butter Paddle. Pine. Light or dark. (Please specify when ordering.) 14″ long, 6″ wide.
8.00 (1.75)
The Mercer Museum, Doylestown, Pennsylvania (member's discount 10% on purchases over 10.00)

Tableware

Ship Captain's Decanter

Before his 1791 whaling voyage, Captain Coffin ordered a fine lead crystal decanter for his spirits chest. The engraving reads: "Ship *Alliance* Property of Captain Bartlett Coffin Nantucket 1791." Crystal decanters of this type were very popular from 1780 to 1820 and were also widely used in homes and inns. Reproduced from an original in Mystic Seaport's collection, this decanter is shaped and hand-blown like the decanters of 200 years ago. Experienced craftsmen faithfully reproduce the delicate 18th-century script by freehand engraving. Custom engraving available. Full lead crystal. 11" high.
50.00 (1.00)
Mystic Seaport (member's discount 10%)

Ship Captain's Decanter

Decanter

The sunburst and diamond pattern on this example of American glass, made in New England c. 1820–40, was achieved through a technique known as blown-three-mold, a full-size mold that forms both shape and pattern simultaneously. Clear. 10½" high including stopper.
25.00 (2.00)
Museum of Fine Arts, Boston (member's discount 10%)

Decanter

Glass Pitcher

Each pitcher is free-blown; no molds or machines are involved in the process. The blower shapes the base of the pitcher, then passes it on to the gaffer, who applies the cobalt-blue rim, forms and finishes the body, and affixes the ribbed handle. The original, in the Chrysler Museum, was produced by the New England Glass Company, Cambridge, Massachusetts, between 1818 and 1890. Clear glass with cobalt-blue rim. 4½" high, 1½" diameter.
10.00 (1.00)
Chrysler Museum at Norfolk (member's discount 10%)

Glass Pitcher

Large Pitcher

Reproduced from a water pitcher made in 1837 by R. Dunham in Westbrook, Maine. Pewter: shiny finish or brushed finish. (Please specify when ordering.) Capacity: 50 ounces. 6¼" high.
75.00 (1.50 east of the Mississippi; 2.25 west of the Mississippi) SV-9
Old Sturbridge Village (member's discount 10%)

Large Pitcher

Tumblers and Pitcher

Glasses

Firing Glass

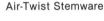
Air-Twist Stemware

Tableware

Tumblers and Pitcher

Variations on a pattern originally made c. 1820 are evident in these blown-three-mold Quilted Diamond and Sunburst American glass reproductions.
Tumblers. A "waffle" sunburst alternates with quilted diamonds between bands of vertical and diagonal ribbing. Clear glass. 3¹/₂" high.
24.00 set of 4 (2.00) F1120
Pitcher. Rectangular sunbursts and panels of diamond quilting. The rim and pouring spout were originally shaped by hand, while the glass was still hot and malleable, and then a second piece of molten glass was deftly shaped by the glassblower into a curving handle. Emerald green glass with crystal handle. Capacity: nearly 1 quart. 6¹/₄" high.
37.50 (2.00) F1152
The Metropolitan Museum of Art, New York (member's discount 25%)

Glasses

Double old-fashioned glasses etched with the design of a human eye combined with a falcon's head. This eye was called *wadjet* in ancient Egyptian and symbolized the eye of Horus, identified with the sun. According to legend, the eye of Horus was injured in a battle with the powers of evil. Thoth, the god of wisdom, separated the combatants and healed the injured eye. Capacity: 14 ounces. Set of 4, boxed.
15.00 the set (1.50)
The Brooklyn Museum (member's discount 15%)

Firing Glass

Firing glasses—stumpy drinking glasses with thick, heavy feet and small bowls—were used by drinkers to express their appreciation of a toast or sentiment by hammering them vigorously on the table. For the most part, they were used on public occasions. When hammered upon the table they produced a sound resembling a volley of musket fire—hence the term "firing glass." The original of this reproduction was made in England during the 19th century. 4" high.
15.00 each (1.95)
27.50 pair (3.50)
Museum of Fine Arts, Boston (member's discount 10%)

Air-Twist Stemware

This spiral air-twist form was developed about 1735 and was popular in the mid-18th century. In making air-twist stemware, a wire is introduced into the molten stem to form a channel. Several channels are successively formed and then combined and twisted into a graceful spiral by the use of wooden paddles and other special tools in the hands of a master craftsman. These reproductions and adaptations are made of lead glass, strong yet translucent, with an extraordinary power to diffuse light.
Left: Sherbet/Champagne. Height 5³/₄". CW 3S
Center: Wine glass. Height 6¹/₂". CW 3W
Right: Goblet. Height 7⁷/₈". CW 3G
34.50 each (0.95)
The Colonial Williamsburg Foundation (does not operate a membership program)

Tableware

Griffin Glasses, Mugs, Plates, and Ashtrays

The fabulous griffin, the emblem of the Philadelphia Museum of Art, and guardian of its treasures, will vigilantly guard any food and libation of which you partake.
Double Old-fashioned glasses. Capacity: 14 ounces. Set of 4, boxed.
15.00 the set (2.50)
Mugs. Capacity: 8 ounces.
4.50 each (1.00)
18.00 set of 4 (2.50)
Plates. 8″ diameter.
4.50 each (1.00)
18.00 set of 4 (2.50)
Ashtrays. 3⅝″ square.
3.75 each (1.00)
15.00 set of 4 (2.50)
Philadelphia Museum of Art (member's discount 10%)

Griffin Glasses, Mugs, Plates, and Ashtrays

Colonial Pottery Reproductions

Henry Piercy, a German potter from Philadelphia, moved his business to Alexandria in 1792. His work, along with that of other potters of the time, has been found in four kiln sites and in three dry wells and privies excavated in the city. Useful household utensils—including chamber pots, mugs, and flower pots—were among the articles unearthed. Inspired by these 18th- and early 19th-century works, several potters have re-created these objects expressly for the Alexandria Bicentennial Museum Shop. Since each piece is handmade and hand glazed, the dimensions and colors will vary slightly.
Chamber pot. Salt glaze. 6″ high, 8″ diameter.
15.00 (3.00)
Small flower pots. Original made 1800–10. Unglazed red clay with incised design. 5″ high.
3.00 (2.00)
Small crock. Salt glaze. 4″ high, 5″ diameter.
10.00 (3.00)
Strawberry pot and pan. Original made 1800–10. Unglazed red clay with grooved and notched rim. 8″ high.
8.00 (3.00)
Alexandria Bicentennial Museum Shop (does not operate a membership program)

Colonial Pottery Reproductions

Barman's Mug

Used in Colonial days, this mug has the ∟ usual feature of a false bottom. A full-pint tip for the barman cost him only half a pint of ale and kept the customer sober until closing. This faithful reproduction will certainly be a conversation piece. Pewter; dull finish. Capacity: ½ pint. 4½″ high.
38.00 (1.75)
Mystic Seaport (member's discount 10%)

Barman's Mug

Mug

Mug, Stein, and Tile

Cup and Mush Bowl

Covered Bowl

Tableware

Mug

The *Gazela Primeiro,* built in 1883, adorns this mug, made expressly for the Philadelphia Maritime Museum. Armetale (metal resembling pewter). 5″ high. **10.00** (1.50) .
Philadelphia Maritime Museum (member's discount 10%)

Mug, Stein, and Tile

Liven up any informal gathering, both indoors and out, with brightly colored mugs and steins bearing the logo of The Franklin Institute, which depicts the various areas of science that can be explored in the museum. The containers of liquid refreshment can be placed on the tile, which is cork-backed to protect your table. Silkscreened. Red, blue, black, and yellow on white ceramic body.

9 ounce Mug **2.50** (0.75)
16 ounce Stein **6.50** (1.00)
6″ square Tile **3.50** (0.75)
The Franklin Institute Science Museum, Philadelphia (member's discount 10%)

Cup and Mush Bowl

American sponge ware resembles the rather coarse and mostly late examples of what in England is commonly called Pratt ware, after one of the Staffordshire manufacturers of this class of ware. Pratt ware is a modern term used for late 18th- and 19th-century cream wares or pearl wares decorated in high-temperature colors, including blue. Those colors were often applied with a sponge. These pieces are being made expressly for The Mercer Museum, Doylestown, Pennsylvania, by a local potter. Each piece is signed. Dimensions will vary slightly. Clay. Mottled blue over white.
Cup: 3″ high, 3¾″ diameter.
5.50 (1.75)
Mush bowl: 2″ high, 5″ diameter.
5.00 (1.75)
The Mercer Museum, Doylestown, Pennsylvania (member's discount not available on these items)

Covered Bowl

Blown-three-mold glass was a milestone in the history of American glass production. Appearing shortly after 1800, it was the ingenious invention of the Early Republic craftsmen in response to the demand for imported cut glass. Originally used as a sugar bowl, this particular piece, dating from the mid-19th century, combines the diamond pattern with diagonal and vertical ribbing. Clear glass. 5⅞″ high.
32.50 (2.00) F1470
The Metropolitan Museum of Art, New York (member's discount 25%)

Tableware

The Annapolis Subscription Plate (Bowl)

This reproduction bowl is an exact copy of the Annapolis Subscription Plate made by John Inch (American, active c. 1720–63). He signed his work with a "II." It is the earliest surviving piece of silver made in Maryland and commemorates the first recorded formal horse race in the state. The original was won at the Annapolis races by Dr. George Steuart's horse Dungannon in 1743. Pewter. Shiny finish. 4½" high, 7½" diameter.
37.50 (2.50)
A smaller version, which is an adaptation of the Annapolis Subscription Plate, is also available. A perfect size for serving nuts or candies. Pewter. Shiny finish. 4" diameter.
16.50 (2.50)
The Baltimore Museum of Art (member's discount 10%)

Delft Bowl

Whether as a centerpiece for fresh flowers or a serving bowl for salads and desserts, this reproduction will be the perfect complement to any table setting. Glazed pottery: Delft blue design on opaque white background. 4" high, 9" diameter.
55.00 (1.50 east of the Mississippi; 2.25 west of the Mississippi) SV2
Old Sturbridge Village (member's discount 10%)

British East India Company Bowl

The original mess bowl, used aboard ship, is one of the few surviving bowls of the era. The seal of the East India Company is shown in full detail. The reproduction is pewter with a shiny finish. 5½" high.
23.00 (1.00)
Mystic Seaport (member's discount 10%)

Bowl

The Kentucky Derby Bowl, made by Wedgwood to celebrate the 200th running of the race. Bone China. White with colorful decals and gold rim. 4½" high, 9½" diameter.
175.00 (3.00)
Buten Museum of Wedgwood, Merion, Pennsylvania (member's discount 20% on this item)

The Annapolis Subscription Plate (Bowl)

Delft Bowl

British East India Company Bowl

The Kentucky Derby Bowl

Slate Trivets

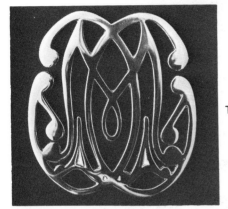

Trivet, Gunston Hall

Trivet, Portland
Museum of Art

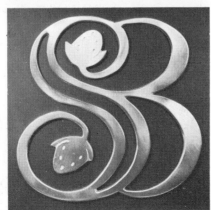

Trivet, The Guild of
Strawbery Banke®

Tableware

Slate Trivets

Three Egyptian hieroglyphs taken from a work in The Brooklyn Museum's collection have been incised on these trivets. Choice of three individual designs: the frog, the ibis, and the owl. (Please specify when ordering.) They are studded on the back to prevent scratching. Each measures 5½" square.
6.00 each (2.00)
The Brooklyn Museum (member's discount 15%)

Trivet

An elegant trivet has been created by using the initials of George and Ann Mason, the owners of Gunston Hall, Lorton, Virginia. It is sure to enhance any table. Solid brass. 8" x 7½".
22.00 (2.25)
Gunston Hall, Lorton, Virginia (member's discount 10%)

Trivet

Create the atmosphere of hospitality with an open door. An illustration of the garden door of the McLellan-Sweat House adorns this trivet. The mansion was built in 1800 and is now a registered historic landmark. White on black slate. (Please specify smooth or rough textured slate.) Rubber feet. 6" x 7½".
8.50 (2.00)
Portland Museum of Art, Maine (member's discount 10%)

Trivet

A graceful design of strawberries and the initials of The Guild of Strawbery Banke was created by Mrs. Alexander Neilson, one of the founders of the Guild. Pewter and slate. 6" square.
26.00 (1.50)
The Guild of Strawbery Banke®, Inc., Portsmouth (member's discount 10%)

Tableware

Trivets

Two works in the Worcester Art Museum have been reproduced on ceramic trivets. They have been felt-backed so they won't scratch your table. If you prefer, use them as wall decorations, since they have tab backs. They may also be purchased with holders. (Please specify when ordering.) 6″ square.
Owl. Detail from a two-handled cup, Greek, 5th century B.C. Black on terra cotta.
3.50 trivet (1.25)
5.95 with wrought-iron holder. 12″ x 6½″. (1.25)
Wishing Well. Reproduction of an antique tile. Lavender on pale blue.
3.50 trivet (1.25)
5.95 with hardwood holder. 8½″ square. (1.25)
Worcester Art Museum (member's discount 10%)

Placemats

During the 18th century, itinerant weavers wandered the countryside plying their trade, with their looms attached to their wagons. These men carried pattern books of designs to show their customers what was available. The design on this placemat is taken from one such pattern book, *Book of Drawings of Weaving Patterns,* Pennsylvania German, late 18th century. The patterns could be reproduced exactly as a double cloth coverlet, usually in two or three colors, in wool, linen, or cotton. The yarns were often spun and dyed by the homemaker herself for the use of the weaver. The bold geometric design looks very contemporary, although it is from the 18th century. Vinyl. Silkscreened. Brown on cream or dark blue on cream. (Please specify when ordering.) Wipe clean. 12¾″ x 17¾″.
2.75 each (1.00)
Philadelphia Museum of Art (member's discount 10%)

Placemats

The Marghab Collection is a group of designs created by Vera Way Marghab from 1934 to the present. The pieces are embroidered by hand on linen or margandie (the rarest of Egyptian cotton spun into threads as fine as a spider's web, then woven, finished, and dyed). The embroidery is executed on the Portuguese island of Madeira. A large part of the collection consists of placemat sets and cloths for the table. They were designed as backgrounds for china, silver, and crystal, and should be viewed as such. The collection, donated by Mrs. Marghab to the South Dakota Memorial Art Center, consists of 261 designs and 1,422 pieces.
Hortensia. Pastel yellow hand embroidery on white margandie. 5½″ diameter.
14.00 (1.50)
Ponto Grega. Hand embroidery on linen. 5½″ diameter. (Please specify color choice when ordering.)
7.00 Dubonnet (1.50)
10.00 White and natural (1.50)
South Dakota Memorial Art Center, Brookings (does not operate a membership program)

Trivets, Worcester Art Museum

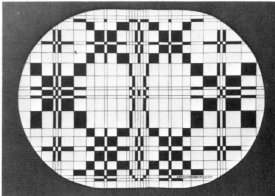

Placemats, Philadelphia Museum of Art

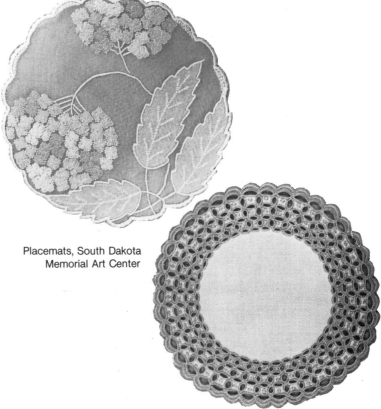

Placemats, South Dakota Memorial Art Center

30

Placemats, The Baltimore Museum of Art

Egyptian Coasters

Candlesticks

Tableware

Placemats

Fun for the kids on a rainy day—they can color their own disposable place mat. The original design, created for The Baltimore Museum of Art, incorporates scenes of Baltimore: The museum, Johns Hopkins Hospital, the zoo, and row houses. Black outline on white paper. Four place mats and box of crayons. 10″ x 16″.
1.50 (1.00)
The Baltimore Museum of Art (member's discount 10%)

Egyptian Coasters

Slate Coasters. Each of the six coasters is incised with a different Egyptian hieroglyph taken from a work in The Brooklyn Museum. The essence of Egyptian art is magic: carved hieroglyphs and sculptured figures actually stand for the kings, noblemen, and divinities depicted and magically impart everlasting life. Each coaster measures 4″ square. They are studded on the back to prevent scratching.
20.00 the set (2.00)
Porcelain Coasters. For a more elegant look, The Brooklyn Museum has reproduced the same Egyptian hieroglyphs on gray porcelain coasters which can double for ashtrays. Set of six. Each measures 4½″ in diameter.
15.00 the set (2.00)
The Brooklyn Museum (member's discount 15%)

Candlesticks

The original, in the collection of Old Sturbridge Village, was made by Freeman Porter from Westbrook, Maine, in 1835. Pewter, brushed finish. 6″ high; base 4″ diameter.
26.00 each (1.30 east of the Mississippi; 1.75 west of the Mississippi) SV-3
Old Sturbridge Village (member's discount 10%)

31

Tableware

Chamber Candlestick

Chamber Candlestick

A pewter adaptation of a sterling silver candlestick with small saucer base and ring handle. The original was made by George W. Riggs (1777-1864), a silversmith who worked in the Baltimore area. It is marked with his last name and the Baltimore Assay Office marks for 1815. 3″ base, 2³/₈″ high.
17.50 (2.50)
The Baltimore Museum of Art (member's discount 10%)

Table Candlestick

Made of handwrought forge-welded ironware by the blacksmiths at the Conner Prairie Settlement, this would be an attractive addition to a table. The original was made in America in the early 19th century. The tools and techniques used in making the candlestick are those used by the early American craftsman. The oil-blackened finish comes direct from the forge. 18¹/₂″ x 13″ x 9″.
90.00 (5.00)
Conner Prairie Pioneer Settlement, Noblesville, Indiana (member's discount 15%)

Table Candlestick

Ship Surgeon's Candleholder

Salvaged from a sunken British warship by Major Symth of Noank. Original bronze holder served well at sea because of its unusual heft (2¹/₂ pounds) and deep sides to catch wax drippings. Reproduction available in solid bronze. 4″ wide.
36.00 each (1.00)
Mystic Seaport (member's discount 10%)

Ship Surgeon's Candleholder

Lined pads, address books, and TV Guide cover

Desk Accessories

Lined pads, address books, and TV Guide cover

A selection of Chinese, Japanese, and Persian works from the Freer Gallery of Art have been reproduced in full color on these helpful organizers.
Flowers, detail from a Japanese screen by Watanabe Shiko. Edo period, Rimpa school. Each accessory has pumpkin cover.
Lined pad. 8″ x 5″.
12.50 (1.00)
Address book. 8″ x 5″.
12.50 (1.00)
TV Guide cover. 7³/₄″ x 5¹/₄″.
12.50 (1.00)
Portrait of a Prince, Persian painting by Muhammad Harawi. Safavid period, 16th century.
Address book. Black cover. 6″ x 4″.
10.00 (1.00)
Cat, Rock and Peonies, Chinese album leaf. Ch'ing Dynasty, 18th century. Reproduced on cream paper. Each accessory has black cover.
Lined pad. 8″ x 5″.
12.50 (1.00)
Address book. 8″ x 5″.
12.50 (1.00)

Birds and Flowers, detail of a Japanese screen by Genga (active early 16th century). Ashikaga period, Muromachi-Suiboku school. Reproduced on green paper.
Address book. Tan cover. 8″ x 5″.
12.50 (1.00)

Desk Organizer and Accessories

Desk organizer, paper and pencil caddy, accordion file, photo frame, address book, TV Guide cover, and bookends

Organization can be fun with these handsome desk accessories from the Freer Gallery of Art. *Peony and Willow,* a Japanese painting of the Momoyama period, early 16th century, is reproduced in full color and gold on each piece.
Desk organizer. 11¹/₂″ x 8³/₄″.
12.50 (1.00)
Paper and pencil caddy. Complete with paper and 10 pencils. 4¹/₄″ x 3¹/₄″ x 2″.
10.00 (1.00). Refills **1.50** per package of 10 pencils
Accordion File. 22-pocket capacity, alphabetical index. 10″ x 12″.
20.00 (1.00)
Photo frame. Space for 4 photographs. 7¹/₄″ x 5¹/₄″.
15.00 (1.00)
Address book. 6″ x 4″.
10.00 (1.00). Refills **2.00** each
TV Guide cover. 7³/₄″ x 5¹/₄″.
12.50 (1.00)
Bookends. 5¹/₄″ x 4¹/₄″.
16.00 the pair (1.00)
All items on this page are from the
Freer Gallery of Art, Washington, D.C. (does not operate a membership program)

Desk Accessories

The Metropolitan Museum of Art Address Book

Address Book

A collection of love letters, letter writers, and letter racks; carrier pigeons, postmen, and mythical messengers; scribes and calligraphers; inkwells, paperweights, and desks enhance this address book. Reproductions of works of art from ancient Egypt to modern times are included. Among the artists represented are Fragonard, Boucher, Corot, Harnett, Cassatt, Utamaro, Holbein, and Eakins. 160 pp.; 40 full-color illustrations; letter index tabs. Cloth cover, spiral binding. Boxed. 6⅝" x 5½".
6.95 (2.00) H7853
The Metropolitan Museum of Art, New York (member's discount not available on this item)

Address Book and Scrapbook

Two handsome desk accessories by To Match, covered in Sabel Ankara, which is one of the patterns from The Brooklyn Museum collection of fabrics, adapted by Jay Yang from a work in the textile collection of the museum. This repeated motif was developed from the edge of a design found on a border fragment of embroidered linen. The pronounced, angular character of the motif derives from the Russian overcast filling or four-sided stitch of the original work, and is of Italian or Persian 16th-century influence. Produced in 100% cotton by P. Kaufmann, Inc., the material is colorfast to water and solvents, and is soil and stain resistant.
Top: Address book with sturdy, loose-leaf mechanism and index with gold-on-black tabs. Sheets are ruled for quick reference to telephone numbers. 6½" x 6".
15.00 (2.00)
Bottom: Scrapbook with heavy white pages. 13¾" x 11".
15.00 (2.00)
The Brooklyn Museum (member's discount 15%)

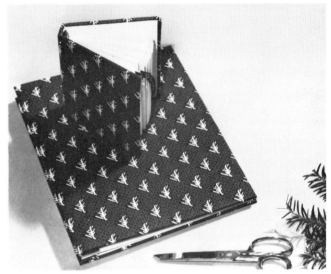

Address Book and Scrapbook

Address Book

In celebration of its 50th anniversary in 1977, the Honolulu Academy of Arts has published a handsome address book containing selections of notable works from the museum's permanent collections. It is lavishly illustrated with paintings, drawings, sculptures, and ceramics of Western and Oriental art. On the cover is a full-color reproduction of *Two Nudes on a Tahitian Beach*, 1892, oil on canvas, by Paul Gauguin (French, 1848–1903). Heavy paper; 120 pp.; 53 illus. (27 color); wire-o-bound; 8½" x 6".
4.95 (0.65)
Honolulu Academy of Arts (member's discount 10%)

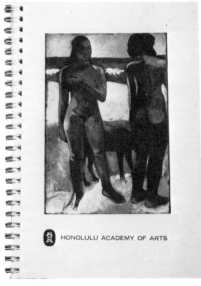

Honolulu Academy of Arts Address Book

Address Book

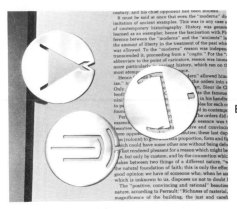

Bookmarks

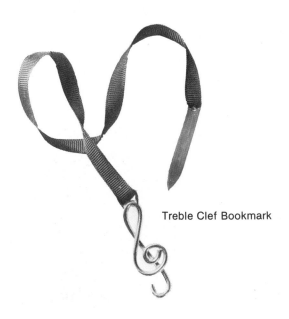

Treble Clef Bookmark

Desk Accessories

Address Book

Great Addresses, designed by Ira Howard Levy with Ben Kotyuk for The Museum of Modern Art, New York. Illustrated with photographs of 23 important residential structures by a diverse group of internationally esteemed modern architects. Among those whose work is represented are: Breuer, Eames, Gaudi, Kahn, Le Corbusier, Mies van der Rohe, and Wright. Pages of lined beige linen-finish paper, with each section conveniently thumb-indexed. Printed in brown and black inks, the book is bound in stain-resistant buckram; the front cover is stamped in bronze and gold-colored metallic inks. Beige, dark red, or dark brown binding (please specify color choice when ordering). 256 pp., 23 illustrations; 7½″ x 6¼″. Boxed for mailing.
10.00 (0.50)
The Museum of Modern Art, New York (member's discount 25%)

Bookmarks

Keep your place easily with brass bookmarks that clip neatly onto the page and point to the correct line. Three original designs by Michael Kalil. 2″ diameter. A set of three, gift-packaged.
10.00 the set (0.50)
The Museum of Modern Art, New York (member's discount 25%)

Treble Clef Bookmark

A perfect way for music lovers to keep their place. Lincoln Center has created a bookmark of bright red grosgrain ribbon with a sterling silver treble clef on one end and a sterling silver arrow on the other. Treble clef 2″ long; arrow 2″ long; ribbon 9″ long.
12.50 (1.75)
Lincoln Center for the Performing Arts, Inc., New York (does not publish a member's discount)

Desk Accessories

Overmantel Bookplates

"George Washington slept here." He also dined and danced in the four 18th-century houses from which these overmantels have been graphically adapted. The originals are to be found in a house at 213 Prince St., Alexandria, Virginia; The Benjamin Dulany Town House, Alexandria; Gadsby's Tavern Ballroom, Alexandria; and Mount Vernon. 3" x 4". (2 are vertical and 2 are horizontal.) Package of 48.
1.75 (0.75)
Alexandria Bicentennial Museum Shop (does not operate a membership program)

Benjamin Franklin Bookends

Benjamin Franklin had a fascination for books. He was a printer, a bookseller, and started a circulating library. The Franklin Institute Science Museum has produced a pair of bookends by adapting a historical caricature of Franklin. Cast metal. Antique gold finish. 6" x 3½" x 2½".
15.00 the pair (1.50)
The Franklin Institute Science Museum, Philadelphia (member's discount 10%)

Shakespeare Bookplates

Your friends will remember from whom they borrowed a book if you inscribe these bookplates with your name. An original pen-and-ink drawing, 1902, by John Byam Lister Shaw (English, 1872–1919) for *The Sonnets* in the Chiswick Press edition of *The Works of Shakespeare* is reproduced in black on cream. Gummed paper. 4" x 3". Box of 50.
2.25 (0.75)
The Folger Shakespeare Library, Washington, D.C. (member's discount 15%)

Scrimshaw Bookends

Scrimshaw, the art of incising or engraving designs on ivory, bone, and whale teeth, was a popular pastime of whalers during lengthy voyages. After spending hours polishing the piece with sharkskin and ash, the design was engraved with a sharp tool. To accentuate the pictures, the lines were then filled with lampblack ink and sometimes colored inks. Whale tooth bookends, sure to please the nautically minded, are faithfully reproduced in polymer to depict the originals in every respect. Tooth 6½" high mounted on 1¼"-thick antiqued solid pine base.
62.50 the pair (5.00)
Peabody Museum of Salem (member's discount 10%)

Overmantel Bookplates

Benjamin Franklin Bookends

Shakespeare Bookplates

Scrimshaw Bookends

Library Lion Bookends

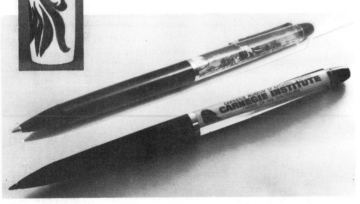
Library Lion Pen

Dinosaur Pen

Inkwell and Quill Pen

Inkwell, Detroit
Historical Museum

Desk Accessories

Library Lion Pen

Designed by Raoul Calabró for The New York Public Library. The lion is the artist's interpretation of the famous lion that guards the entrance of the library. Deep brick red on chunky white ballpoint pen. 5″ long, ³/₄″ diameter.
6.25 (2.00)
The New York Public Library (member's discount 20%)

Library Lion Bookends

The regal lions that guard the main entrance to The New York Public Library have been reproduced in miniature in exact detail for use as bookends. They are certainly a trustworthy pair to support your treasured books. Composite stone. Natural stone color. 7″ high.
32.50 the pair (2.00)
The New York Public Library (member's discount 20%)

Dinosaur Pen

Designed especially for the Museum of Natural History, Carnegie Institute "Home of the Dinosaurs," the pen shows in miniature a mural from Dinosaur Hall. Tilt the pen and a Tyrannosaurus Rex floats back and forth.
2.50 (0.75)
Carnegie Institute, Pittsburgh (member's discount 10%)

Inkwell and Quill Pen

The classic simplicity of this 19th-century pewter inkwell makes it ideal for a modern-day pencil holder or paperweight. It does, however, come with its own quill pen, so for important occasions, both could be used. The reproduction inkwell has an outer chamber that holds water and an inner chamber that holds ink. The quill should be kept in the water when not in use to keep it flexible and ready to write. Perhaps the gracious arts of penmanship and letter writing will be revived. Pewter; shiny finish. 3⁷/₈″ diameter at base.
42.50 (2.50) #323105
Smithsonian Institution, Washington, D.C. (member's discount 10%)

Inkwell

A reproduction of a glass inkwell made in Detroit c. 1840–50. The original is in the collection of the Detroit Historical Museum. Sea-foam green. 2¹/₄″ x 2¹/₂″.
3.00 (1.00)
0.75 White goose quill pen
Detroit Historical Museum (member's discount not available on this item)

Desk Accessories

Inkwell, The Mercer Museum

Inkwell

Henry C. Mercer (1858–1930), founder of the Moravian Pottery and Tile Works and The Mercer Museum in Doylestown, Bucks County, Pennsylvania, was inspired by a 16th-century design when he created this inkwell. The inscription reads, "There is a river, the streams whereof make glad the city of God." Made from Pennsylvania red clay with an overglaze, this handsome reproduction is produced from his original mold. Made to order, each is signed and dated with the year in which it is made. Blue, green, brown, or black. (Please specify color when ordering.) 5″ x 4″.
25.00 (2.50)
The Mercer Museum, Doylestown, Pennsylvania
(member's discount not available on this item)

Animal Paperweights

A collection of animals adapted from works of Egyptian art in the collection of The Brooklyn Museum. 24 karat gold plate on pewter.
Crocodile from a faience figure of a crocodile, Ptolemaic or Roman Period, c. 100 B.C.–A.D. 100.
³/₄″ x 2 ⁵/₈″ x ⁵/₈″.
12.00 (2.00)
Lion from a figure on a glazed faience bowl, Ptolemaic Period, 323–305 B.C.–30 B.C. 1″ x 3¹/₂″ x 1¹/₂″.
14.00 (2.00)
Hedgehog from a glazed faience figure of a hedgehog, XII Dynasty, 1991–1795 B.C. 1¹/₄″ x 2⁵/₈″ x 1³/₈″.
16.50 (2.00)
Cat from a statuette of a cat, Ptolemaic Period, 323–305 B.C.–30 B.C. 2″ x 1⁷/₈″ x 1″.
15.00 (2.00)
The Brooklyn Museum (member's discount 15%)

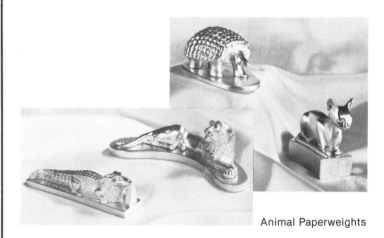

Animal Paperweights

Accelerator Tree

This acrylic cylinder provides a unique and fascinating paperweight. The treelike pattern was produced at the Lawrence Berkeley Laboratory. The cylinder was charged with an electron linear accelerator and then discharged. Each pattern produced by this technique varies slightly. This pattern illustrates two aspects of nature, diversity and uniformity: diversity in the sense that no two patterns are identical, uniformity in the sense that the pattern conforms to the shape and size of the cylinder. Clear acrylic rod with base of red, blue, green, or orange (please specify color choice when ordering). 2″ high, 2″ diameter.
8.95 (1.75)
Lawrence Hall of Science, University of California, Berkeley (member's discount 10%)

Accelerator Tree

Mortar Eprouvette

Originally, this early artillery piece was used to test the strength of black powder. Now its replica has a more peaceful purpose as a unique paperweight. Lead. 2″ x 1¹/₂″ x 2¹/₄″.
5.00 (0.75)
Hagley Museum, Greenville, Delaware (member's discount 10%)

Mortar Eprouvette

Paperweight

Portfolios and Pencil Holder

Dragon Motif Writing Paper

Desk Accessories

Paperweight

A gear, originally used in producing gunpowder, has been reproduced and transformed into a handsome paperweight. Black metal mounted on wood. 5¹/₂" square.
5.00 (0.50)
Hagley Museum, Greenville, Delaware (member's discount 10%)

Portfolios and Pencil Holder

Vibrant purple irises—splendid gravure reproductions in four colors and gold, on covers wrapped with linen and lined in cadet blue. The design is a detail from a six-part screen painted on gold by Ogata Korin (Japanese, late 17th century). Both portfolios have replaceable writing pads and convenient storage pockets. Boxed.
12.50 legal size 14¹/₂" x 9¹/₂". H7850
7.50 8¹/₂" x 5⁵/₈". H7851
7.50 pencil holder with 36 pencils. 4¹/₂" high. H7856
(2.00 per order)
The Metropolitan Museum of Art, New York (member's discount 25%)

Dragon Motif Writing Paper

Handmade paper, produced from the bark of the Daphine bush, is from the Himalayan kingdom of Nepal. The woodblock print is adapted from a tomb tablet, Chinese, Shantung Province, Han Dynasty (206 B.C. to A.D. 220), depicting a Taoist dragon, the symbol of the life force. The original, in the collection of the Museum of Art, Carnegie Institute, was made of clay with impressed and incised designs which have traces of red and white pigments. Red and black on natural. Sheet size: 9" x 7". 26 sheets and 10 envelopes per package.
4.00 per package (0.50)
Carnegie Institute, Pittsburgh (member's discount 10%)

Desk Accessories

Sheet Stationery

Long-overdue letters and thank-yous will be a pleasure to write on this collection of stationery enhanced with ancient motifs from Greek vases in the Museum of Fine Arts collections.

Top left: Leaf design single sheet. Terra cotta and gold on tan with tan envelopes or light blue and silver on white with white envelopes. (Please specify color choice when ordering.) Box of 12. 11″ x 7¼″.
5.00 per box (1.25)
Top right: Same design as above in the same color choices. Box of 12. 9″ x 6¼″.
3.50 per box (1.25)
Bottom left: Greek key border single sheet. White on blue with blue envelopes, terra cotta on tan with tan envelopes, or white on tan with tan envelopes. (Please specify color choice when ordering.) Box of 12. 9″x 6¼″.
3.00 per box (1.25)
Bottom right: Floral design folded note. Terra cotta on tan with tan envelopes, dark blue on light blue with light blue envelopes, or white on tan with tan envelopes. (Please specify color choice when ordering.) Box of 12. 6⅜″ x 5¾″.
3.00 per box (1.25)
Museum of Fine Arts, Boston (member's discount 10%)

Birthday Book

No matter how hard we wish them away, birthdays come every year. Recording those of your friends and relatives will be enjoyable in this charming birthday book. Artists' birthdays are listed alongside the day. There are full-color reproductions of the artists' works on the facing page. Cover design from an original by William Morris (English, 1834–96). The spine is green, stamped in gold. 160 pp., 73 color illustrations; 6¾″ x 5¾″, clothbound.
5.95 (2.00) D0208
The Metropolitan Museum of Art, New York (member's discount 25%)

Photo album, TV Guide cover, and photo frame

An Indian painting of the Deccani school, *Youth Reading,* c. 1610, attributed to Muhammad Ali from the collection of the Freer Gallery of Art has been reproduced on these items. Certain to be an elegant addition to any home or office.
Photo album. Includes 6 magnetic mount pages. Walnut veneer cover. 11″ x 9″.
25.00 (1.00) Refills, 6 pages, **2.00**
TV Guide cover. Tan cover. 7¾″ x 5¼″.
12.50 (1.50)
Photo frame. Space for 4 photographs. Tan cover. 7¼″ x 5¼″.
15.00 (1.00)
Freer Gallery of Art, Washington, D.C. (does not operate a membership program)

Sheet Stationery

Birthday Book

Photo album, TV Guide cover, and photo frame

Shakespearean Characters

Adaptations, Aubrey Beardsley Woodcuts

Stained Glass

Only a small portion of the stained glass produced 700 years ago has survived. Initially, glorious color effects were produced by the use of many small pieces of glass that were colored in the making. Each color was represented by one piece of glass wrapped in lead and attached to the next piece of glass. The only color that the medieval artist was able to paint on was a brownish tint. In the 14th and 15th centuries, there was an increased demand for glass since it was beginning to be used more frequently in buildings other than churches, and clear glass was introduced. Then came the development of glass enameling, whereby the craftsman could paint on either the clear or colored glass, thus creating detail. The stained glass produced for museums today incorporates the techniques developed over the centuries. Most of the pieces are enameled, fired at high temperatures to keep the desired color, and then encased in lead for hanging.

Shakespearean Characters

Hamlet, King Henry VIII, and Ophelia are re-created from the series of stained glass windows—originally executed by Nicola d'Ascenzo in 1929—in the Founder's Room of the Folger Shakespeare Library. Reproduced in the original shades of black, brown, and gold. 8″ high. 18″ pewter chain included.
12.50 each (1.25)
The Folger Shakespeare Library, Washington, D.C.
(member's discount 15%)

Le Morte d'Arthur

Three glass panels adapted from woodcuts by Aubrey Beardsley (English, 1872–98) from Sir Thomas Malory's *Le Morte d'Arthur* (London, 1893–94, two vols.). Includes 18″ pewter chain.
Left: Angel. Red and black. 6¼″ x 2½″.
9.00 (1.00)
Center: Swans. Green and black. 5½″ x 2¾″.
8.50 (1.00)
Right: Peacock. Blue and black. 5¼″ x 3¾″.
8.50 (1.00)
Museum of Fine Arts, Boston (member's discount 10%)

Stained Glass

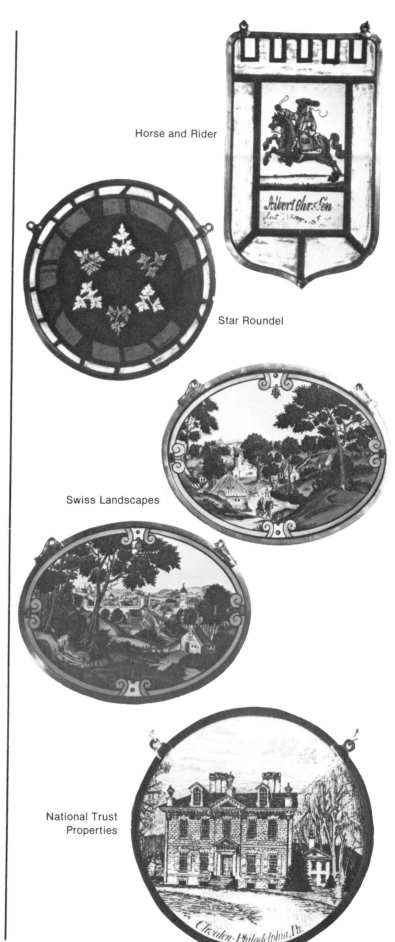

Horse and Rider

The original, dated 1762, was a stained glass panel made to be installed in the windows of a Dutch house. Enameled glass, hand-glazed. Chain provided. Boxed. 8³/₄″ x 5³/₈″.
22.50 (2.00) I1960
The Metropolitan Museum of Art, New York (member's discount 25%

Horse and Rider

Star Roundel

The original is in the Early Gothic Room at The Cloisters, New York. Examples similar to this are to be found in the church of St. Ouen, Rouen, France, dating back to the first quarter of the 14th century. Enameled glass, hand-glazed. Chain provided. Boxed. 6³/₄″ diameter.
22.50 (2.00) I1959
The Metropolitan Museum of Art, New York (member's discount 25%)

Star Roundel

Swiss Landscapes

Both ovals are of enameled glass, hand-glazed, in the colors of the originals, which were of stained and painted glass. They are in the collection of The Metropolitan Museum of Art. Chains provided. Boxed. 6¹/₂″ x 8¹/₂″.
Top: (I1961)
Bottom: (I1962)
25.00 each (2.00)
The Metropolitan Museum of Art, New York (member's discount 25%)

Swiss Landscapes

National Trust Properties

Adapted from drawings by William Wagner, F.A.I.A. The properties that are available on glass: Cliveden (illustrated); Lyndhurst; Woodlawn; and Shadows-on-the-Teche. (Please specify property when ordering.) Black and yellow on stained glass. 6¹/₈″ diameter. Includes 18″ pewter chain.
13.00 (1.50)
National Trust for Historic Preservation, Washington, D.C. (member's discount 10%)

National Trust
Properties

Stained Glass

Red Camellia

Stag

Winter

Red Camellia

Adapted from an album painting, attributed to Wu Ping, Chinese, Ming Dynasty (1368–1644). The original is a watercolor on silk, executed in the 15th century. It has been reproduced in the colors of the original. Red, white, and green on yellowish glass. 5½″ square. Includes 18″ pewter chain.
15.50 (1.50)

Stag

The Regal Stag, a design adapted from a jar with cover manufactured by Royal Doulton, Burslem, England, in 1905. The original is pottery with red flambé glaze. Reproduction: red and black. 5¼″ diameter. Includes 18″ pewter chain.
10.00 (1.50)

Winter

A charming winter scene based on a process print by Ernst Fröhlich (German, 1810–82), after 1849. The print is one of four panels illustrating the seasons, issued as sheet 192 of the *Münchener Bilderbogen* series, published by Braun and Schneider in Munich. Black on white glass. 6½″ diameter. Includes 18″ pewter chain.
11.50 (1.50)

All items on this page are from the **Philadelphia Museum of Art** (member's discount 10%)

Posters

The following are a selection of exhibition posters produced by The Solomon R. Guggenheim Museum, New York:

de Kooning in East Hampton for an exhibition of the work of Willem de Kooning (American, b. Netherlands, 1904) produced from 1962 through the present. The painting, *Untitled XVIII,* was executed in 1977. Full-color offset. Predominant colors are blue, red, and yellow. 33" x 22".

Forty Modern Masters to celebrate the 40th anniversary of The Guggenheim Museum. The illustration is *Football Players,* 1908, oil on canvas by Henri Rousseau (French, 1844-1910). Full-color offset. 37" x 22".

Kenneth Noland: A Retrospective. Whirl, 1960, by Kenneth Noland (American, b. 1924) is illustrated on this poster. Full-color offset. Predominant colors are blue, green, and orange. 29" x 23".

Klee at The Guggenheim Museum for an exhibition of the large collection of the works of Paul Klee (Swiss, 1879-1940) owned by the museum. Illustration: *Runner at the Goal,* 1921. Full-color offset. Predominant colors are brown and green. 32" x 22".

The Evelyn Sharp Collection. Portrait of Thora Klinkowström, 1919, by Amedeo Modigliani (French, b. Italy, 1884-1920) was selected to represent the collection. Full-color offset. 32" x 22".
4.00 each (1.50)
The Solomon R. Guggenheim Museum, New York
(member's discount 25%)

de Kooning in East Hampton

Forty Modern Masters

Kenneth Noland: A Retrospective

Klee at The Guggenheim Museum

The Evelyn Sharp Collection

Admiral Perry Speaking English to the Japanese

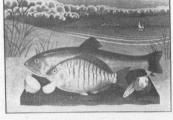

Fish Poster

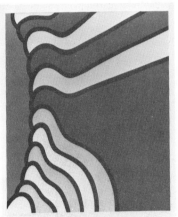

50th Anniversary

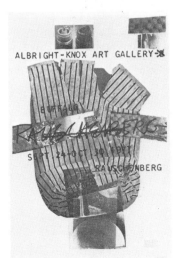

Rauschenberg

Lucy from "The Beggar's Opera"

Stuart Davis: Art and Art Theory

Posters

A selection of posters produced in both signed and unsigned editions exclusively for the Guild Hall, East Hampton, New York:
Admiral Perry Speaking English to the Japanese, 1967, by Saul Steinberg (American, b. Romania, 1914). Brown and black on off-white. 30″ x 40″.
60.00 unsigned (3.50)
500.00 signed (3.50)
Fish Poster by Paul Davis. Full-color. 24″ x 29″.
15.00 unsigned (3.50)
100.00 signed (3.50)
Lucy from "The Beggar's Opera," 1972, by Abraham Rattner (American, b. 1895). Black and white. Edition limited to 100. 28″ x 20″.
50.00 signed (3.50)
Guild Hall, East Hampton, New York (member's discount 10%)

50th Anniversary Exhibition

To celebrate its 50th anniversary, The Minneapolis Institute of Arts commissioned Nicholas Krushenick (American, b. 1929) to design an exhibition poster. The limited edition of 100 is signed and numbered by the artist. Red, yellow, blue-black, and white. Silkscreened. 35″ x 25″.
125.00 (5.00)
The Minneapolis Institute of Arts (member's discount 10%)

Stuart Davis: Art and Art Theory

Sail Loft, 1933, oil on canvas by Stuart Davis (American, 1894-1964) is reproduced in full color on a poster for an exhibition of his works organized by The Brooklyn Museum. Full-color offset. Black background. 45″ x 29½″.
8.00 (2.00)
The Brooklyn Museum (member's discount 15%)

Rauschenberg

R. R. Survey Poster: Most Northern Outbound—Albright-Knox Art Gallery (1977) is the title of the poster designed by Robert Rauschenberg (American, b. 1925) for a traveling retrospective exhibition of his work. Full-color offset. 40″ x 30″.
20.00 (2.50)
Albright-Knox Art Gallery, Buffalo (member's discount 10%)

Posters

Calder's Circus

A bright yellow poster features a wire sculpture executed by Alexander Calder (American, 1898–1976) in 1928. Offset. Black figure, red and blue lettering on yellow background. 36″ x 26″.
5.00 (2.50)
Whitney Museum of American Art, New York (discount not available with regular membership; higher category member's discount 25%)

Ellsworth Kelly

Red Green Blue, 1964, by Ellsworth Kelly (American, b. 1923). Poster produced to accompany a traveling exhibition of Kelly's works. Silkscreen. 37″ x 24″.
10.00 (1.00)
Walker Art Center, Minneapolis (member's discount 10%)

German and Austrian Expressionism

Nudes and Eunuch, an oil painting by Emil Nolde (German, 1867-1956) was selected as the reproduction for this poster to commemorate the exhibition of German and Austrian Expressionism held at the Indiana University Art Museum in 1977. Full color. 31″ x 21½″.
3.50 (0.75)
Indiana University Art Museum, Bloomington (member's discount 10%)

The Cone Collection

The Purple Robe, one of the most popular paintings by Henri Matisse (French, 1869-1954). From The Cone Collection at The Baltimore Museum of Art, it has been reproduced in vivid full color on this poster. Silkscreen. 34″ x 24″.
20.00 (1.50)
The Baltimore Museum of Art (member's discount 10%)

A Panorama of American Painting

This poster provides a reproduction of an original 1897 oil on canvas by Mary Cassatt (American, 1845–926). Motherhood was Cassatt's most frequent theme. Full color on glossy paper. 28″ x 23″.
5.00 (2.00)
Fine Arts Gallery of San Diego (member's discount 10%)

Paris-New York

In 1977 the Wildenstein Gallery, New York, held an exhibition, Paris-New York: A Continuing Romance, for the benefit of The New York Public Library. A charming work, *In the Omnibus,* 1891, by Mary Cassatt (American, 1845–926), from the S. P. Avery collection in the print division of The New York Public Library was selected to be reproduced on the poster which accompanied the show. Full-color offset. 26″ x 19½″.
10.00 (2.00)
The New York Public Library (member's discount 20%)

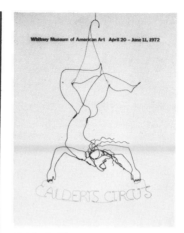
Calder's Circus

Ellsworth Kelly

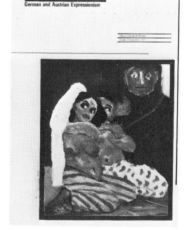
German and Austrian Expressionism

The Cone Collection

A Panorama of American Painting

Paris-New York

Photographs
from the Collection
of Sam Wagstaff

AN EXHIBITION OF PHOTOGRAPHS FROM THE COLLECTION OF SAM WAGSTAFF
THE CORCORAN GALLERY OF ART WASHINGTON, D.C. FEBRUARY 4-MARCH 26, 1978

A Commune Fishpond

No Smoking Sign

The Royal Hunter:
Art of the Sasanian
Empire

Posters

Photographs from the Collection of Sam Wagstaff

Tulips, 1977, by Richard Mapplethorpe (American, b. 1946) appears on the poster prepared by The Corcoran Gallery of Art for their exhibition of "Photographs from the Collection of Sam Wagstaff." Photo-silkscreen. Black and white with peach border. 24" x 32".
5.00 (1.00)
The Corcoran Gallery of Art, Washington, D.C.
(member's discount 10%)

A Commune Fishpond

The painting, *A Commune Fishpond,* 1973, by Tung Cheng-yi has been reproduced in vivid color for this poster to accompany the exhibition, "Peasant Paintings from Huhsien County of The People's Republic of China." Full-color offset. 24" x 36".
8.00 (2.00)
The Brooklyn Museum (member's discount 15%)

No Smoking Sign

The nonsmokers of this world have always had a champion among the Shakers. Among their basic principles was purity of life, which forbade smoking. This sign was originally posted in the buildings of the North Union Shaker Community in Cleveland (Shaker Heights). The original is in the collection of the Western Reserve Historical Society, Cleveland, but has been reproduced by the Shaker Museum, Old Chatham. Black on white cardboard. 9¹⁄₂" x 14".
0.25 (0.25)
Shaker Museum, Old Chatham, New York (member's discount 10%)

The Royal Hunter: Art of the Sasanian Empire

This poster commemorates Asia House Gallery's exhibition, "The Royal Hunter: Art of the Sasanian Empire." It illustrates a splendid silver-gilt rhyton from the Arthur M. Sackler Collections against a royal-blue background. Probably produced by an Iranian craftsman in the 4th century A.D., this horn-shaped, animal-headed vessel exemplifies the objects of luxury created for Sasanian kings. Full-color offset. Laminated. 22¹⁄₂" x 27".
5.00 (member's price 4.00) (0.75)
The Asia Society, Inc., New York

Posters

Broadway is . . .

Popular Theatre and Music Collection show poster with all the spirit of the Great White Way. Black and white newspaper clippings and red on white. 28″ x 20″.
3.00 (1.25)
Museum of the City of New York (member's discount 20%)

5th New York Film Festival

What an appropriate way to celebrate a film festival—a poster in the shape of a giant movie ticket. Artist and filmmaker Andy Warhol (American, b. 1931) designed this ticket superimposed with bright floral patterns. Five fluorescent colors: blue, pink, red, green, and black. Silkscreened. 45″ x 24¼″.
35.00 (3.50)
Lincoln Center for the Performing Arts, Inc., New York (does not publish a member's discount)

Femmes Fatales

A smashing poster for the film buff. Published in conjunction with a film series that presented the great female stars: Louise Brooks, Greta Garbo, Jean Harlow, Claudette Colbert, Bette Davis, Rita Hayworth, Marlene Dietrich, and Jeanne Moreau. Offset. Fuschia printed on gold-foil paper. 35½″ x 22½″.
10.00 (1.00)
Walker Art Center, Minneapolis (member's discount 10%)

Duane Hanson

These are not real people, but an extraordinary lifelike sculpture entitled *Tourists,* 1970, by Duane Hanson (American, b. 1925). This poster was produced in conjunction with a traveling exhibition of the artist's work. Full color. 34″ x 22″.
10.00 (1.50)
Edwin A. Ulrich Museum of Art, Wichita State University (does not operate a membership program)

Turn-of-the-Century America

An exhibition of paintings, graphics, and photographs 1890-1910 was held at the Whitney Museum of American Art in 1977. A poster with a reproduction of a detail from *Central Park,* 1901, watercolor by Maurice Prendergast (American, 1859-1924), was produced to accompany the exhibition. Full-color offset. 28″ x 21¾″.
3.00 (2.50)
Whitney Museum of American Art, New York (discount not available with regular membership; higher category member's discount 25%)

Broadway is . . .,

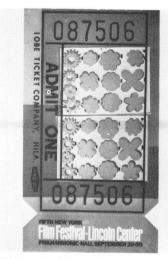

5th New York Film Festival

Femmes Fatales

Duane Hanson

Turn-of-the-Century America

Millet's *Gleaners*

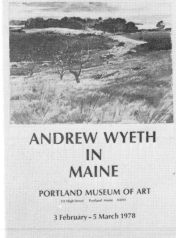

Andrew Wyeth in Maine

The Thinker

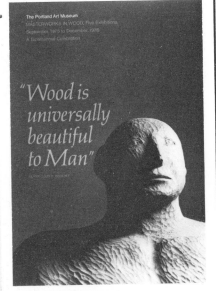

Masterworks in Wood

Master Prints of Japan,
Ukiyo-e Hanga

Posters

Millet's Gleaners

Jean François Millet (French, 1814-75) is well known for his paintings depicting scenes of peasant labor. *The Gleaners* (a detail of which is reproduced on this poster), 1857, oil on canvas, is one of his most celebrated works. The painting hangs in the Louvre and was loaned to The Minneapolis Institute of Arts. Full-color offset. 30³/₄″ x 20¹/₂″.
3.00 (0.75)
The Minneapolis Institute of Arts (member's discount 10%)

Andrew Wyeth in Maine

Broad Cove Farm, Cushing, Maine, 1941, watercolor by Andrew Wyeth (American, b. 1917) has been reproduced on this poster which was produced in conjunction with an exhibition of the artist's work held at the Portland Museum of Art. Full-color offset. Edition is limited to 1,000. 22″ x 17″.
12.00 (2.00)
Portland Museum of Art, Maine (member's discount 10%)

The Thinker

The 50th anniversary poster of the California Palace of the Legion of Honor. This famous work by Auguste Rodin (French, 1840-1917) resides in splendor at the entrance to the California Palace of the Legion of Honor, Lincoln Park, San Francisco. Black-and-white on semi-gloss paper. 24″ x 20¹/₄″.
1.00 (1.50)
M. H. de Young Memorial Museum, San Francisco (member's discount 20%)

Masterworks in Wood

The poster was designed especially for the Portland Art Association. The words are Frank Lloyd Wright's (1869-1959), one of America's most renowned architects: "Wood is universally beautiful to Man." The sculpture, *Hephaestus,* is by Leonard Baskin (American, b. 1922). Offset. Green, brown, and orange. 25″ x 15¹/₂″.
2.00 (1.00)
Portland Art Association, Oregon (member's discount 10%)

Master Prints of Japan, Ukiyo-e Hanga

The image *Sunrise on New Year's Day* is taken from a wood block by Eishōsai Choki from the collection of Mr. and Mrs. Edwin Grabhorn. Ten colors. 32″ x 20″.
15.00 (member's price 12.75) (1.50)
UCLA Art Council, Los Angeles

Posters

Illinois State Museum

An original oil painting by R. G. Larson, 1977, depicts the American Mastodon roaming the spruce forests 16,000 years ago. It has been reproduced in full color on this poster for the Illinois State Museum. Offset. 18″ x 24″.
2.00 (0.75)
Illinois State Museum, Springfield (member's discount 10%)

Tyrannosaurus Rex

The largest and probably the most ferocious dinosaur is thought to have existed for only a short time in the late Cretaceous period, dominating the North American continent. The poster is a reproduction of a mural executed by Ottmar von Fuehrer in Dinosaur Hall, Museum of Natural History, Carnegie Institute. Full-color offset. 36″ x 24″.
2.50 (1.50)
Carnegie Institute, Pittsburgh (member's discount 10%)

Snowy Owl

To celebrate the reopening of The Library Exhibition Hall at the Huntington Library in San Marino, a rarely seen plate *Snowy Owl,* from the elephant folio of John James Audubon's (American, 1785-1851) *Birds of America,* 1827, was reproduced in full color on this poster. 37″ x 25″.
3.00 (0.75)
Huntington Library, Art Gallery, and Botanical Gardens, San Marino, California (members receive a 10.00 annual credit toward purchases)

Animal Camouflage Poster

The poster illustrates animal camouflage; color, shape, and behavior all contribute to disguising an animal in a particular environment. Nature's camouflage allows animals to hide in plain sight, to escape their enemies, or to approach other animals unseen. Can you find the 19 animals hidden in this picture? 3-color offset. 18″ x 22″.
1.50 (1.75)
Lawrence Hall of Science, University of California, Berkeley (member's discount 10%)

Illinois state museum

Tyrannosaurus Rex

Snowy Owl

Animal Camouflage Poster

Library Lion Head

Warehouse Cats

Northwest Coast Mask

Civil War
Recruiting
Poster

Feather

Posters

Library Lion Head

The king of beasts that guards the entrance to the main building of The New York Public Library makes a beguiling poster. Strips of tape on both the top and bottom of the back will adhere easily to wall surface. Full color on glossy paper. 28″ x 21″.
2.50 (1.50)
The New York Public Library (member's discount 20%)

Warehouse Cats

The South Street Seaport Museum has produced several posters which recount the various aspects of the history of the neighborhood through a project called Sidewalk History. *Warehouse Cats* were brought in by the merchants to guard stocks of goods against rodents. Silkscreen. Olive and blue on yellow. 31¾″ x 21″.
4.00 (1.50)
South Street Seaport Museum, New York (member's discount 10%)

Northwest Coast Mask

The ceremonial cedar mask of Komokwa "Lord of the Undersea" was carved in 1977 by Chief Lelooska for the Denver Museum of Natural History. The sea gulls, salmon, and sea urchins on the painted mask reflect the use of animals in Northwest Coast Indian mythology. An information sheet comes with each poster. Reproduced in full color against a black background. Offset. 21″ x 17″.
4.00 (1.50)
Denver Museum of Natural History (discount not available with regular membership; higher category member's discount 10%)

Civil War Recruiting Poster

Times seem not to change. The government still recruits through the use of posters, which have become more elaborate with time. This is a reproduction of a Michigan Civil War poster. Black on cream paper. 25″ x 18″.
2.50 (0.50)
Detroit Historical Museum (member's discount 15%)

Feather

Feather, c. 1965, a photograph by Andreas Feininger (French, b. 1906), was reproduced for a 1976 retrospective of the photographer's work at the International Center of Photography. Black-and-white offset on glossy paper. 24″ x 18″.
4.95 (1.50)
International Center of Photography, New York (member's discount not available on this item)

Posters

The Great American Foot

The foot has been immortalized by an exhibition organized by the Museum of Contemporary Crafts of the American Crafts Council. Americans have a habit of putting their feet into everything. This poster proves the point—everything from cowboy boots to space shoes. Full-color offset. 36″ x 24″.
2.50 (handling and shipping charges included)
Museum of Contemporary Crafts of the American Crafts Council, New York (member's price not available on this item)

The Great
American Foot

Images from Air and Space

The National Air and Space Museum commissioned designer Jim Miho of New York to create a series of posters inspired by the exhibits in the museum. His impressions are expressed in these unique posters. Not only are these posters decorative, they are also educational, commemorating achievements in the air and space fields. Each poster measures 36″ x 24″. (Some are vertical and some are horizontal.)

The Lone Eagle. Lindbergh was the first person to fly solo nonstop across the Atlantic. He made this historic flight on May 20–21, 1927, in his specially built Ryan NYP single-engine plane, "The Spirit of St. Louis." The plane is silver with black markings, and the background is red with white lettering.

35 Phases of Earth. Earth phase photographs taken by a satellite stationed 22,300 miles above the earth show the pattern of daylight and nightfall on the earth. Blue and white photographs on black background.

Kill Devil Hills, N.C. The Wright Flyer was the first heavier-than-air machine to carry a man, take off under its own power, and achieve sustained and controlled flight. The plane is tan; antique brown background with white lettering.

Other posters in the set are:
Pioneers of Flight; The Stars Are in Us; Flight and the Arts; Friend or Foe? Americans Step into Space.

3.00 each
20.00 set of 8
(2.50 per order)
National Air and Space Museum, Smithsonian Institution, Washington, D.C. (Smithsonian Associate member's discount 10%)

The Lone Eagle

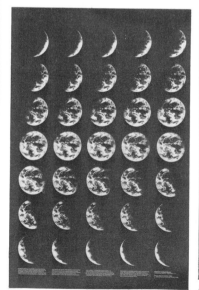

35 Phases of Earth

Kill Devil Hills, N.C.

Reproductions

Mathew Brady Portfolio of Eminent Americans

Mathew Brady Portfolio of Eminent Americans

Mathew B. Brady (American, 1822–96) for more than 50 years was known as Brady of Broadway, excelling in portraiture by daguerreotype, ambrotype, tintype or melainotype, and wet-plate and dry-plate photography. The collection of Civil War portraits, twelve of which are reproduced in this portfolio, are housed in the National Archives. The eminent Americans whose portraits are featured are: Abraham Lincoln, General U. S. Grant, General Robert E. Lee, General William Tecumseh Sherman, Admiral John A. B. Dahlgren, General Philip St. George Cooke, Major General William Mahone, Benjamin Sterling Turner, Clara Barton, Walt Whitman, Horace Greeley, and the Military Commission. The images in this portfolio are printed from the finest quality, unretouched reproductions of the original negatives. The imperfections in the prints reflect the condition of the original plates. Descriptive text is included. Portfolio size: 18″ x 12½″.
7.00 (handling and shipping charges included)
National Archives and Records Service, Washington, D.C. (member's discount 20%)

Dismounted

Dismounted: The Fourth Troopers Moving the Led Horses

Frederick Remington (American, 1861–1909) is best known for his dynamic portrayals of the West. The original oil on canvas was executed in 1890. Full-color offset. 14″ x 20″.
1.00 (1.40)
Sterling and Francine Clark Art Institute, Williamstown, Massachusetts (does not operate a membership program)

Winslow Homer Watercolor Portfolio

One of America's most prominent masters of realism, Winslow Homer (1836–1910) believed that he would best be remembered for his watercolors, and during his long career he developed this medium to an unrivaled level of technical refinement and stylistic sophistication. The National Gallery has selected six watercolors from its collection for inclusion in this portfolio. Full-color offset. Descriptive text is provided. Portfolio size: 22″ x 25″.
The six watercolors:
Girl Carrying a Basket, 1882 (illustrated)
Incoming Tide—Scarboro, Maine, 1883
A Good Shot: Adirondacks, 1892
The Rise, 1900
Key West: Hauling Anchor, 1903
Sketch for Hound and Hunter, 1892
17.95 set of 6 (1.00)
National Gallery of Art, Washington, D.C. (does not operate a membership program)

Winslow Homer Watercolor Portfolio

Reproductions

Brandywine Mills

Bass Otis (American, 1784–1861) traveled America painting portraits; however, he occasionally painted a landscape. This one was executed c. 1840. Full-color offset. 18³/₈″ x 25″.
10.00 (1.50)
The Historical Society of Delaware, Wilmington
(member's discount 10%)

The Carolina Rice Plantation

A series of eight reproductions captures the feeling of plantation living in South Carolina in the 1850s. The original watercolors were painted by Alice Ravenel Huger Smith (1876–1958), born in Charleston. She was influenced by the Japanese wood block print, and she devoted her artistic career to capturing the beauty and atmosphere of the Carolina Low Country. The portfolio is available in a limited edition of 984 numbered sets. Each portfolio includes text relating the history of rice planting and a biography of the artist. Full-color offset. 19¹/₂″ x 24″.
Sunday Morning at the Great House (top)
The Plantation Street, or Settlement
The Sprout-Flow—The First Three to Six Days after Planting
Ready for Harvest
Carting Rice from a Small Field
Shaking the Rice from the Straw after Threshing
Mending a Break in the Rice-Field Bank
The Reserve in Winter
125.00 the set **(3.00)**
Gibbes Art Gallery, Charleston (member's discount 10%)

Roadside Apples

These apples look good enough to eat! A reproduction of a watercolor by Stuart Gentling, in the collection of The Fort Worth Art Museum. Full-color offset. 13¹/₂″ x 22¹/₂″.
35.00 (1.50)
The Fort Worth Art Museum (member's discount 10%)

Brandywine Mills

The Carolina Rice Plantation

Roadside Apples

Sleepy Hollow Portfolio

Reproductions

Sleepy Hollow Portfolio

F. O. C. Darley (American, 1822–88) illustrated *Rip Van Winkle* and *The Legend of Sleepy Hollow*, both by Washington Irving (American, 1783–1859). This portfolio contains a selection of 12 reproductions of these illustrations, accompanied by an introductory booklet. Full-color offset. 8³/₈″ x 10⁵/₈″.
4.50 the set (0.50)
Sleepy Hollow Restorations, Tarrytown, New York (member's discount 10%)

Etchings

The New York Public Library has produced two limited-edition restrikes of etchings by George Cruikshank (English, 1792–1878). He was one of the most popular caricaturists of his day, as well as one of the best illustrators. Each print: 100% rag paper; black and white; edition of 150; 14″ x 10″.
Puss in Boots
Cinderella and the Glass Slipper
35.00 each (2.00)
The New York Public Library (member's discount 20%)

Howard Pyle School of Illustration

Howard Pyle (1853–1911), born in Wilmington, Delaware, was one of America's leading illustrators of the 19th century. His work appeared regularly in *Harper's Weekly.* He illustrated many children's classics. In 1900, he opened a school of art adjacent to his studio in Wilmington. One of his most renowned students was N. C. Wyeth (1882–1945), who also illustrated children's adventure stories and classics. Other pupils included Frank Schoonover, Stanley Arthurs, Ethel P. B. Leach, Clifford Ashley, and Gayle Hoskins. The Delaware Art Museum is offering twelve reproductions of works by the above artists. They may be purchased individually or as a set. Full-color offset. 8″ x 12″. (Some reproductions are vertical and some are horizontal.)
The Springhouse, N. C. Wyeth (illustrated)
The Battle, N. C. Wyeth
The Battle of Bunker Hill, Howard Pyle
The Fight on Lexington Common, Howard Pyle
The Dupont Powder Wagon, Howard Pyle
Through Peaceful Stretches, Howard Pyle
The Sod House of Oklahoma, Frank Schoonover
Study for the First Day of Peace, Stanley Arthurs
Caesar Rodney's Militia, Stanley Arthurs
Howard Pyle's Studio, Ethel P. B. Leach
Getting Fast, Clifford Ashley
At a Rifleman's Shop, Gayle Hoskins
2.50 each (1.00)
25.00 set of 12 (1.00)
Delaware Art Museum, Wilmington (member's discount 10%)

Etchings

Howard Pyle School of Illustration

Reproductions

Saint Francis

The original oil on canvas was painted by Francisco de Zurbarán (Spanish, 1598–1664), c. 1632, at the request of the Count-Duke Olivares, Prime Minister of Spain, for his relative, the Governor of Milan. The work represents Saint Francis (1182–1226) as he appeared in 1449 in a vision of Pope Nicholas V. Full-color offset. 24″ x 13″.
10.00 (1.50)
Milwaukee Art Center (member's discount 10%)

Saint Francis

The Declaration of Independence

Sleepy Hollow Restorations has published a facsimile edition of the Declaration of Independence as originally published in New York State in 1776. Of the five hundred copies printed for distribution in New York, there remain only three known copies, one of which is owned by Westchester County, and another is in the Henry E. Huntington Library in San Marino, California. This facsimile is made from the Huntington copy. The reverse side of this document contains excerpts from minutes of the meeting of the New York Provincial Congress and the names of the delegates attending, all of which have been reproduced.

New York was the last of the original colonies to ratify the Declaration of Independence. The delegates abstained from the voting in which independence from England was declared on July 4, 1776. It was not until July 9 that the New York Provincial Congress voted to approve it. An illustrated information sheet accompanies the facsimile. Black and white. 21″ x 12″.
2.00 (0.50)
Sleepy Hollow Restorations, Tarrytown, New York (member's discount 10%)

The Declaration of Independence

Tournos

A vivid full-color reproduction of a watercolor executed by Stuart Davis (American, 1894–1964) in 1954. Green, black, blue, and white on red background. 30″ x 23¼″.
18.00 (1.50)
Munson Williams Proctor Institute, Utica, New York (member's discount 10%)

Tournos

Vega-Nor

1969 oil on canvas by Victor Vasarely (French, b. Hungary, 1908). Full-color offset.
12.00 22½″ square (2.50)
1.50 8″ square (1.00)
Albright-Knox Art Gallery, Buffalo, New York (member's discount 10%)

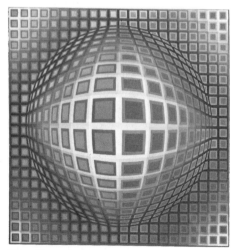

Vega-Nor

May Sartoris

Coco

*Luncheon of the
Boating Party*

Duck Pond

Reproductions

May Sartoris

The original oil on canvas was executed by Frederic Leighton (English, 1830–96), c. 1860, and hangs in the Kimbell Art Museum. Full-color offset. 29$\frac{1}{2}$″ x 17$\frac{3}{4}$″.
12.00 (1.75)
Kimbell Art Museum, Fort Worth, Texas (does not operate a membership program)

Coco

Coco was the nickname of Jean Renoir, the son of Pierre Auguste Renoir (French, 1841–1919). The painting was executed in 1904. It would be a delightful addition to any child's room. Full-color offset. 11″ x 15″.
6.50 (1.50)
Hyde Collection, Glens Falls, New York (member's discount 10%)

Luncheon of the Boating Party

The original oil on canvas was done in 1881 by Pierre Auguste Renoir (French, 1841–1919). The reproduction is full-color offset. 20$\frac{1}{2}$″ x 28″.
15.00 (2.00)
The Phillips Collection, Washington, D.C. (does not operate a membership program)

Duck Pond

Claude Monet (French, 1840–1926) was one of the founders of impressionism and adhered to its principles throughout his life. The original, an oil on canvas, was painted in 1874. Full-color offset. 19″ x 13$\frac{1}{2}$″.
3.00 (1.40)
Sterling and Francine Clark Art Institute, Williamstown, Massachusetts (does not operate a membership program)

Reproductions

The Red Rooster

A reproduction of an oil on canvas by Marc Chagall (French, b. Russia, 1887) which was executed in 1940. Much of Chagall's subject matter is drawn from Jewish life and folklore. He frequently employed flower and animal symbols. Full-color offset. 19" x 23½".
20.00 (1.50)
Cincinnati Art Museum (member's discount not available)

View of Port of Philadelphia

Marine and history buffs will be interested in this reproduction of the port of Philadelphia. The original was published in France about 1840. Full-color collotype. 12" x 17½".
15.00 (1.50)
Philadelphia Maritime Museum (member's discount 10%)

Prints from the Ages of Sail and Steam

The 1th century witnessed the decline of sailing ships and the rise of steam-driven vessels. Both eras are represented in a selection of 6 prints from the collection of the National Archives. The U.S. Steamboat *Col. Thomas* (illustrated here) is one of the prints available. R. F. Loper of Philadelphia offered to build this steamer for $20,000 in 1853. It was to be prefabricated, oiled and packed, and shipped to Oregon for reassembly. It was never built. Each print is full color. Dimensions vary.
U.S. Steamboat *Col. Thomas.* 24½" x 37½"
Ship of the Line. 24½" x 35"
U.S.S. *Congress.* 20½" x 29"
Steamer *Lizzie Davis.* 19" x 26"
Steamer *Corinthian.* 20" x 26½"
Steamer *N. W. Thomas.* 19½" x 26"
3.50 each (handling and shipping charges included)
15.00 set of 6 (handling and shipping charges included)
National Archives and Records Service, Washington, D.C. (member's discount 20%)

Tall Ships

On July 4, 1976, the tall ships sailed up the Hudson River. Tall ships from faraway lands, joined together in the waters surrounding New York City, to celebrate with us our Bicentennial and Operation Sail, 1976. To commemorate the event, Operation Sail commissioned Charles Lundgren, one of this country's finest marine artists, to create 6 original oil paintings. Mystic Seaport offers these reproductions in limited editions of 900. Full-color offset. Each print measures: 24" x 30". (Please order by title.)
U.S.C.G. *Eagle* (illustrated)
Amerigo Vespucci
Christian Radich
Gorch Fock
Danmark
Juan Sebastian de Elcano
60.00 each (1.00)
Mystic Seaport (member's discount 10%)

The Red Rooster

View of Port of Philadelphia

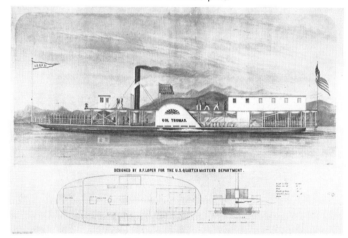

Prints from the Ages of Sail and Steam

Tall Ships

Venice

Brig *Topaz*

Portraits

Reproductions

Venice, The Campo Santo

Joseph Mallord William Turner (English, 1775–1851) traveled abroad extensively, making drawings of subjects he would later execute in oil in his studio. This oil on canvas was painted in 1842. Full-color offset. 19″ x 20¹/₂″.
6.00 (0.50)
The Toledo Museum of Art (member's discount 10%)

Brig *Topaz*

Captain Moses Knight was the commander of the brig *Topaz,* built in Newburyport, Massachusetts, in 1807. The vessel is shown sailing from Marseilles. The original watercolor was done by Antoine Roux, 1808. Offset, hand-colored. Limited edition of 300. 14³/₄″ x 21³/₄″.
30.00 (3.50)
Peabody Museum of Salem (member's discount 10%)

Portraits

The National Air and Space Museum has produced two limited editions, each of 1,000 high-quality reproductions of Paul Calle's graphite pencil portraits of Neil A. Armstrong and James H. Doolittle. Each measures: 29″ x 19″. Each is numbered and signed by both the artist and the subject. The prints are in a handsome portfolio which contains biographies of the artist and the subject. All proceeds are donated to the Charles A. Lindbergh Memorial Fund. $50.00 may be taken as a charitable contribution to the Fund.
Neil Armstrong, 1969. Paul Calle was the only artist to be with the Apollo 11 crew as they prepared for flight at Cape Kennedy on July 16, 1969. This portrait shows astronaut Armstrong four days before he became the first human being to set foot on another planet.
James H. Doolittle, 1977. Calle portrays Jimmy Doolittle in his uniform as Commanding General of the Eighth Air Force and captures his spirit of enthusiasm for aviation.
125.00 each (handling and shipping charges included for orders mailed within the U.S. and Canada; 20.00 elsewhere)
National Air and Space Museum, Washington, D.C.
(Smithsonian Associate member's discount not available on these items)

Reproductions

Gray Squirrels on Hawthorn

The original watercolor was done by the late naturalist and artist, Richard P. Grossenheider. His work appeared in *Life* and *Audubon* magazines. Full-color offset. Predominant colors: varying tones of gray, red, and green. 20″ x 16″.
10.00 (1.50)
St. Louis Museum of Science and Natural History (member's discount 10%)

Gray Squirrels on Hawthorn

Animal Prints

A set of 4 original lithographic prints by D. Noel Smith. This limited edition depicts the Mountain Lion, the Big Horn Sheep, the American Wapiti, and the Mule Deer as they appear in the Denver Museum of Natural History's dioramas. 16″ x 20″.
10.00 the set (1.50)
Denver Museum of Natural History (discount not available with regular membership; higher category member's discount 10%)

Animal Prints

Puppies in the Snow

Detail of *The Twelve Months,* a screen by Katsushika Hokusai (1760–1849), Edo period, Ukiyo-e school. Full-color offset. 22¹/₂″ x 16″.
18.00 (1.00)
Freer Gallery of Art, Washington, D.C. (does not operate a membership program)

Puppies in the Snow

Visions of the Floating World

Six 18th-century paintings of the Ukiyo-e (floating world) School have been reproduced in a portfolio edition. The paintings capture the worldly pleasures of the senses and the natural beauty of the Japanese landscape. The masters of the school are represented: Sharaku, Masanobu, Hokusai, Dohan, Utamaro, and Shunko. The prints are encased in a gold-sealed portfolio with text. Full-color offset on linen-finish paper. Portfolio size: 14″ x 7¹/₂″.
7.50 (1.25)
The Minneapolis Institute of Arts (member's discount 10%)

Iris and Mandarin Ducks

The original ink and pigment on silk was painted by Sakai Hoitsu (Japanese, 1761–1828) during the Late Edo period. Full-color offset. 34″ x 14¹/₄″.
18.00 (2.00)
Dallas Museum of Fine Arts (member's discount 10%)

Iris and Mandarin Ducks

Visions of the Floating World

Reproductions

Maps,
Oregon
Historical
Society

Map of the District
of Maine

The Howe Map

Map of the District of Maine

"Drawn from the latest surveys and other best authorities" by Osgood Carleton and published by Thomas and Andrews in Boston in 1795. Black on off-white. 14½″ x 12″.
3.00 (0.50)
Maine State Museum, Augusta (does not operate a membership program)

The Howe Map

A facsimile of a 1777 map of British and American Army movements and strategies at the important Battle of White Plains in the lower Hudson River Valley, New York. The original was executed by Claude Joseph Sautier and was engraved and printed in England by William Faden. It comes with an illustrated commentary sheet and map key. 3-color offset. 29⅜″ x 20″.
2.50 (0.50)
Sleepy Hollow Restorations, Tarrytown, New York (member's discount 10%)

Maps

The Oregon Historical Society has selected several maps from its collection to reproduce for those interested in the history of this country. They are all suitable for framing.
Trail of Lewis and Clark, 1804–06. This boldly colored map shows the trail followed by these famous American explorers, plus other trails followed by traders and immigrants, including the Oregon, Mormon, Fremont, Santa Fe, and Pony Express trails. 18″ x 30″.
0.50 (0.50)
Indian Tribes and Languages of Old Oregon Territory. Superb full-color map illustrating in color code the original territories of Indian tribes west of the Rocky Mountains. 22″ x 33″.
1.00 (0.50)
Portland, Oregon, 1890. A full-color lithograph with bird's-eye view of a growing, premier western city. It also illustrates fine examples of regional architecture. Available in two sizes.
3.50 29″ x 42″ (0.50)
2.50 20″ x 28″ (0.50)
Oregon Historical Society, Portland (member's discount 10%)

Objects and Ornaments

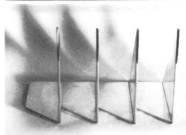

Modular Images

Modular Images

Stephen Godzisz says of his work, commissioned by the Albright-Knox Art Gallery, "I designed these images so that you can become involved in a creative process by manipulating these four elements to suit your own personal expression. By doing so, I hope to bring about a better insight between artist and creator." *Modular Images* (1977) is a set of four aluminum shapes, polished to a chrome luster, designed so that they rest on any of their sides. 5¹/₂" high. Boxed.
38.50 (2.50)
Albright-Knox Art Gallery, Buffalo (member's discount 10%)

1978 Christmas Star

An interpretation of the Christmas star by Linae Frei. The seventh in an annual series designed for The Metropolitan Museum of Art by contemporary artists. There is a ring at the top for hanging as an ornament or pendant. 3¹/₈" diameter. Boxed.
22.50 24 karat gold electroplate on sterling silver (2.00) G7782
9.75 24 karat gold electroplate on copper (2.00) G7783
The Metropolitan Museum of Art, New York (member's discount 25%)

1978 Christmas Snowflake

The eighth in an annual series by contemporary artists. The Metropolitan Museum's 1978 snowflake was designed by Linae Frei. Suitable for hanging on a tree or around the neck. 3¹/₈" diameter. Boxed.
22.50 sterling silver (2.00) G7780
9.75 sterling silver on copper (2.00) G7781
The Metropolitan Museum of Art, New York (member's discount 25%)

1978 Christmas Star

1978 Christmas Snowflake

The Walking Flower

The Walking Flower was executed in 1951 by Fernand Léger (French, 1881-1955) shortly after he started to make ceramics at Blot in southern France. He made only a few free-standing ceramic sculptures. The original, in the Albright-Knox Art Gallery, is 26¹/₂" high. Composite stone painted white, black, red, yellow, and green. Available in two sizes. (Please specify when ordering.)
30.00 8" high (3.00)
85.00 16" high (3.25)
Albright-Knox Art Gallery, Buffalo (member's discount 10%)

Lantern

The Double Sunburst pattern has been adeptly copied from an antique punched tin lantern in the collection of Old Sturbridge Village. The reproductions are handcrafted by artisans working in the village. The door opens and there is a candle holder inside. Tin, shiny finish. 10³/₄" high, 6" diameter.
45.00 (1.30 east of the Mississippi; 2.25 west of the Mississippi)
Old Sturbridge Village (member's discount 10%)

The Walking Flower

Lantern

Objects and Ornaments

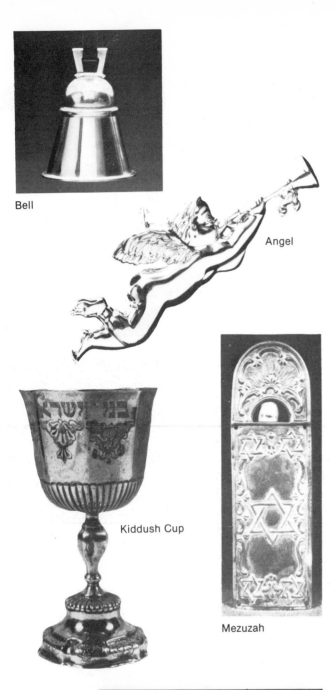

Bell

Angel

Kiddush Cup

Mezuzah

Bell

On its red leather thong, this sterling silver recreation of an Ethiopian bell makes a perfect Christmas ornament. On your own chain, it makes a festive pendant. Bell: 2″ long.
29.75 (1.50) #323113
Smithsonian Institution, Washington, D.C. (member's discount 10%)

Angel

A delightful sterling silver Christmas ornament based on a weather vane representing the archangel Gabriel. 4⁷/₈″ long.
27.50 (1.50) #314278
Smithsonian Institution, Washington, D.C. (member's discount 10%)

Kiddush Cup

This pewter Kiddush cup from The Jewish Museum Collection was engraved and decorated in Augsburg, Germany, in 1791. The Hebrew inscription identifies this as a cup that held wine blessed and shared by the family on festivals such as Sukkot and Shavuot: "So Moses declared to the Israelites the set times of the Lord." (Leviticus 23:44) Pewter. 2¹/₂″ x 4¹/₂″.
75.00 (5.00) #115
The Jewish Museum, New York (member's discount 15%)

Mezuzah

The mezuzah is attached to the doorway of a home according to the commandment "You shall write them upon the doorposts of your house, and upon your gates." (Deut. 6:9) The original 19th-century German mezuzah is decorated with the star of David and a flame that represents divine light. Reproduction, without scroll, available in both pewter and sterling silver. (Please specify when ordering.) 3¹/₂″ x 1¹/₈″.
9.00 Rabinically approved scroll
10.00 pewter (1.50) #P109
40.00 sterling silver (2.50) #S109
The Jewish Museum, New York (member's discount 15%)

Hanukkah Lamp

This medieval Hanukkah lamp from The Jewish Museum's collection burns oil with wicks. It dates from the 12th to the 14th century and was probably made in France or Italy. It is fashioned in the style of a Gothic cathedral with a rose window and the architectural back is meant to represent the temple in Jerusalem. The Hebrew inscription reads: "For the commandment is a lamp, and Torah is light." (Proverbs 6:23) It was originally owned by the destroyed Jewish community of Danzig. Reproduction in bronze. 6¹/₂″ x 6″.
30.00 (2.00) #112
The Jewish Museum, New York (member's discount 15%)

Hanukkah Lamp

Objects and Ornaments

Passover Seder Plate

Pewter plates made by Christian guild members were often bought and decorated by Jewish folk artists. They transformed plain plates into works of art to enrich the Jewish festivals. This reproduction of an 18th-century European Passover plate, in The Jewish Museum's collection, is decorated with a bird holding a matzoh in its mouth. The order of the Seder is engraved around the rim and the Hebrew word *Pesach* in the center. Pewter. 13″ diameter.
90.00 (6.00) #108
The Jewish Museum, New York (member's discount 15%)

Space Medal

Florida's men of discovery: NASA-Apollo astronaut John W. Young, Chief Osceola, and Ponce de Leon. Ercel Jones designed the superimposed profiles. Cathy Carroll designed the tri-hexagonal figure representing man, his environment, and the universe on the reverse of the medal. Limited edition. 1½″ diameter.
3.50 bronze (0.40)
20.00 coin silver (0.40)
John Young Museum, Orlando, Florida (member's discount 10%)

Saudi Arabian Hand Ax

The original, one of the oldest artifacts in the collection of the St. Louis Museum of Science and Natural History, was unearthed near a fossil lake bed in the Rub'al Kahli Desert in southern Saudi Arabia. The original is at least 25,000 years old. Reproduction is a polyester-filled casting. Dark red. 5½″ long.
5.00 (2.00)
St. Louis Museum of Science and Natural History (member's discount 10%)

Pipe Racks and Spoonholder

Handcrafted of pine on the premises of the Shelburne Museum, for distribution exclusively by the museum. Inspired by objects produced in late 18th- and early 19th-century America, and found in the collection.
Left: Double pipe rack. 19″ x 9¾″ x 4½″. Unfinished.
30.00 (2.00)
Center: Spoonholder. 22″ x 13″ x 6″.
30.00 unfinished (2.00)
35.00 waxed (2.00)
40.00 painted red or green (please specify color choice) (2.00)
Right: Single pipe rack with drawer. 18″ x 5″ x 4½″.
40.00 unfinished (2.00)
Shelburne Museum, Inc., Vermont (does not operate a membership program)

Passover Seder Plate

Space Medal

Saudi Arabian Hand Ax

Pipe Racks and Spoonholder

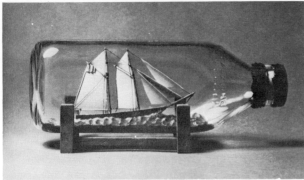
Fishing Schooner in a Bottle

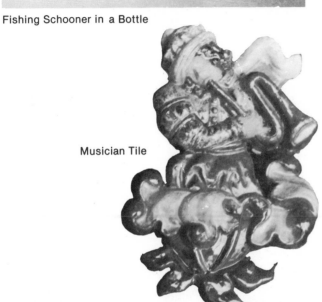
Musician Tile

Canadian Goose and Decoys

Decorative Tile

Objects and Ornaments

Fishing Schooner in a Bottle

Bluenose rides the sea in a bottle. Handcrafted exclusively for the South Street Seaport Museum by Gary Smith, it will certainly delight any nautical enthusiast. Wood ship in glass bottle on mahogany base with a brass nameplate. Beige sails and black hull. 5″ high, 7″ long.
50.00 (3.00)
South Street Seaport Museum, New York (member's discount 10%)

Musician Tile

Using an original mold, designed by Henry C. Mercer, this tile is made by the Moravian Pottery and Tile works in Doylestown. Each tile is signed and dated with the year in which it is made. There is a hole in the back of the tile so that it can be hung from the wall. Ceramic tile with glazes of blue, gold, green, yellow, and brown. This is one of twelve musicians available. 6³/₄″ x 4³/₄″.
12.00 (1.75)
The Mercer Museum, Doylestown, Pennsylvania (member's discount not available on this item)

Canadian Goose and Decoys

Expertly handcrafted in wood by H. Randolph for The Mercer Museum. Each is hand-painted in black and white with variations in the markings. Each piece is signed and dated by the artist. *Canadian Goose* can be hung on the wall, or a metal rod can be inserted in the belly so that it can be free standing. 8″ x 34¹/₄″.
15.00 (1.75)
Left foreground: Decoy. 6¹/₂″ x 15″ x 5″.
18.00 (1.75)
Right foreground: Decoy. 4¹/₂″ x 11¹/₂″.
9.50 (1.75)
The Mercer Museum, Doylestown, Pennsylvania (member's discount 10% on items over 10.00)

Decorative Tile

Henry C. Mercer built the Moravian Pottery and Tile Works and, later, The Mercer Museum, in the early 20th century. The Tile Works continues to make tiles from the original molds designed by Henry C. Mercer. Each sign of the Zodiac is available in several color combinations: buff on a brown, blue, or green background; or red on a brown or green background. (Please specify Zodiac sign and color choice when ordering.) 4″ square.
4.00 (1.25)
The Mercer Museum, Doylestown, Pennsylvania (member's discount not available on this item)

Objects and Ornaments

Kitchen Tiles

Kitchen Tiles

The original labels—picturing cherries, apricots, plums, and currants—used on these tiles were printed by Maison Berthiau in Paris in the 19th century. The tiles are felt-backed and come with reinforced hooks so they may be used either as trivets or as wall hangings. Silkscreened. Six colors on ivory ceramic. 6″ diameter.
22.00 set of 4 (2.00) F0421
The Metropolitan Museum of Art, New York (member's discount 25%)

Totem Poles

A collection of three totem poles in various sizes. The originals were carved in black slate by the Haida Indians of the Queen Charlotte Islands, British Columbia. Composite stone. Black.
Left: 6″ x 1¼″ x 1¼″.
12.50 (2.25)
Center: 11″ x 1¾″ x 1½″.
17.50 (2.25)
Right: 19″ x 3″ x 1¾″.
35.00 (2.25)
The American Museum of Natural History, New York (member's discount 10%)

Totem Poles

Dome-Top Box

Tole—brightly painted metalware—was very popular in the 18th and 19th centuries. With the bold colors and splashy patterns of birds, flowers, and other motifs typical of Pennsylvania German decoration, the painted tinware from Pennsylvania best exemplifies the folk-art tradition. Tin was the most commonly used metal. This decorated box is an adaption of a design by Sarah Upson, American, 19th century. Each box is hand-painted and carefully varnished by Ruth Berkey. Tin. Multicolored on black background.
5¼″ x 8¾″ x 4″.
52.50 (4.00)
The Mercer Museum, Doylestown, Pennsylvania (member's discount 10%)

Dome-Top Box

Ditty Box

Sailors used ditty boxes for carrying small articles such as sewing implements. This box is a reproduction of a mid-19th-century scrimshaw box found in the collection of the Peabody Museum of Salem. Polymer. White, brown, and a touch of green. 3″ high, 6″ wide, 8″ long.
75.00 (5.00)
Peabody Museum of Salem (member's discount 10%)

Ditty Box

Nest of Oval Boxes

Fruit Boxes

Tobacco Box

Benin Box

Objects and Ornaments

Nest of Oval Boxes

The Shakers first made oval boxes at the New Lebanon community in 1798. They were made for sale to the World's people (non-Shakers). They were identified by a numbering system meant to differentiate between the fifteen graduated sizes. The grace and simplicity of the "fingered" lap box is a perfect example of the Shakers' concern for both detail and proportion. The Shaker Museum has the largest collection of oval boxes to be found anywhere. These fine reproductions are almost indistinguishable from the originals, and each is individually stamped to mark it as an authentic reproduction Shaker oval box. Pine and maple. Medium stain.

Top: 2¹/₂″ x 5¹/₄″ x 3³/₄″.	**12.50**
Center: 3″ x 7″ x 4³/₄″.	**16.00**
Bottom: 4″ x 9″ x 6″.	**21.50**

(1.75)
Shaker Museum, Old Chatham, New York (member's discount 10%)

Fruit Boxes

Around the middle of the 18th century, it was fashionable to collect boxes that were realistically modeled and painted as fruits or animals. The originals of these pieces were produced in the Meissen factory, Dresden, Germany, c. 1750, during the directorship of Count Heinrich von Bruhl. The apple was a snuff box, and the smaller lemon was probably intended to contain sweetmeats. Hand-painted porcelain.
29.95 apple box (2.00) F0530
25.00 lemon box (2.00) F0531
The Metropolitan Museum of Art, New York (member's discount 25%)

Tobacco Box

The original pewter box was intended to be used as a humidor. It could still be used for that purpose or as a hiding place for many small things. It was made in the Netherlands by a pewterer named Vos about 1725–50. Pewter. 6¹/₂″ high.
85.00 (2.00) G8093
The Metropolitan Museum of Art, New York (member's discount 25%)

Benin Box

The original of carved ivory was made in the kingdom of Benin, Africa, for the royal court. Two fighting Portuguese, in 16th-century dress, are depicted on this oval box. Composite stone, ivory finish. 2¹/₄″ x 6¹/₂″.
30.00 (2.50)
University Museum, Philadelphia (member's discount 10%)

Objects and Ornaments

Bust of a King

This small bust of a king was a sculptor's model used for preparing royal portraits in ancient Egypt. The original is on display at the University Museum, Philadelphia. Composite stone. White. 5½" x 4".
22.50 (2.50)
University Museum, Philadelphia (member's discount 10%)

Scribe

Statuette sacred to the Egyptian god Thoth, a patron of learning and the arts. As the god of wisdom and magic, he was credited with the inventions of writing, geometry, and astronomy. The original statue was executed in basalt during the XVII Dynasty, c. 1400 B.C. Composite stone, black finish. 3¼" high, including white base. (Base not shown in illustration.)
15.00 (1.95) DT-1
Detroit Institute of Arts (member's discount 10%)

Richard Wagner and Giuseppe Verdi

Sculptor Robert R. Toth having researched the life, philosophy, and moods of the composers and immersed himself with their music, has created these commanding busts, which are on permanent display at the Lincoln Center for the Performing Arts. Each bust is available to order in bronze in an edition of 350. They are cast by the lost wax process. They are also available to order in a composite stone, hand-finished in a bronzelike patina. This edition is limited to 500. Both processes are carefully supervised by the artist. Each is accompanied by a signed certificate of authenticity. They are mounted on a detachable base, and the bust may be turned to display it from various angles. 17" high with 2" high base.
3,600.00 each in bronze (120.00)
225.00 each in composite stone (45.00)
Lincoln Center for the Performing Arts, New York (does not publish a member's discount)

Akua'ba

Made by the Ashanti tribe of Ghana, African fertility dolls of this type were carried around by young girls in their back-cloths, just as they would carry a real child. They were also carried by women who wished to bear children. The original of wood is in the collection of The American Museum of Natural History. Composite stone. Black. 14" (including base) x 6".
40.00 (3.50)
The American Museum of Natural History, New York (member's discount 10%)

Bust of a King

Scribe

Richard Wagner and Giuseppe Verdi

Akua'ba

Basonge Mask

Panther

Chinese
Tomb Dragon

Weathervane

Rooster

Objects and Ornaments

Basonge Mask

A dance mask from the Basonge tribe of the central Congo, Africa, has been reproduced from the collection of the University Museum. Composite stone. Brown and black. 14½″ x 10″.
60.00 (5.50)
University Museum, Philadelphia (member's discount 10%)

Panther

The original silver statuette was cast in Persia in the 2d century B.C. Silver-plated pewter, black base. 2½″ long on base.
15.00 (0.50)
The Art Museum, Princeton University (member's discount 10%)

Chinese Tomb Dragon

A benign dragon which is a replica of a late Han dynasty (A.D. 25–220) earthenware tomb figure, originally painted red and yellow. It would have been placed in an upper-class Chinese tomb. Composite stone. Taupe. 8″ long.
50.00 (4.00) #316513
Smithsonian Institution, Washington, D.C. (member's discount 10%)

Weathervane

The original—much larger—from which this has been reproduced in miniature, was made by an American blacksmith c. 1800, and is in the collection of the Yale University Art Gallery. Gray metal on wood stand. 3″ high.
4.90 (1.00)
Yale University Art Gallery, New Haven (member's discount 10%)

Rooster

Ondori is the tenth sign of the Oriental zodiac. Roosters were believed to be able to forecast the changes in the weather. The original was made in the 19th century of ivory with gold inlaid eyes. Polymer; ivory finish. 1½″ high.
15.00 (1.95)
Peabody Museum of Salem (member's discount 10%)

Objects and Ornaments

Quadruped

Quadruped

A fanciful animal reproduced from an original Chinese bronze statue, late Chou dynasty (6th-5th century B.C.) in the collection of the Freer Gallery of Art. Composite stone, dark green patina. 7¹/₂" long on wood base. (Base not illustrated.)
30.00 (1.00)
Freer Gallery of Art, Washington, D.C. (does not operate a membership program)

Bear Tamer

Statuette of a bear tamer, Chinese, Chou dynasty (6th-5th century B.C.). Original cast in bronze. The figure of a man with upraised arms, balancing a bear on the top of a pole, is a so-called *ming-ch'i* or burial piece. Metal. 6¹/₂" high including base.
37.50 (1.00)
Freer Gallery of Art, Washington, D.C. (does not operate a membership program)

Bear Tamer

Sakhmet

Sakhmet

The lion-headed goddess was associated with medicine and physicians in ancient Egypt. The original is in the University Museum, Philadelphia. Bronze-finished composite stone. 8" high.
25.00 (3.00)
University Museum, Philadelphia (member's discount 10%)

Elephant

Originally carved in wood by the Mende people of Africa, it was used as either an ornament or a toy. Composite stone. Brown. 5¹/₂" x 4¹/₂".
20.00 (2.50)
University Museum, Philadelphia (member's discount 10%)

Elephant

Objects and Ornaments

Panther

Egyptian Cat

Falcon

Elephant

Panther

The original *Panther* was executed by François Pompon (French, 1855–1933), who was one of the first sculptors recognized for his elegantly stylized animals in the Art Deco tradition. This sleek black panther stalks his prey on a thin platform of mahogany (base not illustrated). Composite stone. 15″ long.
37.50 (2.00)
Rosenbach Foundation, Philadelphia (member's discount 20%)

Egyptian Cat

The original, made in bronze, was probably a votive dedication at the temple of the goddess Bastet. Egypt, Late Period (663–332 B.C.). Composite stone, bronze finish. 6³/₄″ high, including base.
18.50 (2.50)
Walters Art Gallery, Baltimore (member's discount 10%)

Falcon

An imposing falcon has been reproduced from an original sculpture in The Cloisters, New York. The original, c. 1200, is probably German or Italian and thought to be from the staff of a German emperor. Gilt bronze on black marble base. 14¹/₂″ high.
395.00 (2.00) F0060
The Metropolitan Museum of Art, New York (member's discount 25%)

Elephant

An elephant you won't forget. It is based on a wooden sculpture found in 1919 during an African expedition sponsored by the Smithsonian. Pewter. 3″ x 4″.
30.00 (2.00) #333179
Smithsonian Institution, Washington, D.C. (member's discount 10%)

Toys and Games

Circus Figures

What a balancing act! The circus figures in this sculptural puzzle can be assembled into an equilateral triangle, 19″ on each side, or they can be balanced in many configurations. Each figure is outfitted in a different brightly colored costume. Wood painted with gloss enamels. Safe for children. Each figure is 8″–10″ high.
40.00 (3.50)

Dragon Puzzle

The fire-breathing dragon, brightly painted on both sides, is a challenge to put together for a child of any age. Pine with leather spikes. Painted with gloss enamels. Safe for children. 13″ x 23″ x 1³/₈″.
22.00 (3.00)

Machinations

This graphic whirligig playfully combines some basic mechanical and visual effects when pulled. Since attachments may be added or removed, a "new" toy is created with each use. Three wheels are left unfinished so the owner can select a color and paint them. Pine, maple, black walnut, and mahogany. Natural wood painted with assorted enamel colors: red, orange, blue, green, and purple. Safe for children. 6″ x 11″ x 8″.
25.00 (3.00)

These three toys were made by Copaesthetic © 1975 especially for the Albright-Knox Art Gallery.
Albright-Knox Art Gallery, Buffalo, New York (member's discount 10%)

Mobile Cards

Two charming mobiles designed by Sherry Tamalonis for the Albright-Knox Art Gallery. Each comes in card form, in a brightly colored envelope, with string and instructions for assembly. 9¹/₄″ long when hanging. Full color on white folder.
Left: Goldilocks and the Three Bears
Right: Natural Forms
1.00 each (0.50)
Albright-Knox Art Gallery, Buffalo (member's discount 10%)

Circus Figures

Dragon Puzzle

Machinations

Mobile Cards

72

Giraffe

Whirligig

Toys and Games

Giraffe

This handsome wooden giraffe on wheels, reproduced in exact detail from a charming 19th-century Pennsylvania German toy, would delight any youngster; it is, however, just as likely to appeal to the connoisseur of folk art. The original was probably made for a Noah's Ark. Each is handcrafted and hand painted by Yesteryear Toy Company especially for the Philadelphia Museum of Art. No two are exactly alike, and the measurements may vary slightly. Wood. Ocher with brown spots. Safe for children. 15″ high.
56.00 (2.50)
Philadelphia Museum of Art (member's discount 10%)

Whirligig

In the 19th century, whirligigs were often mounted on sticks for children to whisk through the air like pinwheels. Larger ones, used as weather vanes, revolved in the wind on top of farmhouses in rural Pennsylvania. The arms of each figure, ending in vanes to catch the wind, were mounted on a rod running through the body. This toy is a replica of a Pennsylvania German whirligig made about 1812–40, carved from wood and brightly painted to resemble the figure of a naval officer in uniform. Each toy is handcrafted and hand painted by Yesteryear Toy Company especially for the Philadelphia Museum of Art. Each piece is slightly different. Wood. Red, gold, and black. Moveable arms. Safe for children. 12″ x 5¼″ x 1½″.
28.50 (2.50)
Philadelphia Museum of Art (member's discount 10%)

Horse Pull Toy

Horse Pull Toy

A charming handcrafted pull toy of white pine with a walnut stain, made specifically for McCall's at Old City Park by one of the area's local craftsmen. 6⅞″ x 7¾″ x 2½″.
6.00 (1.50)
McCall's at Old City Park, Dallas (member's discount not available)

Climbing Bear

Hang the bear on the wall, tug the cord, and the bear will climb the string. This toy is guaranteed to produce a smile from a delighted child. Handcrafted of poplar and stained with a walnut finish, it is made especially for McCall's at Old City Park by a local craftsman. 6″ x 5″ x ¾″.
3.00 (1.00)
McCall's at Old City Park, Dallas (member's discount not available)

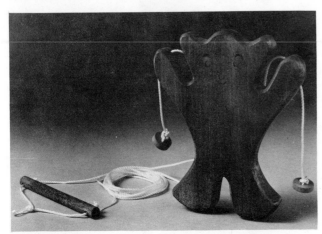

Climbing Bear

Toys and Games

Old-fashioned Top

Tops have been a favorite children's toy for generations. This one is exceptionally well crafted from "scrap" wood for McCall's at Old City Park. Each top consists of a variety of woods including maple and walnut. Not only attractive but an excellent "spinner." 3½" x 5⅜" x 2⅛".
4.00 (1.00)
McCall's at Old City Park, Dallas (member's discount not available)

Rag Toy Reproductions

Reproduced from 19th-century rag toys in the Museum of the City of New York's toy collection. The originals were among the first rag toys produced commercially in America, and each pattern cost a penny. Handscreened in full color on cotton muslin. Each animal is available pre-assembled or as a flat pattern.
Tabby Cat: 13½" high.
13.00 pre-assembled (1.25)
7.00 flat pattern (0.75)
Tabby Kitten: 6½" high.
6.50 pre-assembled (1.25)
3.50 flat pattern (0.75)
Rabbit: 14" high.
13.00 pre-assembled (1.25)
7.00 flat pattern (0.75)
Pug Dog: 11½" high.
13.00 pre-assembled (1.25)
7.00 flat pattern (0.75)
Museum of the City of New York (member's discount 10%)

"William"

The bright blue faience hippopotamus decorated with lotus flowers is Egyptian, XII Dynasty, c. 1940 B.C. "William" has been adapted as a stuffed toy or pillow. Silkscreened cotton. 17" long. Available sewn and stuffed or as a kit with instructions for sewing and assembling.
22.50 sewn and stuffed (2.00) L2420
12.50 kit for sewing and assembling (2.00) L2400
The Metropolitan Museum of Art, New York (member's discount 25%)

Goundie Doll

This reproduction of a Bavarian doll is sure to produce a smile from any child. Originally made in 1840, it is now hand made for the Goundie House Museum Shop. The doll is made of 100% cotton with a dress in an assortment of brightly colored calicos. 16" high.
12.00 (2.00)
Historic Bethlehem, Inc., Pennsylvania (member's discount 10%)

Old-fashioned Top

Rag Toy Reproductions

"William"

Goundie Doll

Toys and Games

Shaker Doll

Doll

Opera Moppets

Shaker Doll

A charming doll which is sure to delight any child. She is dressed in the traditional Shaker garb: blue dress and bonnet with white apron. You have the choice of a blonde or brunette (please specify when ordering). Cotton. 8½″ high.
5.00 (1.00)
Shaker Museum, Old Chatham, New York (member's discount 10%)

Doll

A memory of childhood. Although not an antique, it is reminiscent of times past. The delicately molded face is of an old and durable material known as composition. The beautiful white dress has been fashioned by hand by Southland craftsman Ruth DeNicola. The doll was commissioned by the Museum Shop of the Long Beach Museum of Art.
60.00 (4.00)
Long Beach Museum of Art (member's discount 10%)

Opera Moppets

Mezzo soprano Dora Kartakova has created these delightful Opera Moppets especially for Lincoln Center. The characters come alive through the care given in detailing the facial expressions and colorful costuming. Sure to be of constant enjoyment for opera fans for years to come. Various materials are used.
Top left: Papageno, the comic birdcatcher from Mozart's *Magic Flute,* is dressed in boots and a bright cotton suit of red, blue, or green under felt feathers in a multitude of colors. He balances a wooden birdcage from which hand-sewn birds peek out. (Please specify color of suit when ordering.) 20″ high.
42.00 (3.25)
Top right: Siebel, from Gounod's *Faust,* carries a bouquet of plastic flowers for his Marguerite. Although he is scorned by his love, he will intrigue you with his golden ringlets, floppy beret, tweedy green suit, and enchanting blue eyes. 20″ high.
35.00 (3.00)
Bottom: Octavian, from the Strauss opera *Der Rosenkavalier,* is ready for his role as the rosebearer dressed all in white. He wears a lace-trimmed satin coat and breeches bedecked with seed pearls, sequins, and ribbons. 19″ high.
45.00 (3.25)
Lincoln Center for the Performing Arts, Inc., New York (does not publish a member's discount)

Toys and Games

Soft Sculpture Puppets

Joanne Fox has created these magnificent puppets with lifelike faces and elaborate costumes exclusively for the Lincoln Center for the Performing Arts. Each is 22″ high and comes on a removeable stand.
Top left: Pagliacci, the tragic clown that he is, suffers through an aria grasping his famous hat and wearing a white satin smock with organdy ruffle.
Top right: Shakespeare stands in a scholarly black velvet cloak with a stiff white collar and holds a quill in one hand and a parchment scroll in the other.
Bottom: King Lear rules his domain in a regal robe of purple brocade trimmed with fur at the hem and cuffs. His long white hair cascades out from under his jeweled crown.
95.00 each (5.00)
Lincoln Center for the Performing Arts, Inc., New York (does not publish a member's discount)

Soft Sculpture Puppets

"Puppet-Puppet"

An African mask and pre-Columbian urns ingeniously adapted into colorful felt hand puppets to delight any child.
Left: Pre-Columbian ceremonial urn. Tan, brown, and white with red tongue. 10″ x 9″.
8.50 (1.50)
Center: Bat god incense urn. Gray body; white eyes; purple mouth with red tongue. 10″ x 9″.
8.50 (1.50)
Right: African mask. Bright green head; red face; black hair, nose, eye outline, and tongue; white mouth. 10″ x 6″.
7.50 (1.50)
The Baltimore Museum of Art (member's discount 10%)

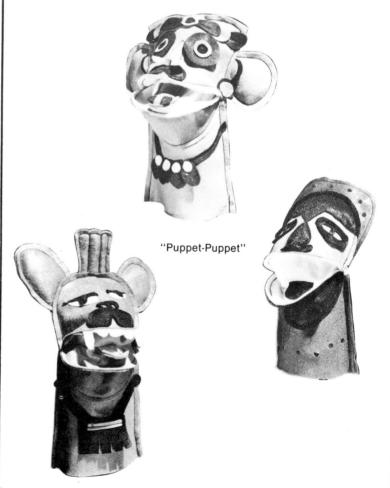

"Puppet-Puppet"

Dinosaur Kits

Griffin

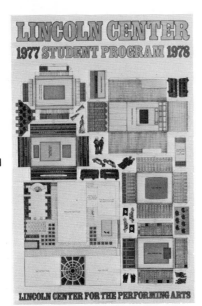

Poster Model

Toys and Games

Dinosaur Kits

Creatures from an extinct era have been re-created in kit form and when completed will be a delightful addition to any collection of stuffed animals. Each contains off-white silkscreened muslin and instructions. Hand washable.
Top: Pteranodon (#314195) Wingspan 50".
Bottom left: Triceratops (#314187) 25" long.
Bottom right: Tyrannosaurus Rex (#320002) 24" high.
8.00 each (1.00)
Smithsonian Institution, Washington, D.C. (member's discount 10%)

Ibo Helmet Mask Kit

A soft sculpture you make yourself: enjoy playing Halloween all year long. When it's not scaring your friends, it makes a handsome wall decoration. The design is based on an Ibo Helmet Mask of Mmwo Society. Kit contains printed gray and brown cotton sheet and detailed instructions. 17" high.
9.50 (1.50)
The Baltimore Museum of Art (member's discount 10%)

Ibo Helmet Mask Kit

Griffin

A soft sculpture of the mythological beast which was half-lion and half-eagle. The original appears on an 18th-century Torah ark curtain at The Jewish Museum in New York. Black on cream. 17" x 18".
28.00 sewn and stuffed (1.50)
9.00 kit for sewing and assembling without stuffing (0.75)
The Jewish Museum, New York (member's discount 15%)

Poster Model

Designed by Victor Lazzaro, the poster for Student Programs at Lincoln Center can be turned into an activity. By following the simple instructions, you can cut out and build a replica of the Lincoln Center complex. Silkscreen. Golds, browns, and greens. 34" x 22".
7.00 (2.50)
Lincoln Center for the Performing Arts, Inc., New York (does not publish a member's discount)

Toys and Games

Model of Gunston Hall

This kit will surely supply hours of fun for the whole family. A scale model of Gunston Hall to be cut out and assembled. Terra cotta and gray on heavy white paper. Scale: 1″ to 10 feet. Assembled size: 2½″ x 6″ x 4″.
2.00 (0.50)
Gunston Hall, Lorton, Virginia (member's discount 10%)

Coloring Books

These bold designs from woodcuts found in rare books in the collection of the Walters Art Gallery provide an ideal introduction to the charm of early printed illustrations. These are not modern redrawn versions, but actual facsimiles of the original woodcuts. Three titles are available: *Noah's Ark; Medieval Parade;* and *Dragons and Other Animals.* (Please order by title.) Black on white paper. 8½″ x 11″.
1.25 each (0.25)
Walters Art Gallery, Baltimore (member's discount not available on this item)

Doll Coloring Book

The Monterey Peninsula Museum of Art has published a coloring book based on the dolls in their folk-art collection. There are 20 pages of dolls to color and short descriptions of the originals. Black on white paper. 8″ x 10″.
1.75 (0.50)
Monterey Peninsula Museum of Art (member's discount 10%)

Model of Gunston Hall

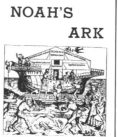

Coloring Books

Doll Coloring Book

78

Mini-puzzle

Jigsaw Puzzles

Cranes Jigsaw Puzzle

Toys and Games

Mini-puzzle

Full-color detail of *Blessing of the Fishing Fleet,* 1900, by Paul Signac (French, 1863–1935) is reproduced on this puzzle of approximately 75 pieces. A perfect gift for people in confined spaces, since it measures 7″ square when completed.
1.50 (0.50)
The Minneapolis Institute of Arts (member's discount 10%)

Jigsaw Puzzles

Merry Jesters (detail), 1906. Oil on canvas by Henri Rousseau (French, 1844–1910).
A detail of a brightly colored and intricately embroidered Chinese woman's robe of the late 19th century is reproduced in full color on this jigsaw puzzle. It is sure to challenge the expert. Shades of pink, blue, green, yellow, white, black, and gold on a dark blue background.
Sunburst Patchwork Quilt. Detail from a quilt made by Rebecca Savery (American, 1770–1885) in 1839. The reverse side of each puzzle is imprinted with a reproduction of an 18th-century marbled paper.
Each contains more than 500 pieces. 14½″ x 23⅜″.
6.50 each (1.00)
Philadelphia Museum of Art (member's discount 10%)

Cranes Jigsaw Puzzle

A challenge! It takes over 500 pieces to put together this elegant puzzle. White and black cranes on a gold background have been reproduced from *Cranes,* a two-paneled screen by Sakai Hoitsu (Japanese, 1771–1828). 18″ x 24″.
6.00 (1.25)
Worcester Art Museum (member's discount 10%)

Toys and Games

Armored Knight Puzzle

Armored Knight Puzzle

This puzzle is inspired by one of the most sumptuous suits of knight's field armor in existence, with etched and gilded ornaments typical of the finest German armor from Augsburg in the mid–16th century. The armor was made about 1560 for a member of the Hapsburg family and comes from the imperial armory. The armor is from the Kienbusch Collection of Armor and Arms at the Philadelphia Museum of Art. Wood. Silkscreened. Silver, black, and gold. 9¹/₂″ x 4¹/₄″ x 1⁷/₈″.
11.75 (1.00)
Philadelphia Museum of Art (member's discount 10%)

Witchcraft Trial

Have fun while re-creating a piece of American history: the famous witchcraft trials of Salem, Massachusetts. *Trial of George Jacobs,* 1855, oil on canvas by Tompkin H. Mattson is reproduced in full color on this puzzle. Jacobs was hanged on Gallows Hill in 1692. 101 pieces. 10″ x 13″.
2.00 (0.50)
Essex Institute, Salem, Massachusetts (member's discount not available)

Witchcraft Trial

Galaxy

A real challenge for the jigsaw puzzle expert! A composition of apparently infinite colored spheres floating in lighted space, *Galaxy,* oil on canvas, was done by Fritz Trautman (American, 1882–1971). It has been reproduced in full color. 23¹/₂″ x 18″.
6.95 (1.75)
Memorial Art Gallery of the University of Rochester, New York (member's discount 10%)

Jigsaw Puzzle

Over 400 pieces to master. The finished picture, *Queen Elizabeth I in Parliament,* is a reproduction of a hand-colored engraving from Robert Glover's *Nobilitas Politica et Civilis,* 1608. 20″ x 12¹/₂″.
5.00 (1.25)
The Folger Shakespeare Library, Washington, D.C. (member's discount 15%)

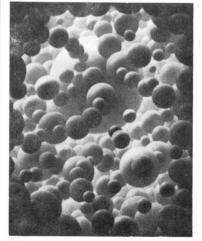

Galaxy

Jigsaw Puzzle

Dinosaur Friends

Samson the
Sabertoothed Cat

Museum Kite

Gaming Board

Toys and Games

Dinosaur Friends

Stegosaurus, triceratops, Dimetrodon, Brontosaurus, Pteranodon, and Tyrannosaurus are a set of friendly dinosaurs that have been handcrafted of natural Canadian birch especially for The Ark in the Park Shop of The Cleveland Museum of Natural History. They will surely be a hit with any child. The toys are finished smoothly. Unpainted wood. 3″ x 5″ x ³/₄″. They are available individually (please specify by name) or as a set.
3.00 each (0.50)
15.00 set of 6 (1.00)
The Cleveland Museum of Natural History (member's discount 10%)

Samson the Sabertoothed Cat

Each puzzle is handcrafted of natural sugar pine and is sanded to remove all burrs. You may add your personal touch by varnishing Samson or coloring him with felt-tip pens. 6″ x 12″ x 1¹/₂″.
8.00 (1.50)
George C. Page Museum of La Brea Discoveries, Los Angeles (member's discount 10%)

Museum Kite

Shop at a museum for the unusual in kites! This striking design, based on a detail from a page in a 15th-century astronomical manuscript (Persian, Timurid) is silkscreened in bright blue, yellow-green, and black on silver mylar in the shape of an eight-pointed star. When not flying, it will make a beautiful wall hanging. The kit includes detailed assembly instructions. You supply the string and reel. The kite measures 36″ across.
Limited edition.
25.00 (2.00)
Museum of Fine Arts, Boston (member's discount 10%)

Gaming Board

The parquet squares of this handsome board are made of rich contrasting woods, meticulously fitted. A complement to your finest chess or checker set. It is copied from an 18th-century antique now in the George Wythe House. 17¹/₄″ square.
70.00 (2.00) AP127
The Colonial Williamsburg Foundation (does not operate a membership program)

Toys and Games

Candle
Molding Kit

Candle Molding Kit

Candle molding provides hours of productive fun for all ages. Make eight 10″ candles, using authentic 18th-century methods and materials. Kit includes a reusable tin candle mold, wicking, beeswax, and complete instructions.
10.25 (1.25) S159
The Colonial Williamsburg Foundation (does not operate a membership program)

Kalah

Used throughout the world, the ancient game of Kalah can be played with many rules. The development of strategy and problem-solving skills is the key to all the variations.
The game consists of a board, 9½″ x 17″, made of high-impact brown polystyrene and ring top cowrie shells.
2.95 (1.75)
Lawrence Hall of Science, University of California, Berkeley (member's discount 10%)

Kalah

Magnet Set

The world of magnets has fascinated children for many, many years. With this well-conceived set, they can spend hours investigating the interactions of magnets and the patterns of magnetic fields.
Case, 4⅜″ x 5⅜″: High-impact polystyrene in brown wood grain color.
Contents: Five magnets; container of iron filings; compass; instructions.
2.95 (1.75)
Lawrence Hall of Science, University of California, Berkeley (member's discount 10%)

Magnet Set

Sunprint Kit

Create photographic-type images without using chemicals! Using only water and specially designed Sunprint paper, children and adults can make successful and imaginative Sunprints each time. The kit includes instructions, a 4″-x-4″ glass plate, and 10 4″-x-4″ Sunprint papers.
1.80 the kit, **0.75** for refill (1.75)
Lawrence Hall of Science, University of California, Berkeley (member's discount 10%)

Sunprint Kit

Block Printing Kit

Playing Cards

Bridge Ensemble, Playing Cards, and Tallies

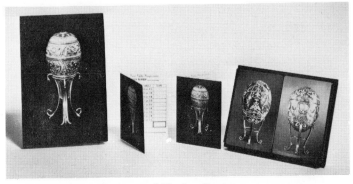

Bridge Score Pad, Tallies, and Playing Cards

Toys and Games

Block Printing Kit

Experience hours of enjoyment creating your own woodblock print designs on stationery and fabric. Contents include: hand-carved animal woodblock from India, two tubes of water-soluble printing ink, brayer, plexiglass tray, paper for block printing, and instructions. All in a wood box. 8″ x 4½″ x 2½″.
4.75 (1.25)
Huntsville Museum of Art (member's discount not available on this item)

Playing Cards

Keep your opponent mesmerized with these brightly colored playing cards. Robert Indiana's *Love*, 1966, acrylic on canvas, has been reproduced on one deck, and the logo of the Indianapolis Museum of Art on the other. Red, green, and blue. Plastic coated. Two decks in a box.
6.50 (1.00)
Indianapolis Museum of Art (member's discount 10%)

Bridge Ensemble, Playing Cards, and Tallies

Bridge anyone? The Freer Gallery of Art has all the aficionados in mind with its complete line of necessities for the game.
Bridge Ensemble
Design in full color is based on *Portrait of a Prince*, Persian painting by Muhammad Harawi, Safavid period, 16th centiry. Boxed set with three bridge score pads and two decks of cards.
9.00 (1.00)
Playing Cards
The design is based on the *Portrait of a Prince* mentioned above. Two decks in a clear plastic box.
6.00 (1.00)
Bridge Tallies
Center: *Portrait of a Prince.*
Lower left: Assorted designs in full color based on sketches by Kanō Tanyū (Japanese, 1602–74). Edo period, Kanō school.
Lower right: Design in full color is based on *An Old Man and a Youth,* Persian painting by Behzad, Herat school, late 15th–early 16th century. 3¼″ x 2½″.
0.75 package of 8 two-table tallies (1.00)
Freer Gallery of Art, Washington, D.C. (does not operate a membership program)

Bridge Score Pad, Tallies, and Playing Cards

Three Imperial Eggs executed by Peter Carl Fabergé (1846–1920) have been selected from the outstanding Lillian Pratt Collection of Russian Jewels at The Virginia Museum, to adorn this attractive bridge ensemble. As Russian court jeweler, Fabergé gained a reputation for his extraordinary work in gold and enamel.
Score pad. Gold egg on black background.
0.70 (0.25)
Tallies. Set of 8.
1.00 (0.25)
Playing cards. The background on one deck is green and the other is blue. Two vinyl-coated decks in plastic box.
4.90 the set (0.50)
The Virginia Museum, Richmond (member's discount 10%)

Toys and Games

Porcelain "Egyptian" Dominoes

Reproduced from works in The Brooklyn Museum's collection, this 28-tile ("Double-Six") set features hieroglyphics chosen for their beauty and for the good fortune each symbolized. The set is made of fine porcelain with incised hieroglyphics and dot values by Vista Alegre, Portugal, for the Block China Corporation. The set comes in a silkscreened canvas container. Each tile measures 2″ x 1″ x ¼″.
80.00 (2.00)
The Brooklyn Museum (member's discount 15%)

Porcelain "Egyptian" Dominoes

Cribbage Board

The original scrimshaw tusk cribbage board was carved for Captain George Comer, commander of the whaling schooner *Era,* during a visit to Hudson Bay in 1905. Detailed carving in relief decorates the entire length of the tusk. Along the pegboard is carved: "Cape Fullerton, ERA, Hudson Bay 1905." A scene depicting the ships in the harbor is outlined with a continuous border of vines. It is an excellent example of Canadian Eskimo folk art. The reproduction, made of Scrim® (synthetic ivory!), has been carefully detailed to include the surface cracks produced from age. 17″ long, supported by 2″ high legs.
40.00 (1.00)
Mystic Seaport (member's discount 10%)

Cribbage Board

Marbles and Jacks

Two favorite games of children spill out of especially designed pouches for The Corcoran Shop. Both are available in either blue or maroon suede pouches with leather drawstring. The word Marbles or Jacks and The Corcoran Shop logo are printed on the pouch. Glass marbles or metal jacks with rubber ball. (Please specify color of pouch and game when ordering.) 5¼″ x 3½″.
2.00 each (0.50)
The Corcoran Gallery of Art, Washington, D.C.
(member's discount 10%)

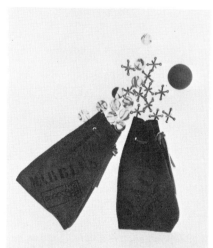

Marbles and Jacks

Dreidel

A dreidel is a four-sided spinning top used in the give-and-take game played during the Jewish holiday of Hanukkah. This top, designed by Merle Steir and commissioned for The Jewish Museum in 1976, is not only a handsome object but actually spins. Test your ability—can you make it spin for five minutes? Brass. 3″ x 3¼″ x 3″.
40.00 (3.00)
The Jewish Museum, New York (member's discount 15%)

Dreidel

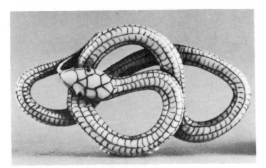
Snake Pendant

Lion

Crowned Sphinx Pendant

Cat Pendant

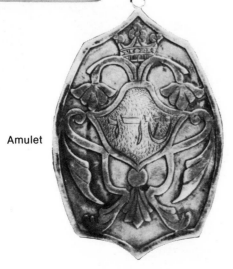
Amulet

Jewelry

Snake Pendant

Hebi, the sixth sign of the Oriental zodiac, is a symbol of woman's jealousy. The 19th-century original was carved from ivory and has inlaid eyes. Polymer. 2¼" long.
15.00 (1.95)
Peabody Museum of Salem (member's discount 10%)

Lion

A replica in miniature of the proud lion that guards the entrance to the main branch of The New York Public Library. Available in bronze on silk cord or sterling silver with sterling silver chain. Lion: ¾" high, 1¾" long.
30.00 bronze (2.00)
70.00 sterling silver (2.00)
The New York Public Library (member's discount 20%)

Crowned Sphinx Pendant

A faience tile said to be from Qantir in the Eastern Delta, Early Ptolemaic Period (300–200 B.C.) was the inspiration for this pendant. The tile depicts a walking crowned sphinx and reflects Persian influence on Hellenistic art. Available in two finishes: 18 karat gold-plated pewter; 18 karat gold-plated pewter with blue cold enamel field. 1⅝" square.
12.00 gold (2.00)
15.50 gold on blue (2.00)
The Brooklyn Museum (member's discount 15%)

Cat Pendant

A smiling cat, adapted from a painted Peruvian textile in the collection of the Philadelphia Museum of Art. Made in the 8th or 9th century by the Tiahuanaco people. The highly stylized cat is probably a puma representing the "puma god" (part man and part puma) worshipped by the Peruvians. 1¼" x 1" with 12" black cord.
45.00 sterling silver; oxidized background (2.50)
25.00 gold-plated over copper (2.50)
Philadelphia Museum of Art (member's discount 10%)

Amulet

A lovely 20th-century Italian charm in the Art Nouveau tradition is the source of this reproduction. Although its style is relatively modern, it is a traditional protection against the evil eye because it is inscribed with the divine name. The central motif may be a stylized "tree of life" and the crown represents the Torah. 2¼" x 1½".
10.00 pewter (1.50) #P111
25.00 silver (2.00) #S111
The Jewish Museum, New York (member's discount 15%)

Jewelry

Hamsa

Hamsa

In the Middle East, the *hamsa,* or hand, traditionally has the power to ward off evil, the way one puts out a hand to protect oneself. Reproduced from a 19th-century Palestinian charm decorated with the flowers of a Persian garden. 2³/₈″ x 1³/₈″.
3.00 pewter (1.50) #P105
15.00 silver (1.50) #S105
The Jewish Museum, New York (member's discount 15%)

Coptic Crosses

The originals of both these crosses are silver, from Ethiopia, post-Axumite style, after 1800. Christianity in Ethiopia dates back to 227, when the dynasty was founded, tracing its ancestry even farther back to Solomon and Sheba. Ethiopia is thus one of the earliest Christian kingdoms in the world.
Left: Silver electroplated on pewter. 3″ x 2³/₄″ with 15″ chain.
15.00 (1.50) PO-1
Right: Silver electroplated on pewter. 3¹/₄″ x 2¹/₄″ with 15″ chain.
15.00 (1.50) PO-2
Portland Art Association, Oregon (member's discount 10%)

Coptic Crosses

Wedgwood Pendants

Jasper, classified as stoneware, has been manufactured by Wedgwood since 1774. Stoneware is usually opaque, and since it is fired at a high temperature, it is watertight and not usually glazed. These pendants, which can also be used as pins, are current reproductions of 18th-century Wedgwood cameos. Each is set in a gold-filled frame and is boxed with an 18″ gold chain.
Left: White on green. 2″ high.
Center: White on blue. 1¹/₂″ high.
Right: Blue on black. 1″ diameter.
47.00 each (1.25)
Buten Museum of Wedgwood, Merion, Pennsylvania (member's discount not available on this item)

Wedgwood Pendants

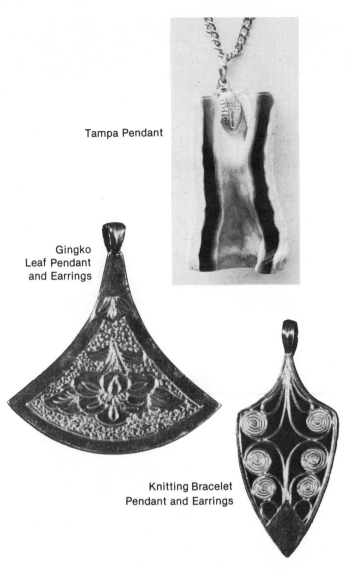

Tampa Pendant

Gingko
Leaf Pendant
and Earrings

Knitting Bracelet
Pendant and Earrings

Stylized Turtle Necklace

Jewelry

Tampa Pendant

This pendant, designed by Laury Marks especially for the John Young Museum in Florida, is made from coral found only in Tampa Bay. It was formed 10 million to 25 million years ago. Due to the mineral content of the matrix, coral went through a process whereby it was replaced by agate, thus producing these beautiful geodes. Each piece will vary slightly in color and size. 1–2^1/$_2$″ x ^{1}/$_2$–1″ with 9″ gold chain.
2.50 (0.40)
John Young Museum, Orlando (member's discount 10%)

Gingko Leaf Pendant and Earrings

The Chinese concern for restraint and harmony of form is captured in these elegant pieces. They have been adapted from a silver gilt hairpin in the shape of a Gingko Leaf from the T'ang dynasty (A.D. 618–906) in the collection of the Philadelphia Museum of Art. 1^3/$_4$″ long, 1^3/$_4$″ wide.
Pendant:
48.00 sterling silver
56.00 24 karat gold gilt over sterling
Earrings (not illustrated). Pierced only.
70.00 sterling silver
74.00 24 karat gold gilt over sterling
(2.50 per item)
Philadelphia Museum of Art (member's discount 10%)

Knitting Bracelet Pendant and Earrings

This shield-shaped filigree jewelry reflects a domestic aspect of America's Federalist period. Originally each such shield was attached by a short chain to a bracelet. Small spurs on the back served to retain balls of knitting wool so that knitting could be continued between household tasks. 1^3/$_4$″ long.
Pendant:
40.00 sterling silver
44.00 24 karat gold gilt over sterling
Earrings (not illustrated). Pierced only.
72.00 sterling silver
80.00 24 karat gold gilt over sterling
(2.50 per item)
Philadelphia Museum of Art (member's discount 10%)

Stylized Turtle Necklace

Inspired by the Senufo tribe of the Ivory Coast, Tzivia Horiuchi has created a handsome necklace, combining faithful reproduction and inventive handwork, for The American Museum of Natural History, New York. The three pendants of this necklace, Stylization of Turtles, are finished in 24 karat gold and are 2^1/$_4$″ high. The collar is made of gold-plated tubular beads, flat gold-plated discs, and serrated black wooden discs.
37.50 (2.50)
The American Museum of Natural History, New York (member's discount 10%)

Jewelry

Grillwork Bracelet, Brooch/Pendant, and Earrings

An elegant collection of jewelry adapted from a
French iron door grill of the 14th to 15th century
which is installed in the Medieval Gallery at the
Virginia Museum. Each piece is handwrought and
signed by William deMatteo and Philip Thorp,
silversmiths from Williamsburg.
Bracelet. Four links. 7" long.
39.00 sterling silver (JVM253)
43.00 gold-plated over sterling (JVM253G)
Brooch/Pendant. 2¼" x 2".
17.90 sterling silver (JVM251)
19.90 gold-plated over sterling (JVM251G)
Earrings. Screw-back or pierced. (Please specify when
ordering.)
16.50 sterling silver (JVM250A)
18.00 gold-plated over sterling (JVM250G)
(1.00 per item)
The Virginia Museum, Richmond (member's discount
10%)

Grillwork Bracelet, Brooch/Pendant, and Earrings

Dragon Necklaces

The dragon, a familiar symbol in the folklore of many
countries, has been depicted in a variety of poses. In
China it was often associated with fertility and
prosperity. Both of these necklaces have been
reproduced from Chinese jade dragon ornaments of
the Warring States Period (480–221 B.C.). Both are gold
electroplated on pewter and come with a 24" chain.
Two-Headed Dragon. 2¾" wide.
15.00 (1.00)
Facing Dragons. 3½" wide.
15.00 (1.00)
Freer Gallery of Art, Washington, D.C. (does not
operate a membership program)

Dragon Necklaces

Little Monkey in a Swing

A pendant reproduced from a gold ornament, Costa
Rica, A.D. 800–1500, in the collection of The Brooklyn
Museum. The goldsmiths of this region probably
learned their trade from the great gold-working
cultures of Colombia, and jewelry (often featuring local
animals) was passed down from generation to
generation—so much so that the Spanish named the
land Costa Rica ("Rich Coast") when they arrived in
1502. Vermeil over sterling silver. Antique finish. With
silk cord. ½" diameter.
14.00 (2.00)
The Brooklyn Museum (member's discount 15%)

Little Monkey in a Swing

Falcon Head Pendant

Holographic Pendants

Baseball Pass Pendant

Jewelry

Falcon Head Pendant

This striking Falcon Head has been adapted from the terminal of an Egyptian broad-collar necklace, probably made during the Ptolemaic Period (330–04 B.C.). Sometimes called "collar of Horus," such necklaces afforded magical protection for their wearers. This adaptation of a work in The Brooklyn Museum's collection has been handcrafted in champlevé enameling by Walter Belzario. As each piece is individually worked, no two pieces will be identical. In champlevé enameling, the design is etched in copper and then gradually filled with enamel and fired. The enameling and firing process is repeated many times before the piece is finished by plating the exposed portions of the metal base in 14 karat gold. White with blue and yellow. 1³/₁₆″ x 1⁹/₁₆″ with black cord.
90.00 (2.00)
The Brooklyn Museum (member's discount 15%)

Holographic Pendants

Something very unusual to add to your jewelry collection and certain to be a topic of conversation. Holographic pendants look like clear glass until you put them on. The three-dimensional image comes into being under any lighting against your clothes. These pendants have been produced by the Museum of Holography in New York. Dichromated gelatin on glass in gold bezel. 1³/₄″ diameter with 18″ gold chain. *Pharaoh,* 1977, by Rich Rallison. Color: white, rainbow colors.
20.00 (1.50)
Rose, 1976, by Rich Rallison. Color: white, rainbow colors.
16.00 (1.50)
Watchworks, 1975, by Rich Rallison. Color: gold.
16.00 (1.50)
Museum of Holography, New York (member's discount 10%)

Baseball Pass Pendant

Three diehard fans are deeply engrossed in the game as the count stands at "2 out; bases full; 3 balls; and 2 strikes." The original Charles Dana Gibson design for the 1930 Giants baseball season pass can be found in the Rare Book Room at The New York Public Library. The pendant has been adapted in bas relief. Gold-plated bronze. 1¹/₈″ x 1⁵/₈″.
15.00 (2.00)
The New York Public Library (member's discount 20%)

Jewelry

Sword Guard (Tsuba) Pendant

Sword Guard (Tsuba) Pendant

The most precious possession of the Japanese warrior was his sword, and for centuries in Japan, schools of metalworkers devoted themselves exclusively to the manufacture and decoration of these swords. The zenith of sword manufacture was reached between the 13th and 16th centuries, a period when the country was ruled by military overlords and frequently torn by internal strife. In later more peaceful times, the various decorative elements became increasingly elaborate. Although the sword guard performed the vital function of protecting the hand of the warrior, it was a completely separate unit that fitted onto the blade and it thus provided two flat surfaces for decoration. Ornamented with an openwork design of cranes, the original is of iron with inlaid bronze eyes, signed Masatsune of Musashi. Japanese, 18th–19th century. Gold electroplated on pewter. 3³/₈″ diameter, with gold chain.
15.00 (1.00)
Newark Museum (member's discount 10%)

Tibetan Lotus

Tibetan Lotus

A stylized motif adapted from a belt worn by the women of Kham province, Tibet, c. 1900. Silver electroplated on pewter. Necklace: choker length. Pin: 1¹/₂″ x 2″.
20.50 necklace (1.00)
7.50 pin (1.00)
Newark Museum (member's discount 10%)

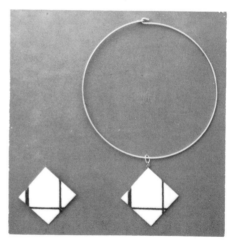

Pin and Pendant

Pin and Pendant

Black-on-white enamel pin and pendant, made expressly for the Yale University Art Gallery, have been based on *Fox Trot A,* an oil on canvas executed by Piet Mondrian (Dutch, 1872–1944) in 1930. The jewelry pieces are in the colors of the original. Enamel. 1¹/₂″ square.
5.00 pin (1.00)
6.00 pendant on neckwire (1.00)
Yale University Art Gallery, New Haven (member's discount 10%)

Cleopatra's Barge Pin and Pendant

Cleopatra's Barge, drawn from plans of the famous Salem ocean-going yacht, built in 1816 for George Crowninshield, Jr. Gold plated.
12.50 pin, 2″ wide (1.95)
18.00 pendant, disc 2¹/₄″ diameter (2.50)
Peabody Museum of Salem (member's discount 10%)

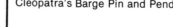

Cleopatra's Barge Pin and Pendant

Collectors Jewellery

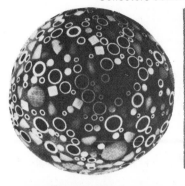

Rooster

Animal Mask Ornament

Jewelry

Collectors Jewellery

The Women's Committee of the Art Gallery of Hamilton has commissioned five of Canada's leading artists to design an original work for *Collectors Jewellery: Five Contemporary Hand Sculptures, three of which are shown here.* Each edition is limited to 150 pieces, which are numbered, registered, and signed by the artist. These works are hand sculptures to be worn and treasured for their beauty and intrinsic value as fine art objects.

Mishipizhew Pendant, 1974, by Dora de Pédery-Hunt (b. Hungary, 1913). Originally Mishipizhew was a "night panther," sometimes called "The Great Lynx," with whiskers and a frightening crest from head to tail. There are many variations of this mythical animal in Objibwa pictographs; some look like serpents, some like lizards, but there are long-legged deerlike ones, too. The artist became fascinated with them and has created her own version which she likes to believe will bring luck and happiness. Sterling silver. 3¹/₈" wide.
185.00 (2.00)

Amulet, Talisman, Bead Sculpture, 1975, by David Chavel (b. Woodstock, Ontario, 1942). His interest explored in this piece was the possibilities of multidimensional responses to pattern, texture, color, and their relationship to small forms. 14 karat gold, sterling silver, ivory, maple, all set in a colored epoxy matrix with a matte finished surface. 2¹/₄" round.
145.00 (2.00)

Ambitious Man Pendant, 1977, by William McElcheran (b. Hamilton, 1927). A disc encircles a man carrying a briefcase and wearing a fedora. Sterling silver. 2¹/₂" diameter with chain.
100.00 (2.00)
Art Gallery of Hamilton, Ontario, Canada (member's discount 10%)

Rooster

Richard Derby ordered a weathervane for the East Church in Salem, Massachusetts. Thomas Drowne executed one in the form of a rooster in 1771, from which this extensive collection of jewelry has been adapted. 24 karat gold plate on brass.

Large Rooster Pin. 2¹/₂" x 2".	10.00
Small Rooster Earrings. Screw back or pierced. (Please specify when ordering.) ⁷/₈" x ³/₄".	8.00
Lapel Pin (not illustrated). ⁷/₈" x ⁵/₈".	3.50
Tie Tack (not illustrated). ³/₄" x ³/₄".	4.50
Tie Bar. Rooster: ⁷/₈" high; bar: 2" long.	5.00

(0.50 per item)
Essex Institute, Salem, Massachusetts (member's discount not available)

Animal Mask Ornament

The original was an iron sleeve-weight overlaid with sheet gold, Chinese, Warring States Period (480–221 B.C.). Gold electroplated on pewter. 2⁵/₈" x 2³/₈" with 24" chain.
15.00 (1.00)
Freer Gallery of Art, Washington, D.C. (does not operate a membership program)

Jewelry

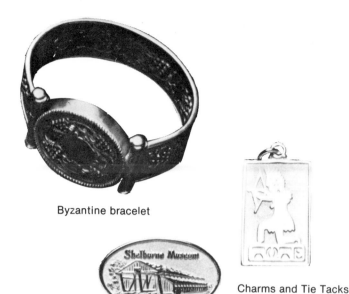

Byzantine bracelet

Byzantine Bracelet

The original of this splendid Byzantine Bracelet was among the jewelry found on the island of Cyprus in 1902. Greek, 6th–7th century.
125.00 24 karat gold electroplate on sterling silver (2.00) G0541
950.00 24 karat gold electroplate on 14 karat gold (2.00) G5299
The Metropolitan Museum of Art, New York (member's discount 25%)

Charms and Tie Tacks

Charms and Tie Tacks

The Shelburne Museum, in the rolling hills of Vermont, is an outdoor museum devoted to the American heritage. Three special attractions on the museum's premises have been selected for charms, and in the case of two of them, they are also available as tie tacks.
Covered Bridge: Sterling silver. ¹/₄″ x ³/₄″.
5.00 charm (1.50)
3.50 tie tack (1.50)
Weather Vane: Sterling silver. ³/₄″ x ¹/₂″.
5.00 charm (1.50)
3.50 tie tack (1.50)
Ticonderoga: A replica of the day lake steamboat, built in 1906 and retired in 1954, that cruised the waters of Lake Champlain. Sterling silver. ¹/₄″ x 1¹/₄″.
7.00 charm (1.50)
Shelburne Museum, Inc., Vermont (does not operate a membership program)

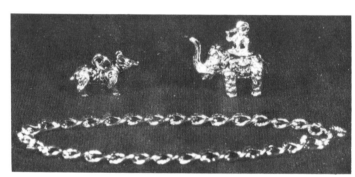

Quadruped and Two Elephants

Quadruped and Two Elephants

Two delightful animals to add to your silver or gold charm collection. And if you are just beginning, there is the added bonus of purchasing the bracelet at the same time.
Left: Quadruped, Chinese bronze, late Chou Dynasty, 5th–4th century B.C.
6.00 sterling silver (1.00)
7.00 gold filled (1.00)
Right: Two Elephants, Chinese ritual vessel, late Shang Dynasty, 12th century B.C.
10.00 sterling silver (1.00)
10.00 gold filled (1.00)
Bracelet.
10.00 sterling silver (1.00)
10.00 gold filled (1.00)
Freer Gallery of Art, Washington, D.C. (does not operate a membership program)

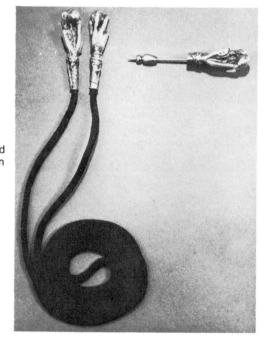

Lariat and stickpin

Lariat and Stickpin

Originally this graceful hand was the decoration to a bronze hairpin from Egypt (after 30 B.C.).
Lariat of black silk can be worn around the neck or waist. Hands are silver-plated. 36″ long.
16.00 (1.50)
Stickpin: Silver-plated
12.00 (1.50)
The Brooklyn Museum (member's discount 15%)

Griffin
Stickpin

Sabertoothed Cat Charm

Gold Scarab

Scarf Pins

Jewelry

Griffin Charm, Stickpin, and Tie Tack

In ancient times, this mythical creature with the head and wings of an eagle and the body of a lion was said to know by instinct where buried treasure lay and to guard it vigilantly. Each piece is three-dimensional. Griffin: 5/8″ high.
Charm. Jump ring included.
25.00 solid sterling silver
115.00 solid 14 karat gold
Tie Tack. (not illustrated)
27.50 solid sterling silver
Stickpin.
27.50 solid sterling silver
130.00 solid 14 karat gold
(1.50 per item)
Philadelphia Museum of Art (member's discount 10%)

Sabertoothed Cat Charm

The Sabertoothed Cat is now extinct but a stylized version is available to wear as a charm on a bracelet or on a chain. Sterling silver. 3/8″ x 1″.
5.00 (0.75)
George C. Page Museum of La Brea Discoveries, Los Angeles (member's discount 10%)

Gold Scarab

Gold Scarab inscribed for Queen Mutnodjemet, wife of Pharaoh Horemheb (reigned 1350–1315 B.C.), from Egypt, XIX Dynasty. Worship of the life-giving sun and belief in rebirth were central to the religion of the ancient Egyptians. Thus almost every inhabitant of the Upper and Lower Kingdoms possessed a polished stone or glazed faience scarab, the symbol of these two primary forces in daily life. Only the wealthiest or most powerful could hope to possess a scarab as rare or as fine as this gold masterpiece. This 22 karat gold (6 pennyweight) reproduction was cast using the lost wax process. 3/4″ x 1/2″ x 5/16″.
410.00 (1.50)
The Brooklyn Museum (member's discount 15%)

Scarf Pins

Secure your scarf or enhance your lapel with one or more of these elegant scarf pins, reproduced from works of art in the collections of the Museum of Fine Arts, Boston.
Left: Ibex Head, finial of a gold necklace, Hellenistic, 3rd century B.C. 24 karat gold gilt on silver. 2″ long.
48.00 (3.50)
Center: Lily, Japanese gold pouch ornament, 19th century. Gold-plated on pewter. 2 1/8″ long.
7.50 (1.25)
Right: Butterfly, detail from a Japanese lady's hair ornament. Gold-plated on pewter. 1 3/8″ long.
7.50 (1.25)
Museum of Fine Arts, Boston (member's discount 10%)

Jewelry

French Horn
Stickpin and
Earrings

French Horn Stickpin and Earrings

This brass wind instrument, developed after a small
hunting horn in the 17th century, has been produced
in miniature especially for the Lincoln Center for the
Performing Arts, Inc. These realistically detailed horns
will surely be of interest to music enthusiasts. 1″
x 1½″.
Stickpin. 14 karat gold-plated sterling silver
20.00 (2.50)
Earrings. Available as clip-ons or pierced. (Please
specify when ordering.)
35.00 14 karat gold-plated sterling silver (3.00)
30.00 sterling silver (2.75)
Lincoln Center for the Performing Arts, Inc., New York
(does not publish a member's discount)

Spiral Pendant and Earrings

An exquisite set of jewelry for a special person.
Reproduced from a gold Greek earring of the 4th
century B.C., the pendant is the exact size of the
original, and the earrings are slightly reduced. An
elongated spiral form is enhanced by beautifully
decorated finials, reflecting Eastern design. The gold-
bead filigree work is an ancient technique called
granulation.
Pendant: 1¼″ long.
780.00 22 karat gold (2.50)
690.00 18 karat gold (2.50)
Earrings: Screw-back or pierced. (Please specify when
ordering.) 1″ long.
760.00 22 karat gold (2.50)
604.00 18 karat gold (2.50)
**Museum of Art, Rhode Island School of Design,
Providence** (member's discount 10%)

Late Roman Earrings

The original from which these elegantly simple
earrings have been reproduced in exact detail is
Roman, 1st–3rd century A.D. The upper end of the
crescent is drawn out into a fine curved gold pin,
ending in a widened conical point designed to pass
through the wearer's earlobe. Gold and cultured
pearls. 1⅛″ long.
400.00 22 karat gold (2.50)
380.00 18 karat gold (2.50)
**Museum of Art, Rhode Island School of Design,
Providence** (member's discount 10%)

Fan-shaped Earrings

The originals were found in the Greater Sinu
archaeological area in northeast Colombia. Pre-
Columbian period. Pierced only.
35.00 24 karat gold electroplate (2.00) G1401
325.00 14 karat gold (2.00) G5405
The Metropolitan Museum of Art, New York (member's
discount 25%)

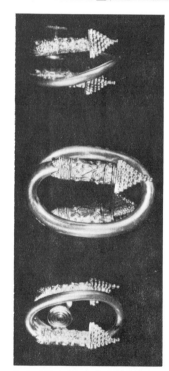

Spiral Pendant and Earrings   Late Roman Earrings

Fan-shaped
Earrings

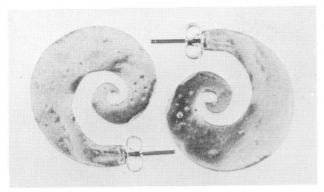
T'ang Dynasty Earrings

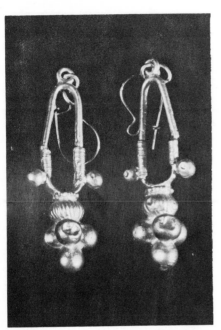
Greco-Roman Earrings

Ceremonial
Wedding Ring

Scarab Pendant and
Crocodile Ring

Jewelry

T'ang Dynasty Earrings

Cast from an original Chinese, T'ang Dynasty (7th to 10th century) earring, these reproductions are elegant in their simplicity. Gold-plated metal. Pierced only. 1″ wide.
5.00 (0.75)
The Minneapolis Institute of Arts (member's discount 10%)

Greco-Roman Earrings

A grape cluster design of golden balls hangs from the lower end of the graceful, elongated oval thread. The original gold earrings were discovered in Syria and date from A.D. 300–400. Screw-back or pierced. (Please specify when ordering.) Gold electroplated on pewter. 1⅝″ long.
8.50 (1.25)
Museum of Art, Rhode Island School of Design, Providence (member's discount 10%)

Ceremonial Wedding Ring

Ornate wedding rings were often owned by a synagogue and lent to the bride to wear during the first week of her marriage. The house on the top symbolizes the wish that the wearer will be blessed with the joys of a good home life. A reproduction of an 18th-century Italian ring, this can be worn by any bride, since the size is adjustable.
5.00 pewter (1.50) #P102
20.00 silver (2.00) #S102
The Jewish Museum, New York (member's discount 15%)

Scarab Pendant and Crocodile Ring

Both pieces of jewelry have been adapted from works in the collection of The Brooklyn Museum.
Scarab Pendant from a glazed faience scarab, Egypt, probably XXVI Dynasty (664–525 B.C.). 24 karat gold plate on beryllium copper. 1⅜″ x 1″ x ½″.
10.00 (2.00)
Crocodile Ring reproduced from a gold ring with a figure of a crocodile, Egypt, New Kingdom, or later. Ring size adjustable. 24 karat gold plate on beryllium copper. Crocodile: 1¼″.
7.00 (2.00)
The Brooklyn Museum (member's discount 15%)

Jewelry

Gold Signet Ring and Trapezoidal Gold Necklace Spacer

Two beautiful pieces of jewelry reproduced in 22 karat gold from originals in The Brooklyn Museum's collections.

Gold Signet Ring from Egypt, XXVI Dynasty. Though inscribed with the name of Cheops, the pharaoh who built the Great Pyramid of Giza before 2500 B.C., Neferibre, named as owner of the ring, was not his contemporary but a priest who lived during the XXVI Dynasty and was connected to a cult of the goddess Isis, which was itself associated with the famous pharaoh. 22 karat gold (9 pennyweight). Available in ring sizes: man's 10, woman's 6. (Please specify when ordering.) Width of face $^{15}/_{16}$".
380.00 (2.00)

Trapezoidal Gold Necklace Spacer from the Sudan, 6th century B.C. Though this type of trapezoid appears to be a Sudanese form of adornment, the hieroglyphs are Egyptian, reflecting the cultural influence Egypt exerted over the Sudan. The inscription also reflects this influence, styling the Sudan's King Aramatelgo "Son of Re, King of Upper and Lower Egypt." This 22 karat gold (29 pennyweight) reproduction was cast using the lost wax process. With black silk cord. $1^{3}/_{4}$" high.
990.00 (2.00)
The Brooklyn Museum (member's discount 15%)

Gold Signet Ring and Trapezoidal Gold Necklace Spacer

Ship Buckles

Charles W. Morgan, the last of the wooden whaling ships, built in 1841, is a national historical landmark, docked at Mystic Seaport. The buckle is set off with a deep intaglio effect (no protrusions) and is made in two different sizes for both men and women. Pewter.
Man's buckle. 2" x 2". Will fit belt up to $1^{3}/_{4}$" wide.
9.00 (1.00)
Lady's buckle. $1^{1}/_{4}$" x 2". Will fit belt up to 1" wide.
6.75 (1.00)
Mystic Seaport (member's discount 10%)

Ship Buckles

Gunston Hall Belt Buckle

The United States 3¢ commemorative stamp of Gunston Hall, issued in 1959, has been adapted in pewter as a belt buckle. Gunston Hall in Lorton, Virginia, was the home of George Mason, the author of the Fairfax Resolves, the first Constitution of Virginia, and the Virginia Declarations of Rights. This document, adopted by the Convention of Delegates at Williamsburg on June 12, 1776, was to become the basis of the Federal Bill of Rights. Pewter. $1^{1}/_{2}$" x 3".
6.00 (2.00)
Same design also available as:
3.00 key ring (1.00)
5.00 money clip (1.00)
7.50 stamp box (2.00)
Gunston Hall, Lorton, Virginia (member's discount 10%)

Gunston Hall Belt Buckle

Butcher Apron and Claw Mitts

Textiles and Fashion Accessories

Butcher Apron

You certainly will be head chef in the kitchen or at the grill wearing a unique apron featuring the giant of the dinosaur world, Tyrannosaurus Rex. Designed expressly for the Museum of Natural History, Carnegie Institute, by June Critchfield. Silkscreened natural seed canvas (adult). Silkscreened light-weight canvas (children). Brown on natural. Machine washable. Available for adults (one size fits all) and for children (one size fits all).
17.95 adult (1.50)
12.95 child (1.50)

Claw Mitts

To accompany the butcher apron, dinosaur claw mitts to protect your hands from hot pots and pans. Silkscreened canvas. Quilted palm; loops to hang. Dark brown on natural. Machine washable. One size fits all.
10.00 a pair (1.50)
Carnegie Institute, Pittsburgh
(member's discount 10%)

Chef Apron

These proud chefs on parade hold aloft trays bearing a bountiful feast for the gourmand. The silhouetted figures are part of a print by the 19th-century German artist Kaspar Braun entitled *The Banquet* in the collection of the Philadelphia Museum of Art. 50% cotton, 50% polyester. Denim weave. The ties and neck strap are faced with grosgrain ribbon in the same color as the design. The apron is adjustable to the height of the wearer by the gold-colored metal rings on the neck strap. Silkscreened. Black design and ribbon on natural or rust design and ribbon on natural. (Please specify color choice when ordering.) Machine washable. One size fits all.
14.50 (1.00)
Philadelphia Museum of Art
(member's discount 10%)

Barnyard Calico Apron

Brighten up kitchen capers with mother-and-daughter aprons. Functional yet festive, these aprons add a rustic touch to cookouts and casual dining affairs. 100% cotton calico. Blue or red calico (please specify) with yoke inset of contrasting colors. Mother: one size fits all. Daughter: one size fits 6–10, skirt length 25″. Machine washable, warm: dry on warm temperature.
24.00 mother (1.00)
16.00 daughter (1.00)
National Trust for Historic Preservation, Washington, D.C. (member's discount 10%)

Chef Apron

Barnyard Calico Apron

Textiles and Fashion Accessories

Needlework Charts

The Textile Museum Shop commissions fine line drawings based on the museum's extensive collection of handwoven, braided, knotted, and embroidered fabrics, assembled by George Hewitt Myers as a detailed record of the finest textile skills. Hand-drawn or printed needlework charts for use as lace, needlepoint, tapestry weaving, and cross-stitch patterns are not a recent invention but have been a textile designer's tool throughout the centuries.

#101: Persian Chart. Authentic 16th–17th-century Persian rug chart.

3.00 (0.50)

Florentine (Bargello) Charts: Carefully charted from authentic Renaissance silk fragments, they lend themselves to both traditional muted shades and vibrant contemporary colorings. Although each symbol represents a specific color, there is no reason why the individual cannot choose his own shades.

Top: Chart #10

Bottom: Chart #16

2.75 each (0.50)

The Textile Museum, Washington, D.C. (member's discount 20%)

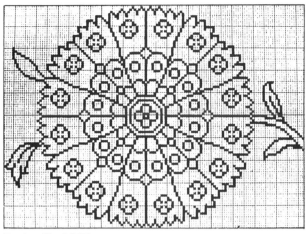

Persian Chart #101

Florentine Bargello Chart #10

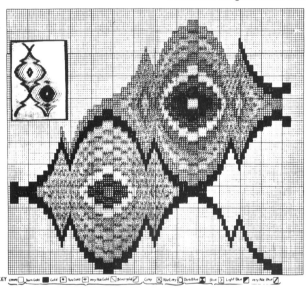

Florentine Bargello Chart #16

Design Transfer #123

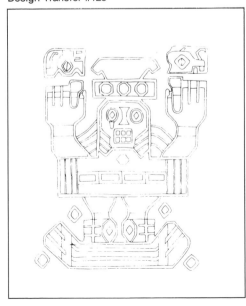

Textiles and Fashion Accessories

Hot Iron Line Design Transfers

Each transfer bag includes a copy of Textile Museum Bulletin #1, a description of the original piece of fabric or source of design, and stitch suggestions for either the needlepoint or crewel interpretation of the pattern. The dimensions given are of the actual design.

#123: Human Figure on Balsawood Raft, tapestry band, classic Tiahuanaco, about 700–1100. Textile Museum, 12¹/₂″ x 10″.
3.00 (0.50)

#121: Cranes, Mandarin Square, Ming dynasty, late 16th-early 17th century. Textile Museum. 12″ x 14″.
3.50 (0.50)

#103: Tent Band, Yomud Turkoman, 19th century. Textile Museum. 12″ x 20″.
3.50 (0.50)

#126: Tapestry Banner, Fon people, African, Dahomey. Museum of African Art. 14″ x 26″.
5.25 (0.50)

#116: Elizabethan Botanical Slips from the *Pictorial Common Place Book* of Thomas Trevelyon. Folger Shakespeare Library. Each slip measures 5″ square.
3.50 (0.50)

The Textile Museum, Washington, D.C. (member's discount 20%)

Design Transfer #126

Design Transfer #116

Design Transfer #121

Design Transfer #103

Textiles and Fashion Accessories

Quilted Wall Hangings

Marcia Aasmunstad has created these beautiful quilted cotton wall hangings for the Alexandria Bicentennial Museum Shop by adapting old quilt designs. As each piece is handmade, they will vary; however, you may request a border of polka dots or flowers. She has used earth colors: brown, rust, orange, green, and black. You may specify which color you would like to predominate. (Please indicate your preferences clearly.) 11″ square.
18.00 (2.00)
Alexandria Bicentennial Museum Shop (does not operate a membership program)

Lucretia Hall Fabric

The original coverlet from which this fabric was adapted may be seen in Tavern Hall in the Village of Old Deerfield, Massachusetts. Lucretia Hall, the innkeeper's wife, wove and embroidered the coverlet of her own design in the mid–1800s. 54% linen, 46% cotton. Spice (rust, tan, and gold) on charcoal. Repeat 36″.
14.60 per yard (1.50 for first yard plus 0.50 for each additional yard)
Historic Deerfield, Inc., Massachusetts (member's discount 10%)

Velveteen Pillows

Decorative pillows created exclusively for the Philadelphia Museum of Art, which have been inspired by works in the collection. They are batiked, using the Indonesian wax process of printing. In addition, there is hand quilting on the *Iris* pillow. 100% cotton. Removable slip-on covers. Dry clean for best results. 17″ square.
Iris. Detail of a handscroll *Flowers of the Four Seasons* by Sōsen (Japanese, active Kanei Era, 1624–43). Colors on paper. Shades of blue with touch of green and dark blue backing or blue flower on shades of moss greens with darker green backing. (Please specify color choice when ordering.)
Carousel Figure of a Pig. The first merry-go-rounds in Philadelphia were built in the 18th century, and amusement parks with carousels were well established by the 1860s, when steam power became widely available. This fanciful *Pig* is one of the best carousel figures that the Dentzel Company (American, 1867–1928) produced. It was carved by Salvatore Cernigliano, 1903–09, an immigrant Italian woodcarver. Painted basswood. Pink, red, green, and brown on off-white background with brown backing.
21.00 each (2.50)
Philadelphia Museum of Art (member's discount 10%)

Quilted Wall Hangings

Lucretia Hall Fabric

Velveteen Pillows

Pillow and Wall Hanging

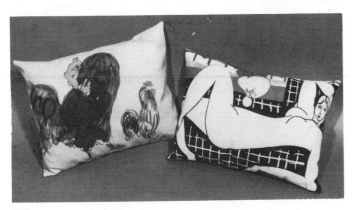

Pillows

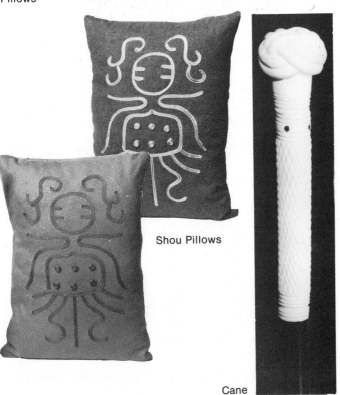

Shou Pillows

Cane

Textiles and Fashion Accessories

Pillow and Wall Hanging

Is it the year of the fish fossil? Why not?—there seems to be a year for everything. Be the first in your neighborhood to start your collection. The Natural History Museum, Carnegie Institute has commissioned artist Bill Godfrey to adorn both a pillow and wall hanging with his interpretation of a fish fossil from the collection.
Top: Pillow. Silkscreened cotton. Black design on white, with light gray backing. 15″ square.
20.00 (2.50)
Bottom: Trapunto Wall Hanging. Velvet. Silkscreened and quilted. Grays, browns, and black. 28″ x 28″ x 5″.
200.00 (8.00)
Carnegie Institute, Pittsburgh (member's discount 10%)

Pillows

Hand-painted canvas pillows, adapted from works in the permanent collection of The Baltimore Museum of Art.
Left: Two Roosters, based on a watercolor by Pablo Picasso. Tan canvas. Black roosters with red combs. Wipe clean only. 13″ x 17″.
Right: Pink Nude, based on a painting by Henri Matisse. Colors are basically pink, white, and yellow. Navy backing. Wipe clean only. 12″ x 17″.
27.50 each (1.75)
The Baltimore Museum of Art (member's discount 10%)

Shou Pillows

This symbol—the Chinese character *shou,* signifying longevity—is one of a hundred variations that appears on an embroidered satin tapestry from the Ch'ing Dynasty (1644–1911) in the collection of the Philadelphia Museum of Art. The tapestry, a birthday hanging, was embroidered with these symbols to wish the recipient good luck and a long life. Perhaps you would like to give such a gift and carry on the tradition. Pillows with removable zippered cover. Rayon ribbon on wool and rayon blend material. Light gray ribbon on medium gray or rust ribbon on burnt orange. (Please specify when ordering.) Dry clean. 18″ x 14″.
25.00 (2.50)
Philadelphia Museum of Art (member's discount 10%)

Cane

Turk's Head Knot carved cane head, reproduced in manmade "ivory"—Seaport Scrim©—from a 19th-century piece in the Mystic Seaport collection. Cane: 36″ long. Please specify black or mahogany.
25.00 (1.00)
Mystic Seaport (member's discount 10%)

Textiles and Fashion Accessories

Shoe Buttons

Shoe Buttons

High-grade shoe buttons from the era of spats, gaiters, and high button shoes. These are authentic early 1900s buttons, repackaged especially for McCall's at Old City Park, Dallas, waiting to be used in the 1970s. Package of 25.
0.75 (0.50)
McCall's at Old City Park, Dallas (member's discount not available)

Buttons

Buttons

Lost buttons always present a problem, but perhaps that problem has now been solved. You could replace the buttons on a blazer or coat with a set of handsome pewter ones. These have been copied from the uniform buttons worn by members of Col. John Haslet's Delaware Regiment, Continental Line (Delaware Blues) in 1776–77. 1″ diameter.
0.75 each (1.00)
The Historical Society of Delaware, Wilmington (member's discount 10%)

Patterns of History

These patterns have been precision drafted from originals in the 19th-century costume collection of The State Historical Society of Wisconsin. These are the first of a series which when complete will cover every major style from the period 1835–99. Patterns are well documented and clearly marked. Full directions are given for required undergarments such as hoops or bustles. Commentary drawn from contemporary fashion magazines is included; many small engravings are actually reproduced to show hair, hat, and wrap style proper for the dress. In the tradition of the 19th century, these patterns provide the basic cut; use of varied fabric and trimming will produce the kind of costume desired—anything from a house dress to a dinner or wedding gown. Each pattern is available in sizes 10, 12, and 14. (Please specify size when ordering.) Please order by the date of the pattern: 1865; 1893; 1835; 1840; 1857; or 1876.
10.00 each (0.75)
The State Historical Society of Wisconsin, Madison (member's discount 10%)

Patterns of History

Lion Head Belt

This belt buckle is an interpretation of the head of the famous lion that guards the main entrance to The New York Public Library. The beast is indeed proud with its elegant mane. Bronze buckle: 2½″ x 3¾″ on dark brown leather. Belt available in the following sizes: petite (26–28); small (30–32); medium (34–36); large (38–40). Please specify size when ordering.
40.00 (2.00)
The New York Public Library (member's discount 20%)

Lion Head Belt

Paper Billfolds

Umbrella

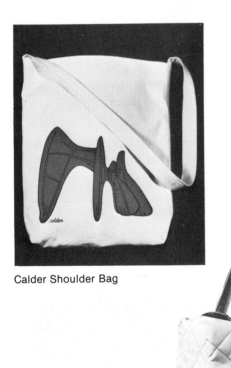

Calder Shoulder Bag

The Brooklyn
Museum
Garb Bag Kit

Textiles and Fashion Accessories

Paper Billfolds

Tired of the "leather look"? Then buy one of these durable sturdy paper billfolds, made in Japan for the Freer Gallery of Art. The full-color designs printed on the exteriors are based on works by Japanese Rimpa school artists with contrasting traditional Japanese textile designs on the interiors. 3⅝" x 7⅜".
Left: Thirty-Six Master Poets, by Sakai Hoitsu
Right: Cranes in Flight, by Nonomura Sotatsu
2.00 each (1.00)
Freer Gallery of Art, Washington, D.C. (does not operate a membership program)

Umbrella

The New York Botanical Garden celebrated the reopening of its Conservatory in March 1978. This crystal palace, an Italian Renaissance landmark, originally opened in 1901 but was closed to the public in 1975. As part of the celebration, the Botanical Garden produced this handsome umbrella, which adapts the architectural structure of the building as an overall design. Nylon. Tropical green on white. Hardwood cane-shaped handle. 34" high.
22.50 (3.00)
The New York Botanical Garden (member's discount 10%)

Calder Shoulder Bag

Alexander Calder (American, 1898–1976) produced many representational sculptures; however, following a visit to Mondrian's studio in 1930, he abandoned this work for abstract geometrical constructions involving primary colors. The reproduction on this bag is that of *La Grande Vitesse,* a stabile erected in 1969 in the Grand Rapids City Plaza. Canvas. Red on natural. Hand washable. 13" x 10" x 1".
10.00 (1.50)
Grand Rapids Art Museum (member's discount 10%)

The Brooklyn Museum Garb Bag Kit

You will be truly amazed with the versatility of this incredibly spacious and fashionable Garb Bag, which measures a full 11½" high by 20" wide by 9" deep. This commodious quilted bag is designed in natural cotton canvas with The Brooklyn Museum symbol, silkscreened in deep brown, on the front pocket. The kit comes complete with pre-cut fabric including lining, zipper, and easy-to-follow, step-by-step, illustrated instructions. Hand or machine washable.
16.50 (2.00)
The Brooklyn Museum (member's discount 15%)

Textiles and Fashion Accessories

Gift Tote and Briefcase

The Corcoran Shop logo appears on two very stylish bags. One or both will surely meet your needs, whether it be to carry your shoes and purchases, or to carry your work home and back again to the office.
Gift Tote. Navy on white canvas. 5″ x 7″ x 3″.
3.75 (1.00)
Briefcase. Black on beige canvas with black handles and front pocket. 10½″ x 14½″ x 3″.
12.00 (1.00)
The Corcoran Gallery of Art, Washington, D.C.
(member's discount 10%)

Gift Tote and Briefcase

Briefcase/Tote

Sling this bag over your shoulder as a tote or remove the strap and carry it to work as a briefcase. A bold geometric design is taken from a *Manuscript of Weaver's Draughts,* dated 1766, belonging to a Johann D. . ., from Darmstadt, Germany. During the 18th century, itinerant weavers wandered the countryside plying their trade, with their looms attached to their wagons. These men carried pattern books of designs to show their prospective customers what was available. The patterns would be reproduced exactly as a double cotton coverlet, usually in two or three colors in wool, linen, or cotton. Textured light khaki. Silkscreened. Dark blue on khaki. Zipper. Bonded blue lining. 3 small inside pockets. Removable shoulder strap. Hand wash or gentle machine wash. 12″ x 15″ x 3″.
21.50 (2.50)
Philadelphia Museum of Art (member's discount 10%)

Briefcase/Tote

Opera Evening Bag

Attend the opera in style by carrying your lorgnettes, program, and other necessities in an evening bag announcing the titles of your favorite operas. Gold lettering on black satin. Zipper closing and long shoulder strap. 5″ x 5½″.
12.95 (1.75)
Lincoln Center for the Performing Arts, Inc., New York (does not publish a member's discount)

Opera
Evening Bag

The IMA Bag

What does IMA stand for? Indianapolis Museum of Art. It's their bag and could be yours! The logo of the museum makes an attractive repeat design. Canvas. Inside zippered pocket. Navy on natural with navy trim or brown on natural with brown trim. (Please specify color choice when ordering.) 15″ x 13″.
12.00 (2.00)
Indianapolis Museum of Art (member's discount 10%)

The IMA Bag

"To, Te"

"To Be" Tote Bag

Ark in the Park

St. Louis Art
Museum Tote Bag

Yale Tote Bag

Textiles and Fashion Accessories

"To, Te"

Design inspired by an early 18th-century American weather vane in the collection of the Shelburne Museum, Inc. Canvas. Brown design on white. 14½" x 13".
8.50 (1.50)
Shelburne Museum, Inc., Vermont (does not operate a membership program)

"To Be" Tote Bag

In a quandary? This tote bag will not solve your problem, as it only states it more clearly "To be or not to be." A consolation might be that you are in the same predicament as Shakespeare's famous character Hamlet. The calligraphy is bold and gives the bag a very contemporary look. 100% cotton duck. Silkscreened. Black on rust with white trim. 12" x 16" x 3".
9.95 (1.00)
The Folger Shakespeare Library, Washington, D.C. (member's discount 15%)

Ark in the Park

The Cleveland Museum of Natural History tote bag features the animals as they march two by two to the Ark in the Park, which is the shop in the museum. Get into step by using this carry-all. 100% cotton duck. Silkscreened. Black on tan. 15" x 13" x 7½".
19.00 (1.50)
The Cleveland Museum of Natural History (member's discount 10%)

Yale Tote Bag

The Yale is a mythological beast with double horns and a forked tail. Another charming creature to add to your collection of fanciful animals. Canvas. Blue design on white with blue straps. Available in two sizes.
6.50 14" x 16" x 3" (1.00)
6.00 12" x 14" x 3" (1.00)
Yale University Art Gallery, New Haven (member's discount 10%)

Tote Bag

Ideal for carrying the groceries, a picnic, books, etc. A stylized beast adapted from a bronze Horse's Cheek Piece, Iranian, Luristan, c. 1000 B.C. Silkscreened canvas. Red on natural. Metal snap for closing. 14" x 10" x 5".
6.95 (1.00)
The St. Louis Art Museum (member's discount 10%)

Textiles and Fashion Accessories

Double-Headed
Eagle Tote Bag

Double-Headed Eagle Tote Bag

In Panama the Double-Headed Eagle, from which this motif was adapted, was employed to placate the gods and ward off evil spirits. Its magic will work for you as well when you carry the bag. Canvas. Inside pocket. Silkscreened. Navy on gray or brick on natural. (Please specify color choice when ordering.) 11″ x 15″.
13.50 (1.95)
Pin shown on bag. Gold-plated pewter.
10.00 (1.95)
Worcester Art Museum (member's discount 10%)

Sabertoothed Cat Tote Bag

A stylized version of the sabertoothed cat, which is now extinct, has been adopted as the logo for the Los Angeles County Museum of Natural History. Silkscreened canvas. Black stripes and rust cats on taupe with black handles. 14″ x 16″ x 4″.
11.00 (1.50)
Los Angeles County Museum of Natural History (member's discount 10%)

Sabertoothed Cat Tote Bag

Tabby Tote Bag

Especially for cat lovers! The Tabby Cat is a reproduction of a 19th-century lithographed rag toy in the Museum of the City of New York's toy collection. Canvas. Black printing on natural. 14″ x 12″ x 3″.
12.00 (1.25)
Museum of the City of New York (member's discount 20%)

Tabby Tote Bag

Dragon Tote

The perfect size to hold that extra pair of shoes. The dragon motif is adapted from a piece of Chinese pottery, dating from the Six Dynasties Period. Silkscreened canvas. Chinese red on natural or white on navy. (Please specify color choice when ordering.) Gentle machine wash. 11″ x 7½″ x 3½″.
10.00 (1.50)
Museum of Art, Rhode Island School of Design, Providence (member's discount 10%)

Strawbery Banke Tote Bag

The Guild of Strawbery Banke®, has selected its logo as an all-over design to enhance this bag. Canvas. Handscreened. Red straps. Red on white or red on putty. (Please specify color choice when ordering.) 10″ x 14″ x 5″.
17.00 (1.50)
The Guild of Strawbery Banke®, Inc., Portsmouth (member's discount 10%)

Dragon Tote

Strawbery Banke Tote Bag

National Trust
Tote Bag

The Detroit
Institute of
Arts Bag

The Newark
Museum Bag

Museum of Fine
Arts Tote

Textiles and Fashion Accessories

National Trust Tote Bag

The eagle appears as the logo of the National Trust in trapunto appliqué on a natural canvas bag. Inside pocket. Blue design and trim or gold design and trim. (Please specify color choice when ordering.) 13″ x 11½″ x 5″.
15.00 (2.00)
National Trust for Historic Preservation, Washington, D.C. (member's discount 10%)

The Detroit Institute of Arts Bag

Charles J. Byrne executed the design of *Renaissance Arches* (the entrance to the museum) in 1976. Silkscreened canvas. Black on taupe. Removable lacquered wooden dowels. 13″ x 15″ x 7″. Hand wash or dry clean.
15.00 (1.50)
Detroit Institute of Arts (member's discount 10%)

The Newark Museum Bag

Embellished with the names of famous stars of the silent screen, this bag's design was created in conjunction with the museum's major bicentennial exhibition, "Making Movies in New Jersey." The exhibition was a tribute to achievement in America—especially New Jersey—in the technical and artistic development of movies. New Jersey was the movie capital of the world in the early days. Silkscreened canvas. Black on white. Removable lacquered wooden dowels. 15″ x 15″ x 7½″. Hand wash or dry clean.
10.00 (1.50)
Newark Museum (member's discount 10%)

Museum of Fine Arts Tote Bag and Scarf

MFA, the museum logo in a striking all-over design, enhances this ensemble.
Tote Bag. Heavy canvas. Navy blue and green with white on navy. 13½″ x 10½″ x 3½″.
10.50 (1.95)
Scarf. 100% polyester. Navy blue and green on white. 22″ square.
6.50 (1.25)
Museum of Fine Arts, Boston (member's discount 10%)

Textiles and Fashion Accessories

Art Scarves

Art Scarves

Two distinctive scarves to add to your collection. Both have been adapted from favorite works in the collection of the Museum of Arts, Carnegie Institute. Each is 100% cotton. Silkscreened.
Left: The Thousand and One Nights. In the last years, Henri Matisse (French, 1869–1954) created brilliant, strong, and gay paper cutouts and stencils. The original, a gouache on cut and pasted paper, was executed in 1950. 8 colors: black, light and dark blue, yellow, green, purple, red, and fuchsia on white. 24″ square.
25.00 (2.00)
Right: Composition (Constellation), 1955, by Jean Arp (French, b. Germany, 1887–1966). Black and gray on white. 26″ square.
20.00 (2.00)
Carnegie Institute, Pittsburgh (member's discount 10%)

Unicorn Scarf

Of all the fabulous creatures, the unicorn is the one most familiar to the modern world. It has never ceased to fascinate mankind. One such unicorn prances around on this scarf designed exclusively for The Folger Shakespeare Library. As it is available in several colors, you are sure to find one that will complement your wardrobe. Cotton and polyester blend. Silkscreened. Navy, cocoa, teal, or burgandy on natural. (Please specify color choice when ordering.) 22″ square.
5.95 (1.00)
The Folger Shakespeare Library, Washington, D.C. (member's discount 15%)

Unicorn Scarf

Chinese Rug Scarf

The Textile Museum has reproduced an elegant 19th-century Chinese rug on a scarf. The dark blue symmetrical all-over blossom and vine design is on a pale gold background with light blue stripe and dark blue fret borders. Certain to enhance any wardrobe. Cotton and polyester. 20″ square.
7.95 (0.55)
The Textile Museum, Washington, D.C. (member's discount 20%)

Chinese Rug Scarf

Worcester Art Museum Scarfs

Two bold abstract designs inspired by contemporary works in the museum's collections. Cotton and polyester. Each scarf measures 22″ x 21½″.
Top: Blue leaf on white.
Bottom: Terra cotta abstract on white.
6.50 each (1.25)
Worcester Art Museum (member's discount 10%)

Worcester Art Museum Scarfs

Gunston Hall Scarf

Museum
Draculas

Indonesian Scarf

Butterfly Shawl

Textiles and Fashion Accessories

Gunston Hall Scarf

A prominent feature at Gunston Hall is the splendidly carved woodwork of William Buckland. Created by Claudia Wuigk, the design on this scarf was taken from the wood carvings in the Palladian Drawing Room. 77% dacron, 23% cotton. Red on bone. 29″ square.
10.00 (2.00)
Gunston Hall, Lorton, Virginia (member's discount 10%)

Museum Draculas

The design of this multicolored silk scarf in brilliant red, blue, yellow, white, black, and green was originally conceived by Los Angeles artist Billy Al Bengston for a large museum banner. The Modern and Contemporary Art Council then commissioned him to adapt the striking iris motif as a handsome scarf. Pure silk. Limited edition; signed and dated by the artist. 50½″ x 13¼″.
27.50 (1.50)
Los Angeles County Museum of Art (member's discount 10%)

Indonesian Scarf

An Indonesian sarong in the Los Angeles County Museum of Art's textile collection has been reproduced on this scarf. Polyester. Sepia and indigo blue on an ivory ground. 27″ square.
7.50 (1.50)
Los Angeles County Museum of Art (member's discount 10%)

Butterfly Shawl

This magnificent shawl derives its exuberant pattern of butterflies and flowers from a mid-19th-century porcelain platter made for the Chinese export trade. A fine wrap for cool summer evenings, its generous size and vibrant colors make it a lovely decorative addition to the house as well—as a table cover or wall hanging. Multi-colored. Silkscreened. Pure wool challis. Fringed, 51″ square.
27.50 (2.00) K1897
The Metropolitan Museum of Art, New York (member's discount 25%)

Textiles and Fashion Accessories

Brooklyn Museum Ties

Fashion statements for men, translated from 16th-century textile designs from The Brooklyn Museum collection of fabrics. Choose from two versatile and timely patterns. 100% cotton which is colorfast to water and solvents, soil and stain resistant, vat-dyed, and preshrunk. Double-lined. 4″.

Left: Izmir. The first European record of Indian polychrome silks worked in chain stitch on cotton attributes this style to immigrant Moorish washerwomen in the 16th century. The dissected, stylized flowers of this example were adapted to a printed fabric from a square cushion cover thought to be Indian embroidery of the mid-19th century. Blue or brown. (Please specify color choice when ordering.)

Right: Ankara. This repeated motif was developed from the edge of a design found on a border fragment of embroidered linen. The pronounced, angular character of the motif derives from the Russian overcast filling or four-sided stitch of the original work, and is of Italian or Persian 16th-century influence. Salmon or sable. (Please specify color choice when ordering.)

8.50 each (2.00)
The Brooklyn Museum (member's discount 15%)

Apollo Tie

In commemoration of space flight, the Smithsonian has produced a tie depicting the Apollo Module which is on permanent display at the National Air and Space Museum. Woven polyester. White and red on navy blue.

6.50 (1.00) #336560
Smithsonian Institution, Washington, D.C. (member's discount 10%)

National Trust Necktie

This tie features the eagle, which is the logo used by the National Trust for Historic Preservation. 100% polyester. White on navy, white on burgundy, gold on green, or red on black. (Please specify color choice when ordering.) Hand washable. 3¹⁄₂″ wide.

8.00 (1.00)
National Trust for Historic Preservation, Washington, D.C. (member's discount 10%)

Fish Fossil Tie

This contemporary bold design is not what it seems! It is actually a rendering of a fish fossil, adapted from a fossil in the Museum of Natural History, Carnegie Institute. 100% polyester. Silkscreened. Black design on bone. 3¹⁄₂″ wide.

10.00 (2.00)
Carnegie Institute, Pittsburgh (member's discount 10%)

Brooklyn Museum Ties

Apollo Tie

National Trust Necktie

Fish Fossil Tie

Brontosaurus
Necktie

Textiles and Fashion Accessories

Brontosaurus Necktie

The Brontosaurus, a dinosaur thought to have measured over 70 feet long and weighed over 30 tons, has been miniaturized on a necktie. The tie was woven in England exclusively for the American Museum of Natural History. 100% texturized polyester. Cream dinosaur on dark blue, brown, burgundy, or forest green. (Please specify color choice when ordering.) 3³/₄″ wide.
12.00 (1.00)
American Museum of Natural History, New York (member's discount 10%)

Five Senses Tee-shirt

A striking adaptation of an Egyptian cartouche depicting the five senses: seeing, hearing, smelling, tasting, and touching. 100% cotton. White design on navy. Adults' sizes: 34–36, 38–40, 42–44. Children's sizes: 6–8, 10–12, 14–16. (Please specify size when ordering.)
3.25 adults, **2.75** children (1.25)
Huntsville Museum of Art (member's discount not available on this item)

Five Senses
Tee-shirt

Alexander Calder Tee-shirt

Design based on Alexander Calder's whimsical drawings. The artist has even lent his signature. Cotton and polyester. Silkscreened. Red, blue, and black on white. Washable. Adults' sizes: small, medium, large, extra large. Children's sizes: 6, 8, 10. (Please specify size when ordering.)
5.00 adults, **4.50** children (1.50)
Whitney Museum of American Art, New York (discount not available with regular membership; higher category member's discount 25%)

Alexander
Calder Tee-shirt

Dinosaur Tee-shirts and Sweatshirts

Don your favorite dinosaur from the selection offered by the Carnegie Institute: Diplodocus; Pteranodon (illustrated); Stegosaurus (illustrated); Triceratops; and Tyrannosaurus. 92% cotton, 8% acrylic. Silkscreened. Black on white. Both tee-shirts and sweatshirts are available in the following sizes: adults' sizes small, medium, large, extra large, children's sizes 8, 12, 16. Please specify which shirt you want and the size when ordering.
5.95 adult's tee-shirt (1.25)
4.95 child's tee-shirt (1.25)
9.95 adult's sweatshirt (1.25)
8.95 child's sweatshirt (1.25)
Carnegie Institute, Pittsburgh (member's discount 10%)

Dinosaur Tee-shirts and Sweatshirts

Textiles and Fashion Accessories

Wagonette Tee-shirt and Sweatshirt

Wagonette Tee-shirt and Sweatshirt

The original Wagonette—or early bus—was made in America in the 1830s, and is now on display at the Carriage Museum at Stony Brook.

Tee-shirt. Silkscreened cloth. White on navy. Adult sizes: small, medium, and large. Children's sizes: small, medium, and large. (Please specify size when ordering.)
5.95 adults, **4.50** children
Sweatshirt. Silkscreened cloth. Brown on yellow. Cold water wash; do not put in dryer. Sizes: small, medium, and large. (Please specify size when ordering.)
8.50
(1.00 per order)
The Museums at Stony Brook, New York (member's discount 10%)

Bear Tee-shirt

The Grizzly's Last Stand, a bronze statue executed by sculptor Louis Paul Jonas, has been adopted as the logo of the Denver Museum of Natural History. He stands proudly on this tee-shirt. 100% cotton. Color choice: white on black or red, blue on yellow or tan, or navy blue on heather blue. Sizes: Adult's or children's small, medium, large, and extra large. (Please specify color and size when ordering.)
3.90 adults, **3.00** children (1.25)
Denver Museum of Natural History
(discount not available with regular membership; higher category member's discount 10%)

Bear Tee-shirt

Tee-shirts and Tote Bags

Several museums have followed the coordinated look in the world of fashion and produced both the easy-to-wear tee-shirt and the matching tote in the same design.

Mostly Mozart Tee-Shirt and Tote Bag

These coordinates were produced in conjunction with the 1978 Mostly Mozart Festival held at the Lincoln Center for the Performing Arts in the summer of 1977, honoring the Austrian composer.
Tee-shirt. 100% cotton. Silkscreened. Black Gothic lettering, white notes on red. The main theme of the slow movement, Piano Concerto No. 21, appears on both the front and back. Adults' sizes: small, medium, large, extra large. Children's sizes: small, medium, large. (Please specify size when ordering.)
6.00 adults, **5.00** children (1.20)
Tote bag. Polycanvas. Silkscreened. Red lettering, black notes on off-white. Hand wash. 14″ x 17″.
10.00 (1.50)
Lincoln Center for the Performing Arts, Inc., New York
(does not publish a member's discount)

Mostly Mozart
Tee-shirt and
Tote Bag

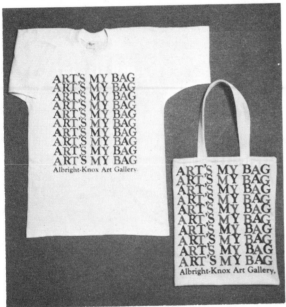

The Franklin Institute
Tee-shirt and Tote Bag

Art's My Bag Tee-shirt and Tote Bag

Loch Haven Tee-shirt and Tote Bag

Textiles and Fashion Accessories

The Franklin Institute Tee-shirt and Tote Bag

An original design by Frank Nofer, depicting the various areas of science which may be explored at The Franklin Institute Science Museum, is vividly produced in four colors: red, blue, yellow, and black.
Tee-shirt. 100% white cotton. Silkscreened. Adults' sizes: small, medium, large. Children's sizes: small, medium, large. (Please specify size when ordering.)
4.95 adults, **3.95** children (0.75)
Tote bag. Natural canvas. Silkscreened. Warm water wash. 13″ x 14½″.
5.75 (1.00)
The Franklin Institute Science Museum, Philadelphia (member's discount 10%)

Art's My Bag Tee-Shirt and Tote Bag

The Albright-Knox Art Gallery commissioned Tony and Eleanor Paine of Canada to produce this bold repeat design.
Tee-shirt. Cotton and synthetic. Silkscreened. Alternate red and black letters on white. Machine washable. Adults' sizes: small, medium, large, extra large. Children's sizes: small, medium, large, extra large. (Please specify size when ordering.)
6.00 adults, **5.00** children (2.00)
Tote bag. Canvas. Silkscreened. Alternate red and black lettering on natural. Machine washable in lukewarm water and mild soap. 15½″ x 13¼″.
10.00 (2.00)
Albright-Knox Art Gallery, Buffalo (member's discount 10%)

Loch Haven Tee-Shirt and Tote Bag

Before you head for the sunny South, bedeck yourself with this tee-shirt and tote from one of Florida's museums, the Loch Haven Art Center. The museum's logo appears on both. In addition the National Art Education slogan "You Gotta Have Art" appears on the tee-shirt.
Tee-shirt. 50% cotton, 50% polyester. Silkscreened. Red, tan, yellow, orange, and light blue. Sizes: small, medium, large, and extra large. (Please specify size when ordering.)
5.00 (1.00)
Tote Bag. 100% cotton canvas. Silkscreened. Navy on white, with 26″ white webbing straps. Washable. 11½″ x 11½″ x 3″.
10.00 (1.25)
Loch Haven Art Center, Orlando, Florida (member's discount 10%)

Needlework

Florentine Pillow

Florentine Pillow

A vibrant design, to be worked in bargello, has been taken from a large European carpet made around 1730, and is now on display in the Dwight-Barnard House at Historic Deerfield. Gradating shades of yellow, green, blue, and brown. Contains #13 canvas, Paterna Persian yarn, and instructions. 12″ square.
12.00 (1.25) #2
Historic Deerfield, Inc., Massachusetts (member's discount 10%)

The St. Louis Art Museum Collection

Four bold designs have been adapted for needlepoint kits for you to work from original works in the St. Louis Art Museum. Includes hand-painted canvas, Paterna Persian yarn, needle, instructions, and information regarding the original work of art.
Top left: Oceanie, La Mer, silkscreen stencil on linen by Henri Matisse (French, 1869-1954). Tan and cream. #14 canvas. 15″ square.
36.00 (1.00)
Top center: Flowers, detail from a *Friendship Quilt,* Baltimore, 1848. Quilted and appliqued cotton. White, red, green, and gold. #14 canvas. 15″ square.
45.00 (1.00)
Top right: Composition of Red and White, 1938-42, oil on canvas by Piet Mondrian (Dutch, 1872-1944). White, red and black. #10 canvas. 14″ square.
22.50 (1.00)
Bottom: Kalota, 1963, oil on canvas by Victor Vasarely (French, b. Hungary 1908). Red, blue, and orange. #14 canvas. 14″ square.
36.00 (1.00)
The St. Louis Art Museum (member's discount 10%)

The St. Louis Art Museum Collection

Oriental Needlepoint Kits

Flowers and animals from the Orient have been adapted from various media for needlepoint kits. The original works of art are in the distinguished Oriental collection of the Freer Gallery of Art. Contents of each kit: silkscreened cotton canvas, Persian yarn, needle, and instuctions.
Chrysanthemums. Detail of a Japanese fan painting, by Ogata Korin (1658-1716), Edo period, Rimpa school. Blue, green, and lilac on gold background. #14 canvas. 12″ square.
25.00 (1.00)
Foo Dogs. Detail from a Chinese silk chair cover. Ch'ing Dynasty, Ch'ien-lung period (1736-95). Green, blue, tan, and coral on light coral ground. #18 canvas. 14½″ x 16½″.
37.50 (1.00)
Phoenixes. Chinese silk tapestry. Ming Dynasty, 15th century. Shades of blue, taupe, beige, sienna, and green. #18 canvas. 14½″ x 16½″.
37.50 (1.00)
Flying Goose. Chinese pottery dish. T'ang Dynasty (A.D.618–906). Blue, gold, and green on white ground. 14″ diameter.
30.00 (1.00)
Freer Gallery of Art, Washington, D.C. (does not operate a membership program)

Oriental Needlepoint Kits

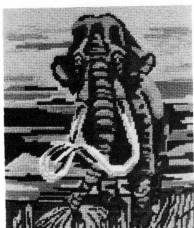

Imperial Mammoth

Sabertoothed Cat

Chinese Cat

Bear Cub

Needlework

Imperial Mammoth

The Imperial Mammoth, an extinct elephant, roamed the North American continent in the Pleistocene epoch. The majesty of the beast will certainly be felt when the canvas is worked as either a hanging or a pillow. It is adapted from a mural by Elma and Jerome Connolly in the George C. Page Museum. The mammoth is worked in browns and oranges against a background of blues, oranges, and greens. Contents: #12 cotton canvas, wool yarn, needle, and instructions. 12″ x 10″.
15.00 (1.50)
George C. Page Museum of La Brea Discoveries, Los Angeles (member's discount 10%)

Sabertoothed Cat

Three sleek sabertoothed cats of white, beige, and tan, the logo of the Los Angeles County Museum of Natural History, stalk across a brown needlepoint canvas. Kit includes handscreened cotton canvas, wool yarn, needle, and instructions. 12″ square.
14.00 (1.50)
Los Angeles County Museum of Natural History (member's discount 10%)

Chinese Cat

The original Chinese porcelain cat was hollow, open on the bottom, with a slit on the back and eye sockets empty to let light shine through. It was made during the Ch'ing Dynasty, K'ang Hsi period, 1662-1722. The adaptation in needlepoint is worked in purple, lavender, sea green, and beige with a touch of white. The tweed effect is achieved by combining the purple and beige. Kit includes handpainted #14 interlocking canvas, Paterna Persian yarn, needle, and instructions. The finished cat is shaped. 10″ x 14″.
25.75 (1.50)
Philadelphia Museum of Art (member's discount 10%)

Bear Cub

Hook an adorable cuddly bear cub. It is sure to delight any child, and many grown-ups too. He is adapted from a color lithograph, 1938, by Elveyenii Ivanovich Charushin (Russian, b. 1901). He is worked in three shades of brown with touches of white, green, and orange. Red felt tongue. Kit includes: silkscreened polyester washable rug canvas, precut acrylic rug yarn, rug wool for eyes, nose, and claws, felt, latch hook, needle, and instructions. 24″ x 18″.
28.00 (1.50)
Philadelphia Museum of Art (member's discount 10%)

Needlework

Pillow and Lamb

Pillow and Lamb

Two crewel kits adapted from The Mercer Museum collection of early Americana.

Pillow: Except for the rooster in the center of the pillow, which was originally a weather vane, the designs were inspired by butter molds. Worked in brown on natural homespun fabric. Kit includes hand-screened fabric, yarn, and instructions. 10″ square.
6.00 (1.75)

Lamb: In its original form, this toy lamb would have been a piece of candy, since it is adapted from an early-20th-century candy mold used by Thomas Mills & Son, Philadelphia. Worked in gray wool on charcoal gray fabric. Kit includes hand-screened fabric, yarn, and instructions. 8″ x 10″.
6.00 (1.75)

The Mercer Museum, Doylestown, Pennsylvania (member's discount not available on these items)

Sun or Lion's Head

Sun or Lion's Head

A Spanish glazed earthenware ceiling tile, dating from the late 15th century, was the inspiration for this needlepoint kit. Such tiles *(socarrats)* were decorated with animals—both real and fanciful—and geometric patterns, ships, and figures of men and women. Painted by artists working in simple earth tones, the plaques were set in rows in the ceiling between the supporting beams of the roof. The designs, executed in vigorous broad brushstrokes, reflect their Moorish or Islamic ancestry. The center of production for the tiles was Paterna in the province of Valencia. The bold design is worked in red-brown, beige, and dark brown. Includes screened #12 interlocking canvas, Paterna Persian yarn, two needles, and instructions. Design area 14″ square. Canvas size 18″ square.
25.00 (2.50)

Walters Art Gallery, Baltimore (member's discount 10%)

Elephant and Horse

Elephant and Horse

These designs are adapted for needlepoint from the resplendent woven silk tapestry robe of a Buddhist priest (Chinese, K'ang-hsi period, 1662-1722). They are worked in 11 or 12 colors. Each kit contains silkscreened #13 canvas, Persian yarn, instructions, and a description of the original work of art.

Elephant (L1392). Design size: 15″ x 15½″.

Horse (L1393). Design size: 13″ x 16½″.
25.00 each (2.00)

The Metropolitan Museum of Art, New York (member's discount 25%)

Knight on Horseback

Needlework

Knight on Horseback

Put your talent to work and create your own knight in shining armor. This embroidery kit was inspired by armor from the Kienbusch Collection of Armor and Arms in the Philadelphia Museum of Art. The knight's suit is armor for the tilt, Austrian, Innsbruck, c. 1560. It is made of steel and bears the armorer's mark of Anton Hörburger. The horse is bedecked in composed horse armor of etched steel, German, 1510-60. Quilt as you embroider. Worked in black with red plume on gray. Contents: silkscreened polyester fabric, quilt batting, cheesecloth, DMC cotton embroidery thread, needle, and instructions. 25″ x 21″.
17.00 (1.50)
Philadelphia Museum of Art (member's discount 10%)

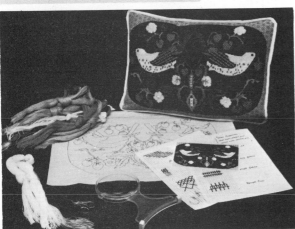

The Strawberry Thief

The Strawberry Thief

William Morris (English, 1836-96) is considered one of the great Victorians. He was a poet, artist, craftsman, designer, social reformer, and printer. He founded the famous design firm of Morris and Co. of London, well known for its wallpaper, chintzes, furniture, tiles, and stained glass. He worked his first embroidery himself at the age of 21. He executed many embroidery designs including *The Strawberry Thief,* from which this needlepoint kit has been expertly adapted. Since the design is only outlined on the canvas, you can create your own color scheme with the 18 colors of yarn provided. A sufficient quantity of each color is available, so they are interchangeable. For the purists who want an exact rendering of the original, a full-color reproduction is included. Contents: #16 canvas, yarn, history of design, full-color picture, and instructions. 14″ x 21″.
50.00 (1.00)
Delaware Art Museum, Wilmington (member's discount 10%)

Hand-painted Canvas

Hand-painted Canvas

The Boat Builders, 1873, by Winslow Homer (American, 1836-1910), has been adapted for needlework. The colors used on the canvas are those of the original painting: blue, yellow, sand, brown, and rust. This is not a kit. You are purchasing only the hand-painted #12 canvas. You supply the yarn and the ingenuity. 10″ x 17″.
18.75 (0.50)
Indianapolis Museum of Art (member's discount 10%)

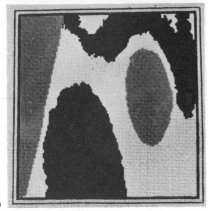

Rooftop

Rooftop

Alexander Calder (American, 1898-1976) was known for his use of primary colors. A bold design, worked in red, black, and white, adapted from a painting executed for the rooftop of the County Building in Grand Rapids in 1974. Kit includes hand-painted rug canvas, wool rug yarn, needle, and instructions. 12″ square.
24.95 (1.00)
Grand Rapids Art Museum (member's discount 10%)

Needlework

Doorstop

From one house to another. Keep your door open, letting in the sun and clean air, with a needlepoint doorstop, a replica of Gunston Hall. The house is worked in dark and light terra cotta, and the detailing is worked in brown, gold, green, and shades of gray. Includes #12 canvas, yarn, wool, and instructions. You will need to supply the brick and stuffing for the roof. 7″ x 8″ x 2½″.
35.00 (2.00)
Gunston Hall, Lorton, Virginia (member's discount 10%)

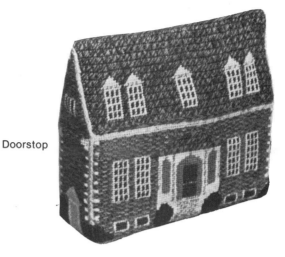

Doorstop

The Medieval Town

Many a hilltop of France and Flanders wears a crown of walls and towers. Such a town surmounts the tapestry *Mille Fleurs Armorial,* Franco-Flemish (Tournai), c. 1500, bearing the arms of an unknown nobleman. The original hangs in the collection of The Fine Arts Museums of San Francisco. Three details, *The Church, The Bird,* and *The Castle,* have been adapted for needlepoint and are worked in 19 colors of yarn: greens, reds, tans, and white. Basket weave stitch is recommended for execution, the design area being worked first. Included in each kit: #18 canvas, Paterna Persian yarn, and instructions. 13½″ x 16″. Please specify by design when ordering.
Top center: The Church
Bottom left: The Bird
Bottom right: The Castle
45.00 each kit (1.50)
M. H. de Young Memorial Museum, San Francisco (member's discount 20%)

The Medieval Town

Drake House Sampler

A charming sampler to be worked in red, green, gold, blue, and brown. It has been recently adapted from an original in the Drake House Museum. Kit contains silkscreened linen, needle, thread, instructions, and a history of the museum. 10″ x 13″.
10.00 (1.00)
Drake House Museum, Plainfield, New Jersey (member's discount not available)

Drake House Sampler

Sampler

The Martha Stearns Sampler was designed exclusively for The Guild of Strawbery Banke. It features stitches and motifs used in Early American crewel work. The sampler is worked in multicolored yarns on white linen. Contents: linen, Appleton yarn, transfer, and instructions. 20″ x 12″.
10.00 (1.00)
The Guild of Strawbery Banke®, Inc., Portsmouth (member's discount 10%)

Strawbery Banke Sampler

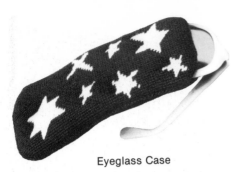

Eyeglass Case

Floral Pillows

Tennis
Racquet Cover

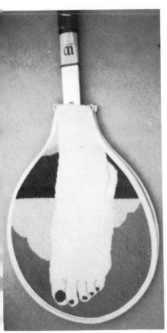

Latch-Hook Rug

Needlework

Eyeglass Case

Stars taken from decorative details employed by architect Frank Furness in the historic Pennsylvania Academy of Fine Arts, Philadelphia, completed in 1876. Stars are worked in either silver and white on light blue background, or white on navy background. (Please specify color choice when ordering.) Kit includes canvas, yarn, needle, and instructions. 6″ long, 2″ wide.
10.00 (1.00)
Pennsylvania Academy of Fine Arts, Philadelphia (member's discount 10%)

Floral Pillows

Taken from the many floral decorations used by architect Frank Furness on the architectural elements in the historic Pennsylvania Academy of Fine Arts. The building, completed in 1876, has recently been restored.
Left: Needlepoint flower worked in olive green, maroon, rust, yellow, and black on beige background. Kit includes canvas, yarn, needle, and instructions. 12″ square.
40.00 (1.00)
Right: Crewel flower worked in green, ivory, beige on off-white background. Kit includes fabric, yarn, needle, and instructions. 10″ diameter.
35.00 (1.00)
Pennsylvania Academy of Fine Arts, Philadelphia (member's discount 10%)

Tennis Racquet Cover

Be the envy of your court set. Protect your racquet with this unique needlepoint cover, inspired by *Seascape #21,* 1967, an oil on canvas by Tom Wesselmann (American, b. 1931), which hangs in his home town in the Cincinnati Art Museum. Kit includes preassembled pastel plastic and canvas cover with zipper, which opens flat for working, hand-painted #10 canvas, and yarn color guide, matched to the colors of the original. Yarn is not supplied. 15½″ x 11″.
35.00 (1.35)
Cincinnati Art Museum (membership discount not available)

Latch-Hook Rug

With a design adapted from a 9th-century Peruvian tapestry fragment, representing Puma-headed conventionalized figures, the hooking of this kit is sure to occupy many enjoyable hours. The figures are worked in earth colors of rust, gold, yellow, brown, beige, white, and black against a beige background with rust border. Includes hand-painted #4 rug canvas, precut acrylic rug yarn, latch hook, and instructions. 3′ x 5′.
200.00 (3.00)
Philadelphia Museum of Art (member's discount 10%)

Needlework

Evening Bag

A combination of 16th- and 17th-century Italian woven silk ribbons, known as coach laces, have been used to produce this subtle decorative design, worked in shades of gold, rose, dark blue, and beige. Kit includes black faille bag with gold chain (bag opens flat for working), #14 canvas with outline, chart for working ribbon designs, DMC cotton floss, needle, and instructions. Bag size: 6¹/₂″ x 9″ x 2¹/₄″ with 28″ chain.
35.75 (1.50)
Philadelphia Museum of Art (member's discount 10%)

Pillow or Pocketbook

A geometric design from a Ghanian shopping bag. The original is made of woven grass with the design embroidered in raffia. The kit is available in two color combinations: bone and charcoal gray or navy and terra cotta. (Please specify color choice when ordering.) Contents: painted #12 canvas, Paterna Persian yarn, needle, and instructions for making up the kit as either a pillow or pocketbook. 15″ square.
26.00 (1.00)
Monterey Peninsula Museum of Art (member's discount 10%)

Clutch Bag

In 1745, Sarah Franklin Ripely embroidered a double clutch pocketbook for her father. The floral motif has been transferred to needlepoint canvas so that you can make a single-envelope clutch bag. The flowers are worked in shades of red, pink, violet, green, olive, gold, and blue on a golden-brown background. A variety of stitches are used: basket weave, stem, and mosaic. Includes heat-transfer design on #18 canvas, Persian yarn, needle, brown lining fabric, and instructions. Bag folded: 5″ x 7″.
20.00 (1.00)
The Old State House (The Bostonian Society)
(member's discount not available)

Evening Bag

Pillow or Pocketbook

Clutch Bag

Tote Bag

Klokkestreng
(Bell Pull)

Wall Hanging,
Norwegian-American

Wall Hanging,
Colorado Springs
Fine Arts Center

Needlework

Tote Bag

A design in brown, red, beige, and two shades of green, adapted from a woven wool coverlet in the collection of the Norwegian-American Museum. *Klostersom,* like needlepoint, is worked with wool yarns on canvas, but the stitches cover several threads and go vertically rather than diagonally. Kit includes #12 double-thread canvas, yarn, needle, pattern, and instructions. Bag: 10¾" x 14".
Handle: 15" x 3".
10.00 (0.75)
Norwegian-American Museum, Decorah, Iowa
(member's discount 10%)

Klokkestreng (Bell Pull)

Although this striking design, worked in red, green, gold, white, and several shades of blue, is reminiscent of the bold weavings of the American Indians, this kit is actually adapted from an early Norwegian textile. This type of needlework, *Klostersom,* is worked with vertical stitches rather than with diagonal ones. Includes #12 double-thread canvas, yarn, needle, pattern, and instructions. 25" x 5¼".
8.50 (0.75)
Norwegian-American Museum, Decorah, Iowa
(member's discount 10%)

Wall Hanging

Klostersom has been a popular form of needlework in Norway for about a century. Like needlepoint, it is done with wool yarn on canvas, but the stiches cover several threads and go vertically rather than diagonally. The bride and groom have been adapted from an early Norwegian tapestry in the Norwegian-American Museum. Red and blue on white background. Kit includes #12 double-thread canvas, yarn, needle, pattern, and instructions. 23½" x 10½".
10.00 (0.75)
Norwegian-American Museum, Decorah, Iowa
(member's discount 10%)

Wall Hanging

A Navajo Yei figure adapted from a contemporary sand painting from the Taylor Museum of the Colorado Springs Fine Arts Center. The needlepoint piece is worked in tan, Indian red, and white with touches of green, black, copper, and gold. Kit includes hand-painted interlocking #13 canvas, Persian yarn, instructions, and a brief historical note about the design. 13" x 6".
19.00 (2.00)
Colorado Springs Fine Arts Center (member's discount 10%)

Needlework

Crewel Kits

A pictorial commonplace book by Thomas Trevelyon, published in 1608, in the collection of The Folger Shakespeare Library, was the inspiration for these two charming crewel kits. Each contains printed linen, wool crewel yarn, needle, instructions, and a history of the book.
Tree of Life. The colors are predominantly shades of brown green. 11″ square.
15.00 (1.25)
Strawberry and Acorn Vine. Multicolored yarns. 11″ square.
15.00 (1.25)
The Folger Shakespeare Library, Washington, D.C. (member's discount 15%)

Crewel Kits

Crewel Flower Pillows

Create a pair of pillows which are based on 18th-century bed hangings in the Smithsonian collections. They have been designed to complement each other. The intertwining vine and flower patterns are worked in red, yellow, blue, and green on an off-white background. Each kit contains printed linen, Persian wool, backing, piping, zipper, and instructions. 15″ square. (Please order by number.)
Top: #338491
Bottom: #333773
11.00 each (1.00)
Smithsonian Institution, Washington, D.C. (member's discount 10%)

Crewel Flower Pillows

Portfolio

A splash of color is created by this design of gradating hues of yellow, blue, red, and green, with outlines of white and black, worked in bargello. The adaptation was inspired by an early-18th-century needlepoint chair seat worked by Elizabeth Coates Paschall in Philadelphia. The kit includes a preassembled black canvas portfolio with wooden handles and double zipper, which opens flat for working, #12 canvas, Paterna Persian yarn, needle, chart, and complete working instructions. Portfolio size 12″ x 15″.
45.00 (1.50)
Philadelphia Museum of Art (member's discount 10%)

Portfolio

122

Vest

Unicorn

T'ang Tray

Needlework

Vest

A bargello vest, worked both front and back in subtle earth tones of gold, terra cotta, denim blue, and gray-green with touches of white, was inspired by Turkish embroideries—Karaman, early 19th century—in the museum's textile collection. The canvas is marked for small, medium, and large. Adjustments for width for the three sizes and for the length can be made right on the canvas, before working the garment. Kit includes #10 interlocking canvas, chart, Paterna Persian yarn, needle, and instructions. Finished lengths from underarm: small $11^1/_2$″; medium $12^1/_2$″; large $13^1/_2$″.
62.75 (2.50)
Philadelphia Museum of Art (member's discount 10%)

Unicorn

A needlework kit adapted from the celebrated Unicorn Tapestries at The Cloisters, New York, which is worked in approximately 12 colors, matching the original. Contents: hand silkscreened #18 canvas, Persian yarn, basic stitch instructions, and a description of the original work. Design size: $22^1/_4$″ x $15^3/_4$″.
65.00 (2.00) L1416
The Metropolitan Museum of Art, New York (member's discount 25%)

T'ang Tray

This ancient design, adapted for canvaswork, was inspired by a three-legged ceramic tray, Chinese, made during the height of the T'ang Dynasty (A.D. 680–750). The stylized lotus pattern incised into the plate is accentuated by brightly colored glazes, themselves a uniquely Chinese development of the T'ang period. This type is an offshoot of the popular san-ts'ai, or the three-colored glaze wares which are frequently found as tomb furniture in northern China. The original tray is in the Asian Art Museum of San Francisco. The needlepoint is worked in four colors: beige, mustard, dark green, and light green. The kit includes heat-transferred design on #13 canvas, yarn, and instructions. $14^1/_2$″ diameter.
25.00 (1.50)
M. H. de Young Memorial Museum, San Francisco (member's discount 20%)

Needlework

Matzah Cover

A design of flowers and vines encircled by Hebrew letters is worked in 16 colors. It was inspired by a 19th–century Matzah Cover made in Galicia, which is in the collection of The Jewish Museum. Includes: off-white linen, Persian wool yarn, and instructions. 14″ diameter.
15.95 (1.50)
The Jewish Museum, New York (member's discount 15%)

Matzah Cover

Stencils

Two wall stencils, executed around 1800, which decorate the ballroom of the Tavern Hall Museum at Historic Deerfield, have been re-created as needlepoint kits. They become useful as well as decorative when they are placed under glass and inserted into a walnut trivet. Each contains #14 canvas, Paterna Persian yarn, and instructions. Finished size of needlepoint: 6″ x 6″.
Horse #9. Green on gold background.
Flower #10. Green, rust, brown on antique gold background.
6.00 each (0.75)
Trivet. #250. Walnut and glass. 6″ x 6″.
7.00 (1.25)
Historic Deerfield, Inc., Massachusetts (member's discount 10%)

Stencils

Black Work Flower Kits

Black work, a form of embroidery which historically uses black silk and gold thread on cream linen, originated in Spain and reached its peak of popularity in 16th-century England. It was used in abundance to decorate neck ruffs, shirt cuffs, sleeves, stomachers, bodices, and caps. It was often used on elaborate bed hangings. Patterns are stylized, since the design is worked with geometric repeat fillings. The finished work gives the appearance of being simultaneously bold and lacy. Through the years other colors have been substituted for black, as in the case of the bed rug, worked in blue and white by Abigail Foot around 1780. It is on display in the Wells-Thorn House at Historic Deerfield. Three flowers from the bed rug, to be worked in three shades of blue on white, have been selected for these black work kits. Each includes 100% cotton Aida cloth, embroidery floss, and instructions. Finished size: 12″ x 10″. (Please order by number given below.)
Top. #3A. Design size: 6″ x 6″.
Center. #3B. Design size: 6″ x 6″.
Bottom: #3C. Design size: 5½″ x 5″.
4.00 each kit (0.50)
Historic Deerfield, Inc., Massachusetts (member's discount 10%)

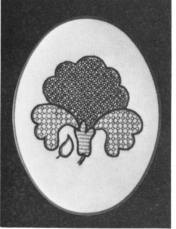 

Black Work Flower Kits

Flowers in a Vase

Greeting and Note Cards

Albright-Knox Art Gallery, Buffalo (member's discount 10%) (1.00)
Flowers in a Vase, 1909, by Henri Rousseau (French, 1844–1910). Full-color on white folder. 7" x 5". Without greeting.
6.00 12 cards with envelopes

Museum of the American Indian, New York (member's discount 15% on purchases over $5.00) (0.50 per order)
Fish Mask, 1960, by Gabriel Monignok (Eskimo). Full-color on white folder. 6" x 4". Without greeting.
3.00 12 cards with envelopes

Arizona Historical Society, Tucson (member's discount 10%) (0.50)
Military Notes. A selection of 5 subjects: Jeff Davis hat, 1856; Small Horn, after 1875; Dress Shako, 1872; Officer's boots; Boots with wooden-pegged shoes, 1876. Black on buff folder. 5¹/₈" x 4¹/₈". Without greeting.
1.75 10 cards (2 per design) with envelopes

Fish Mask

Military Notes

Greeting and Note Cards

The Baltimore Museum of Art (member's discount 10%) (1.00)
In the Garden, by Mary Cassatt (American, 1845–1926). Full-color on white folder. 6½" x 4½". Without greeting.
2.50 10 cards with envelopes

The Brooklyn Museum (member's discount 15%) (2.00 per order)
Flower-like lovers walking under a partially closed umbrella, 1753, by Torii Kiyohiro (Japanese, active 1737–76). Full-color on white folder. 7" x 5". With "Season's Greetings" or without greeting. (Please specify when ordering.)
2.50 10 cards with envelopes

Carnegie Institute, Pittsburgh (member's discount 10%) (0.75)
The Large Cat, engraving by Cornelis Visscher (Dutch, mid-17th century). Black on off-white folder. 5" x 7". Without greeting.
3.00 10 cards with envelopes

Museum of the City of New York (member's discount 20%) (1.25)
New York Dolls' Houses. An assortment of 12 note cards depicting the dolls' houses in the Toy Gallery at the Museum of the City of New York. Full-color on white folder. 4⅞" x 6¾". Without greeting.
5.95 12 cards with envelopes

In the Garden

Flower-like lovers walking...

The Large Cat

New York Dolls' Houses

Sunset, Saco Bay

Greeting and Note Cards

Sterling and Francine Clark Art Institute, Williamstown, Massachusetts (does not operate a membership program) (0.60 per box)
Sunset, Saco Bay, 1896, oil on canvas by Winslow Homer (American, 1836–1910). Full-color on white folder. 4¼" x 5¼". Without greeting.
2.60 12 cards with envelopes

The Corcoran Gallery of Art, Washington, D.C. (member's discount 10%) (0.50 per box)
Victorian America, designed by Ted Naos exclusively for The Corcoran Gallery of Art. Die cut, white paper. Triple fold. Color envelope. 6¼" x 4⁵⁄₁₆" closed. Without greeting.
8.00 10 cards with envelopes

Detroit Institute of Arts (member's discount 10%) (1.50)
The Gardener, oil on canvas by Jean Honoré Fragonard (French, 1732–1806). Full-color on white folder. Without greeting.
4.00 10 cards with envelopes

Victorian America

The Gardener

Greeting and Note Cards

Free Library of Philadelphia (member's discount 10%) (1.50)
Spring, 1974, etching by George Stuemfig. Brown on ivory folder. 6¹/₂″ x 4¹/₄″. Without greeting.
3.00 8 cards with envelopes

The Solomon R. Guggenheim Museum, New York (member's discount 25%) (0.50)
Preparedness, 1968, magna on canvas, three panels by Roy Lichtenstein (American, b. 1923). Full-color on white folder. 6³/₄″ x 4³/₄″. Without greeting.
3.00 10 cards with envelopes

Huntington Library, Art Gallery, and Botanical Gardens, San Marino, California (members receive a 10.00 annual credit toward purchases) (0.75)
Nine Beasts from a French manuscript encyclopedia, c. 1430. Full-color on white folder. 4⁵/₈″ x 5³/₄″. With a Christmas message or without greeting. (Please specify when ordering.)
6.50 25 cards with envelopes

Spring

Preparedness

Nine Beasts

Mille-Fleur
with Animals

Greeting and Note Cards

Hyde Collection, Glens Falls, New York (member's discount 10% on purchases over 3.00) (1.00)
Mille-Fleur with Animals. Detail from a French tapestry, c. 1400. Full-color on white folder. 4½" x 6". Without greeting.
2.00 10 cards with envelopes

Lycoming County Historical Society and Museum, Pennsylvania (member's discount not available on purchases) (0.50)
Fruit Still-Life, oil on canvas by Severin Roesen (b. Germany, active in America). 4¾" x 5⅜". Full-color on white folder. Without greeting.
1.50 6 cards with envelopes

National Trust for Historic Preservation, Washington, D.C. (member's discount 10%) (0.50)
Patchwork Quilt Detail, by Beverly Bancroft Davis. Blue, purple, and terra cotta on white folder. 6" x 5". With "Greetings" or without greeting. (Please specify when ordering.)
6.00 20 cards with envelopes

North Carolina Museum of Art (member's discount 10%) (0.50)
Winter 1946, tempera on board, by Andrew Wyeth (American, b. 1917). 4½" x 6½". Full-color on white folder. Without greeting.
2.50 10 cards with envelopes

Fruit Still-Life

*Patchwork
Quilt Detail*

Winter 1946

Greeting and Note Cards

Norwegian Recipes

Norwegian-American Museum, Decorah, Iowa
(member's discount 10%) (0.75)
Recipe Note Card of Norwegian delicacies:
Julekake, Fattigmand, Sandbakkels, Krumkake,
S-shaped Spritz, and Rosettes are pictured. These
cookies and Christmas bread were served to Crown
Prince Harald of Norway on his visit to the
Norwegian-American Museum in 1966. Full-color
on French fold note paper. 5″ x 6¹/₂″. Recipes for
the pastries are found on the inside fold of the
note paper. Plenty of room to write your message.
1.75 6 cards with envelopes

Topsail Schooner *Baltick*

Peabody Museum of Salem (member's discount
10%) (1.25)
Topsail Schooner Baltick *of Salem,* 1765,
watercolor. Full-color on white folder. 4¹/₄″ x 6¹/₄″.
Without greeting.
4.00 10 cards with envelopes

Philadelphia Museum of Art (member's discount
10%) (1.00)
The Kiss, 1899, color woodcut by Peter Behrens
(German, 1868–1940). Full-color on white folder.
6¹/₂″ x 5″. Without greeting.
3.00 10 cards with envelopes

The Kiss

The Phillips Collection, Washington, D.C. (does not
operate a membership program) (1.00)
Snow at Louveciennes, 1874, oil on canvas by
Alfred Sisley (English, 1839–99). Full-color on white
folder. 7¹/₄″ x 5¹/₄″. Without greeting.
5.00 10 cards with envelopes

Snow at Louveciennes

Brig *Boxer* at Marseilles

Snow-Covered Tree

Still Life

Madonna and Child

Greeting and Note Cards

Portland Museum of Art, Maine (member's discount 10%) (0.50 per order)
Brig Boxer at Marseilles, William McLellan, Jr., Master. A late 19th-century engraving after an 1815 watercolor by Joseph Ange Antoine Roux (1765–1835). Sepia on ivory folder. 4¹/₂″ x 6″. Without greeting.
3.50 10 cards with envelopes

The Art Museum, Princeton University (member's discount 10%) (0.50)
Snow-Covered Tree, Yosemite National Park, photograph by Ansel Adams (American, b. 1902). Black on white folder. 4¹/₄″ x 5³/₈″. With "Season's Greetings."
2.00 10 cards with envelopes

Norton Simon Museum of Art at Pasadena (member's discount 20%) (1.00)
Still Life with Cherries, Strawberries and Gooseberries, 1630, oil on panel by Louyse Moillon (French, 1610–96). Full-color on white folder. 5″ x 7″. With "Greetings of the Season" or without greeting. (Please specify when ordering.)
3.50 10 cards with envelopes

The J. B. Speed Art Museum, Louisville (member's discount 10%) (0.75)
Madonna and Child, tempera on panel by Francesco Granacci (Italian, 1477–1543). Full-color on white folder. 4¹/₄″ x 5¹/₄″. With "May the blessings of Christmas be with you" or without greeting. (Please specify when ordering.)
3.50 10 cards with envelopes

Greeting and Note Cards

The Museums at Stony Brook, New York (member's discount 10%) (0.50 per order)
Carriages. An assortment of 8 drawings of carriages in the Carriage Museum at Stony Brook. Among the designs: *Boston Chaise,* c. 1840; *Basket Phaeton,* c. 1810; *Conestoga Wagon,* c. 1840; *Extracts and Perfumes Wagon,* c. 1900; *Oil Tank Wagon,* c. 1900; and *Fire Parade Hose Carriage,* c. 1875. Brown on tan folder. 5" x 7". Without greeting.
1.25 8 cards with envelopes

The Toledo Museum of Art (member's discount 10%) (handling and shipping charges included)
Reeds and Geese, 1928, color woodcut by Ohara Shoson (Japanese, 1877–1945). Full-color on white folder. 7¹/₈" x 5". Without greeting.
4.00 10 cards with envelopes

Walters Art Gallery, Baltimore (member's discount not available on this item) (1.25 per order)
La Beale Isoud at Joyous Gard. From *Le Morte d'Arthur* in *A Book of Fifty Drawings,* by Aubrey Beardsley (English, 1872–98). Black on white folder. 4³/₄" x 6³/₄". Without greeting.
2.00 10 cards with envelopes

Worcester Art Museum (member's discount 10%) (1.25)
Collector's Packet. An assortment of 24 note cards reproduced from works in the Worcester Art Museum. Full-color on white folders. Various sizes. Without greeting. Boxed.
6.50

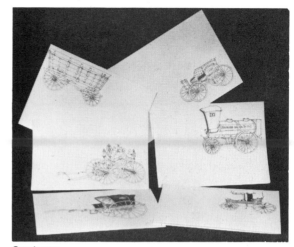
Carriages

Reeds and Geese

La Beale Isoud

Collector's Packet

Sight and Sound

Recordings of Asian Music

The Asia Society's Performing Arts Program offers the finest of Asia's traditional theater, music, and dance, performed by the leading exponents of these arts. The 33⅓ rpm record albums briefly described below were recorded during four different tours across the United States.

A Persian Heritage: Classical Music of Iran
The classical music of Iran is an independent and distinct type that must be understood in its own terms. Dating back to the Sassanian Empire of ancient times, Persian music made significant contributions to both Middle Eastern and Greek musical theory. This record presents virtuoso performances by Faramarz Payvar and his ensemble during his national tour in 1973.

Japan: Traditional Vocal and Instrumental Music
Diversity of instruments, vocal techniques, formal construction, rhythmic patterns and activity, and style all make a definitive impression on the listener to Japanese music. This recording presents four of Japan's most important traditional instruments: the *koto,* a large zitherlike instrument; the *shamisen,* a three-stringed instrument; the *shakuhachi,* a bamboo vertical flute; and the *biwa,* a Japanese flute with four or five strings. The musicians are members of the Ensemble Nipponia, who toured the nation in 1976.

Shakuachi: The Japanese Flute
The slow, haunting music of this delicate wind instrument was originally conceived of for chamber ensembles. In recent years, however, many of the original solo pieces have been revived as aids to meditation, both for the player and the listener. The musicians in this recording are Kohachira Miyata and several accompanists, members of the Ensemble Nipponia. The recording was made during their tour in 1976.

P'ansori: Korea's Epic Vocal Art and Instrumental Music
The demanding art of the P'ansori requires virtuosity and power; a single performer must impersonate and enact all of the roles of an epic folk tale, conveying the entire saga with his voice alone. He is aided by none of the usual theatrical trappings; only his dramatic entrances and exits are accompanied by a drummer playing the *pook* (a kind of barrel drum). P'ansori is a unique synthesis of song and speech in which phonemes and speech sounds become musical events. The musicians—Kim So Hee and three accompanists—were brought to the United States by The Asia Society for a national tour in 1972.

China: Shantung Folk Music and Traditional Instrumental Pieces
The music featured on this record is representative of the ancient heritage of the Chinese. Originally performed by itinerant professional musicians, it is the music of festivals, funerals, weddings, and spirited parties. The music is performed by the Lu-Sheng Ensemble and recorded during its tour in 1972.
(Please order records by title.)
3.95 each (member's price 3.00 each) (0.75)
The Asia Society, Inc., New York

Recordings of
Asian Music

Sight and Sound

Record

The Language and Music of the Wolves, narrated by Robert Redford. Actually recorded in the wilds.
5.95 (1.25)
The American Museum of Natural History, New York
(member's discount 10%)

American Indian Music

Music of the Pueblos, Apache and Navaho, recorded by David P. McAllester and Donald N. Brown. Edited by Donald N. Brown. Included are selections from the Pueblos of Taos, Santa Clara, and Zuni; Apache instrumental and vocal music; and several Navaho pieces. Each 33¹/₃ rpm record is accompanied by the booklet "Indian Music in the Southwest" and a set of notes explaining the role of music in each of these cultures, translations of the songs, and information about each selection.
7.00 (1.50)
Colorado Springs Fine Arts Center (member's discount 10%)

Faded Memories—Songs of Deerfield

Nine original songs by John Wesley Hardin retelling a part of Deerfield's colorful 300-year history beginning with the 1704 massacre. Sometimes serious, mostly humorous, the songs will provide many hours of entertainment and have you tapping your foot and humming along. Record: 33¹/₃ rpm.
5.00 (0.75)
Historic Deerfield, Inc., Massachusetts (member's discount 10%)

Record

American Indian Music

Faded Memories—Songs of Deerfield

Slide Set

Sight and Sound

Slide Set

The Huntington consists of a library of manuscripts and rare books, an art collection emphasizing British and French art (including Thomas Gainsborough's *Blue Boy* and Thomas Lawrence's *Pinkie*), and a dozen specialized botanical gardens within park-like grounds. This slide set contains 40 color slides (35 mm) illustrating a selection of book and manuscript pages, paintings, sculpture, plants, and landscape views. Each slide measures 2″ square.
9.00 (0.75)
Huntington Library, Art Gallery, and Botanical Gardens, San Marino, California (members receive a 10.00 annual credit toward purchases)

Holographic Movies

Your friends will be in for a big surprise when you invite them over to view your latest movies. Holographic movies can be viewed with an ordinary light bulb. Rainbow colors. Photographic emulsion. Each measures 4″ x 7″.
Venus, 1976, by Hart Perry and Christos Tountas. A beautiful computer-generated image adapted from one of the first holographic movies.
Fred's Flower, 1977, by Rudie Berkhout. A time-lapse sequence of the opening of a lily.
Night at the Movies, 1977, by Dan Schweitzer. Three-dimensional movies pop out of this film strip. The illustration here shows a screen star reaching out and plucking up a man from the audience.
35.00 each (1.50)
Museum of Holography, New York (member's discount 10%)

Holographic Movies

Sight and Sound

Projecting Train Hologram

The original hologram, *Engine No. 9,* 1975, was created by Stephen Benton. Holograms look like photographs, but they are totally three-dimensional and project out into space. Although they are made with laser light, they are viewed with an ordinary light bulb, and are easily displayed in the home. Bright yellow-orange. Photographic emulsion on glass. 4″ x 5″.
120.00 (1.50)
Museum of Holography, New York (member's discount 10%)

Projecting Train Hologram

Images of Man

Images of Man is a series of 9 audiovisual journeys into the life of 20th-century man through the photographs and personal spoken narration of nine significant photographers. The program, produced in cooperation with the International Center of Photography and in cooperation with the International Fund for Concerned Photography, Inc., reviews some of the most important human events of the last decade and explores the values underlying the human experience. Each kit includes 70–80 slides in a carousel tray, a tape narrated by the photographer, and an illustrated booklet containing transcripts, biographies, and text. 10″ x 14″.
Toward the Margin of Life: From Primitive Society to Population Crisis, by Cornell Capa
Voyages of Self-Discovery: Unknown Worlds Close to Home, by Bruce Davidson
The Uncertain Day: A War Photographer's Journal, by Don McCullin
Between Birth and Death: An Affirmation of Life, by W. Eugene Smith
Morning of Creation, by Eliot Porter
A Sense of Place: Life on the Edge of Modern Civilization, by William Albert Allard
Kansas, by Brian Lanker
The Decisive Moment: The Photographer as Artist, by Henri Cartier-Bresson
The Life That Disappeared: A Jewish Experience in Eastern Europe 1935–1939, by Roman Vishniac
75.00 each (2.50)
International Center of Photography, New York (member's discount not available on these items)

Images of Man

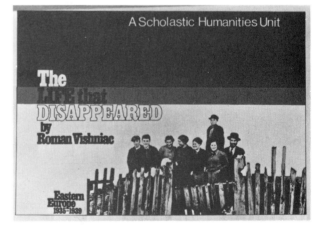

Sound/Slide Library

The Metropolitan Museum of Art, in an effort to share the treasures of both its permanent collections and temporary exhibitions, has developed a *Sound/Slide Library*. The library currently consists of 9 individually packaged sets, each consisting of approximately 40 full-color 35 mm slides, and a 30–minute cassette tape, usually narrated by a curator and often accompanied by music.

Treasures of Early Irish Art (I2042). Featured are stunning gold and silver ornaments and illustrated manuscripts, including the celebrated Book of Kells. Ancient Irish harp music is in the background.

Late Antique and Early Christian Art (I2045). Masterpieces of art from the 3rd to the 7th centuries gathered from over 100 collections around the world. Highlights include rare ivory, silver, gold, and stone treasures from Byzantium and Rome and re-creations of architectural monuments.

Monet at Giverny: 1883–1926 (I2047). A dazzling and illuminating study of the Impressionist's late work.

Scythian Gold: From the Lands of the Scythians (I2051). Luxurious gold artifacts made by Greek craftsmen for Scythian royalty and remarkable objects of Urartian, Altaic, and Sarmatian cultures. Collection on loan from museums of the U.S.S.R.

The Heritiage of American Art (I2054). Collection of 40 major American paintings by this country's finest artists from 1730 to 1916 from the permanent collections of The Metropolitan Museum of Art.

Christmas Story (I2055). The story of Christmas visually re-created through medieval and Renaissance paintings, narrated in the words of Matthew and Luke with a background of authentic Renaissance music.

Two Worlds of Andrew Wyeth: Kuerner's and Olson's (I2059) Studies and paintings of the land, buildings, and people of Karl Kuerner's farm in Pennsylvania and Christina Olson's house in Maine—the most important environments of the artist's life.

Thracian Treasures from Bulgaria (I2060). Exquisite gold and silver artifacts, including drinking vessels, armor, and jewelry, from ancient Thrace.

The Treasures of Tutankhamun (I2706). Beautiful and representative objects from the tomb of the boy-king Tutankhamun (1334–1325 B.C.) including statuettes, masks richly inlaid with jewels, and funerary jewelry and furniture. Collection on loan from the Cairo Museum in Egypt.

14.95 each (2.00)

The Metropolitan Museum of Art, New York (member's discount 25% on all sets except *The Treasures of Tukankhamun,* to which member's discount does not apply)

137

Calendars

Art of Our Time

Great examples of modern art by Jasper Johns, Henri Matisse, Georgia O'Keeffe, Pablo Picasso, Frank Stella, Robert Delaunay, Mark Rothko, Robert Indiana, Marisol, Sam Francis, Victor Vasarely, and Fernand Leger are illustrated on the postcards that comprise this 1979 calendar. All of the original art is in the Albright-Knox Art Gallery. 13 full-color illustrations (12 cards plus cover); spiral bound; easel-back for desk use plus wall hanger; 9" x 5½".
3.50 (1.00)
Albright-Knox Art Gallery, Buffalo, New York (member's discount 10%)

Art of Our Time

History Lives 1979

Arizona at work and play as illustrated in photographs of the past. An appointment calendar for 1979 for you to keep your current engagements, and at the same time learn a bit of Arizona history from the state's important dates that are included. 55 pp.; 53 sepia photographs; plastic ring binding; 9" x 6½".
5.00 (1.00)
Arizona Historical Society, Tucson (member's discount not available on this item)

Peach Blossom Spring

An innovation in wall calendars for 1979. *Peach Blossom Spring* is a scroll calendar, which comes in a plastic sleeve and unfurls into a 13" x 60" (horizontal) picture with the 12-month calendarium printed under the full color illustration. A Chinese landscape in spring—peach trees in blossom, fields and mountains in a glorious burst of turquoise and green, villagers boating and strolling near lakes and streams. The segment of a rare and beautiful scroll was painted by Ch'iu Ying (16th century) and illustrates a poem by T'ao K'an. The original scroll is in the collection of the Museum of Fine Arts, Boston.
7.95 (1.25)
Museum of Fine Arts, Boston (member's discount 10%)

History Lives 1979

Peach Blossom Spring

Calendars

To Each Her Own

Chinese Flowers and Birds

Metamorphoses

To Each Her Own

Woman, in all her diversity and beauty, portrayed by great artists through the ages, is the theme for this wall calendar for 1979. The innocence of youth, the tenderness of motherhood, the sparkle of adulthood, the wisdom of old age—women at work and at play—their many moods have been captured. The works included are Cassatt's *The Letter;* Toulouse-Lautrec's *Jane Avril;* Renoir's *Nude;* Breton's *The Lark;* Melchers' *Mother and Child;* Courbet's *Mère Gregoire;* Picasso's *Sylvette;* Rembrandt's *Young Girl at Open Half-Door;* Master of Moulins' *The Annunciation;* van Dongen's *Lady Against White Background;* Bouguereau's *The Bathers;* and Choki's *Two Women by a Stream.* All of the originals are in the collection of the Art Institute of Chicago. 12 pp. plus cover; 13 full-color illustrations; spiral bound; 17″ x 11″.
7.95 (0.75)
Art Institute of Chicago (member's discount 10%)

Chinese Flowers and Birds

Brilliantly colored birds and richly colored flowers from a rare early 19th-century album of Chinese watercolors have been reproduced in postcard form for this 1979 calendar. The original, painted on silk, is in the collection of the Indianapolis Museum of Art. 13 full-color illustrations (12 cards plus cover); spiral bound; easel-back for desk use plus wall hanger; 9″ x 5½″.
3.50 (0.75)
Indianapolis Museum of Art (member's discount 10%)

Metamorphoses

A mask that changes identity, a sculpture that comes alive, people who become beasts and beasts who become people: a woman turns into a tree, a daddy into a dragon, a king into a rock, and a beauty into a hag. All of these transformations, accompanied by stories from myths, fairy tales, and folklore, take place in this 1979 wall calendar. 13 color illustrations; spiral bound with hole for hanging; 13¾″ x 11¾″; boxed.
3.95 (2.00) H7855
The Metropolitan Museum of Art, New York (member's discount not available on this item)

Calendars

A Treasury of Far Eastern Art

A selection of 56 outstanding examples of art from the Metropolitan's Far Eastern department are reproduced in full color in this 1979 engagement calendar. Reproductions of sculpture, painting, textiles, ceramics, and decorative objects, spanning a time period of many centuries, are interleaved with the weekly appointment pages. 116 pp.; 56 color illustrations; spiral bound; 7″ x 9″.
3.95 (2.00) H7854
The Metropolitan Museum of Art, New York (member's discount not available on this item)

The Floating World

The world of beautiful women and elegant men in 18th-century Japan is exquisitely portrayed in this handsome engagement calendar for 1979. Scenes depicting worldly pleasures of the senses, the natural beauty of the Japanese landscape, and the graciousness of the Japanese way of life are captured by masters of the Ukiyo-e style (floating world) of art. The original works are in the collection of The Minneapolis Institute of Arts. There is ample space to record your daily schedule on the weekly appointment pages. 120 pp.; 52 illustrations (26 color); spiral bound; 10″ x 5½″.
5.95 (1.00)
The Minneapolis Institute of Arts (member's discount 10%)

50 Years

To celebrate its 50th anniversary, The Museum of Modern Art has compiled a festive commemorative edition of its appointment calendar for 1979. There are 50 illustrations of works of art from the collections, one important acquisition for each year from 1929 to 1979. Among the artists, photographers, and sculptors represented are: Pablo Picasso, Paul Cézanne, Piet Mondrian, Marc Chagall, Robert Motherwell, Frank Stella, Jasper Johns, Walker Evans, Alfred Stieglitz, Edward Weston, Henry Moore, and David Smith. Full-color and black-and-white illustrations. Spiral bound. 8½″ square.
7.95 (0.50 for the first calendar plus 0.20 for each additional)
The Museum of Modern Art, New York (member's discount 25%)

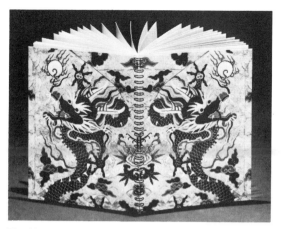
The Metropolitan Museum of Art Engagement Calendar

The Floating World

50 Years

MoMA Postcard Calendar

Louis
Comfort
Tiffany

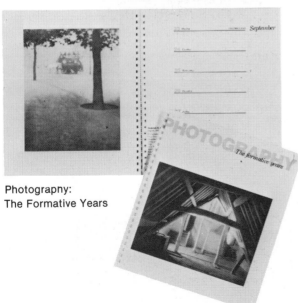

Photograpny:
The Formative Years

Calendars

Postcard Calendar

12 of the most frequently requested works of art in the collection of The Museum of Modern Art have been selected to be reproduced in postcard form as a calendar for 1979. The works are Cézanne's *Still Life with Apples;* Dali's *The Persistence of Memory;* Hopper's *Gas;* Léger's *Three Women;* Magritte's *False Mirror;* Matisse's *Dance;* Miro's *The Hunter;* Picasso's *Three Musicians;* Rousseau's *Sleeping Gypsy;* Seurat's *Entrance to the Harbor;* van Gogh's *The Starry Night;* and Wyeth's *Christina's World.* The calendarium is perforated on each picture; when it is removed, the cards are ready to mail. 12 full-color illustrations. Spiral bound. 8″ x 6″.
3.95 (0.50 for the first calendar plus 0.20 for each additional)
The Museum of Modern Art, New York (member's discount 25%)

Louis Comfort Tiffany

Twelve full-color photographs of the opulent work of Louis Comfort Tiffany (American, 1848-1933) in the design collection of The Museum of Modern Art enhance this wall calendar for 1979. The selection includes vases, lamps, a bronze and glass candlestick, a pen tray of bronze and glass mosaic, and a peacock handmirror of silver, enamel, and jewels. Introduction by J. Stewart Johnson. Photography by Phil Marco. Design by Peter Bradford. 12 color illustrations. 18″ x 12″.
6.95 (0.50 for the first calendar plus 0.20 for each additional)
The Museum of Modern Art, New York (member's discount 25%)

Photography: The Formative Years

This 1979 appointment calendar, containing 55 remarkable images selected from the Alfred Stieglitz Center for Photography at the Philadelphia Museum of Art, is a tribute to pioneers of the art of photography. Each spacious weekly page is accompanied by a classic photograph notable for its originality. The calendar includes Parisian street scenes by Atget, Gothic cathedrals by Frederick Evans, Steichen's studies of Rodin, Frank Sutcliffe's observations of fishermen in the Yorkshire village of Whitby, John Thompson's record of travels in China, portraits of American Indians by Edward Curtis, and some rarely seen early photographs by Alfred Stieglitz. 55 illustrations; wire-o bound; 9″ x 7³/₄″.
6.95 (1.00)
Philadelphia Museum of Art (member's discount 10%)

Calendars

Japanese Landscapes

Enjoy the beauties of Japanese landscape painting all year with a distinctive 1979 wall calendar. Reproduced from the Philadelphia Museum of Art's collection are six works by such masters of the field as Hiroshige, Hokusai, and Kuniyoshi. Each of these reproductions is suitable for framing at the year's end. Decorative cord hanger; 14″ square.
8.95 (1.00)
Philadelphia Museum of Art (member's discount 10%)

Art of the Flower

The Smithsonian's engagement calendar for 1979 is in full bloom! Iris, pansies, roses, carnations, mums, and imaginary blossoms depicted by artists and craftspeople through the centuries. An elegant and delightful album celebrating the glorious colors and charming intricacy of flowers in many moods and modes. From paintings and folk works, porcelain and song sheets, carpets and embroidery, fans and screens, quilts and tiles, tiaras and bracelets, greeting cards and beadwork, an all-color calendar combining beautiful images and apt quotations on a theme that has inspired artists, poets, songwriters, and artisans since time began. Weekly appointment pages are interleaved amidst the blooms. 120 pp.; 52 full-color illustrations; spiral bound; 8″ x 7″.
5.95 (0.50) #539247
Smithsonian Institution, Washington, D.C. (member's discount 10%)

Splendors of Nature

Rare gems, delicate seashells, exquisite flowers, colorful butterflies, woven reeds, feathers, and shells from the Smithsonian's diversified collections enhance this postcard calendar for 1979. 13 full-color illustrations (12 cards plus cover); spiral bound; easel-back for desk use plus wall hanger; 5½″ x 9″.
3.50 (0.50) #539239
Smithsonian Institution, Washington, D.C. (member's discount 10%)

Japanese Landscapes

Art of the Flower

Splendors of Nature

The Artist
in the Kitchen

The Portland
Art Museum
Cook Book

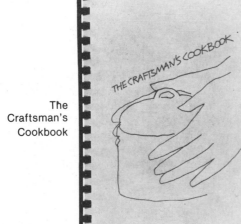

The
Craftsman's
Cookbook

Cookbooks

The Artist in the Kitchen

This lavishly illustrated volume, with 400 recipes, is sure to tempt any cook. In addition to the usual sections covering hors d'oeuvres, soups, meats, poultry, fish, vegetables, and breads, there are three special sections. Unusual and delicious dishes can be prepared in the Microwave, which the modern cook bought basically for fast food service and convenience: Rice and Artichoke Salad; Crab-stuffed Fillet of Sole; Continental Chicken Breasts with Mushroom-Cheddar Sauce; Cheesecake with Flaming Cherry Sauce. For the chocolate lovers—a special section including Chocolate-Cinnamon Torte, Starlight Double Delight Cake, and Chocolate Meringues. Many people enjoy cooking for friends and preparing delicacies as gifts for all occasions—a special section for them: Old Curiosity Pate, Old English Nut Toffee, and French Peach Sauce. A cookbook that from the cover, *Wheat Field,* 1958, serigraph with watercolor by Ben Shahn (American, 1898–1969) right through to the end, will inspire many to become artists in the kitchen. 296 pp., 60 illustrations (13 color); 9″ x 6″, wire-o bound.
8.95 (0.55)
Don *The Artist in the Kitchen* apron and you won't soil your clothes while mixing ingredients. 50% cotton, 50% polyester. White with black embroidery. One size fits all.
6.00 (1.00)
The St. Louis Art Museum (member's discount 10%)

The Portland Art Museum Cook Book

An innovative approach to cookbook design. Instead of the traditional bound format, there are 60 loose-leaf recipe pages, each with an illustration by René Rickabaugh, suitable for framing. The pages are boxed with an easel, clip, and clear plastic sheet for working display of the recipe. Each page measures 11¼″ x 15″.
20.00 (1.50)
Portland Art Association, Oregon (member's discount 10%)

The Craftsman's Cookbook

Craftsmen have been making both utilitarian and decorative objects for the table and kitchen for many years. When the American Crafts Council was organizing the exhibition "Objects for Preparing Food" it seemed appropriate to produce a cookbook of recipes gathered from contemporary craftsmen across the United States. The result is a collection of 160 imaginative recipes, including: No-Knead Cottage Cheese Bread; Egyptian Fathia; Pul Kogi (Korean Barbecued Meat); "Chinese" Turkey; Sweet Potatoes with Orange-Rum Glaze; and Rose Geranium Pound Cake. Biographies of the craftsmen are included. 192 pp.; 7″ x 10″, spiral bound.
6.35 (member's price 5.35) (handling and shipping charges included)
Museum of Contemporary Crafts of the American Crafts Council, New York

Cookbooks

To the Queen's Taste

Forty delicious recipes from Tudor England adapted for the modern cook by Lorna J. Sass. For your Elizabethan banquet, you could begin with "Livering Puddinges" (liver-currant paté with nutmeg), proceed to "Minst Pyes" (mincemeat of ground veal, suet, fruits, and rose water), add the side dish "Quelchechose" (parsnips and marigold cooked in orange juice), and finish with "Finer Jumbals" (almond cookies scented with rose water and garnished with anise seeds). Illustrated with engravings from contemporary gastronomic books. 144 pp., illustrated; 4³/₄" x 8¹/₂", clothbound.
5.95 book only (2.00) D2006

Queen Elizabeth's Herb Box

As a supplement to the cookbook, a box of five rare and exotic herbs: Strawberry Leaves, Marigold Flowers, Violet Leaves, Whole Nutmeg, and Powdered Licorice.
9.75 box of herbs and book (2.00) D2007

To the King's Taste

Lorna J. Sass has adapted for modern cooking 40 recipes from Richard II's 14th-century book of feasts and recipes. 136 pp., illustrated; 4³/₄" x 8¹/₂", clothbound.
5.95 book only (2.00) D2004
9.75 box of six herbs and book (2.00) D2005
The Metropolitan Museum of Art, New York (member's discount 25%)

Herb Boxes and Cookbooks,
The Metropolitan Museum of Art

Dinner with Tom Jones

Over 60 18th-century recipes adapted for the modern kitchen by Lorna J. Sass. Lavishly illustrated with charming scenes of English life by caricaturist Thomas Rowlandson (English, 1756–1827). 196 pp., illustrated; 6" x 7", clothbound.
7.95 (2.00) D0425
The Metropolitan Museum of Art, New York (member's discount 25%)

Dinner with Tom Jones

Cook Box

A handy and attractive way to organize your recipes: The Cook Box contains 60 new goodies and you can use it to file your own favorite recipes. The recipes, which include appetizers and snacks and barbecues, have been culled from the staff of The Baltimore Museum of Art. A reproduction of *Two Roosters,* a watercolor by Pablo Picasso, adorns the top of the ivory vinyl (easy to keep clean!) box. The name of the museum appears in chocolate brown lettering. 3³/₄" x 5¹/₂" x 4".
9.95 (2.00)
The Baltimore Museum of Art (member's discount 10%)

Cook Box

Cookbooks

The Cookbook

Portfolio of Culinary Art

Joslyn Presents Bernard Schimmel's Masterpieces

The Cookbook

A collection of more than 460 ethnic, regional, and gourmet recipes from members, friends, and staff of the Worcester Art Museum. *The Cookbook* is divided into chapters relating to the progression of the meal, from beverages to candy. Included are: Avocados with Hot Crab Acapulco; Pheasant Casserole; Meatballs Harunobu; Syrian Bread; Macadamia Nut Pie. All recipes have been tested and tasted. Other features include an article entitled "What About Wine?" by John J. Maginnis, member, Confrêrie des Chevaliers du Tastevin; "Herbs with a Light Touch," a guide for using herbs to the best culinary advantage; and a guide to metric conversion.
The book is enhanced with both color and black-and-white illustrations. The color plates reproduce paintings from the museum collection in which food was the source of inspiration for the artist. The black-and-white plates focus on the museum collection of Early American silver. 208 pp., 42 illustrations (15 color); 9″ x 9¹/₂″, spiral bound.
9.95 (1.00)
Worcester Art Museum (member's discount 10%)

Portfolio of Culinary Art

The international scope of this cookbook reflects the wide range of the museum's collections. It is divided into categories that correspond to the major departments of the museum, including Native America, Latin America, Africa, and Southeast Asia. Reflecting the western mode of life, there are recipes for patio parties, mountain picnics, and open-air cooking for camping trips. "Collector's Choice" is a special section featuring favorite recipes of renowned artists, writers, and cooks. Lavishly illustrated with reproductions of works from the museum's permanent collections. 194 pp., 138 illustrations (10 color); 8¹/₂″ x 8″, spiral bound.
9.95 (0.50)
Denver Art Museum (member's discount 10%)

Joslyn Presents Bernard Schimmel's Masterpieces

Reputed to have originated the famous Reuben Sandwich, Schimmel was a master chef from the Midwest. The wide selection of gourmet recipes gathered in this volume is basically French. In addition, there is a complete section on wines by Bern C. Ramey. Sumptuously illustrated with color reproductions of works in the Joslyn Art Museum, especially their renowned Netsuke collection. Many of the works have never before been reproduced. 216 pp., illustrated; 8¹/₂″ square, clothbound.
11.95 (.75)
Joslyn Art Museum, Omaha (member's discount 10%)

Cookbooks

Gourmet Gallery

What is "Aggravation"? According to this cookbook, it is a milk punch, just one of over 800 recipes featured in *Gourmet Gallery.* Others are of French, Chinese, Italian, Greek, Spanish, and Polynesian origin. There are special sections on "Good-for-you Foods," award-winning restaurant menus and recipes, citrus cooking, one-dish meals, and men's cooking. 465 pp., illustrated; 6" x 9", spiral bound.
6.95 (0.60)
Museum of Fine Arts, St. Petersburg (member's discount not available on this item)

Gourmet Gallery

The Fine Arts Cookbook

This cookbook, carefully compiled by the Ladies Committee of the Museum of Fine Arts, Boston, has the distinction of being one of the first cookbooks published by a museum and is now in its seventh printing. It features almost 400 European, Oriental, and American recipes, and is sumptuously illustrated with reproductions of paintings, graphics, and decorative arts. 196 pp., 43 illustrations (16 color); 7" x 9", spiral bound.
7.95 (0.75)
Museum of Fine Arts, Boston (member's discount 10%)

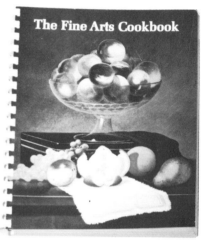

The Fine Arts
Cookbook

Entertaining Is An Art

A committee of nine women from the Art Museum Council of the Los Angeles County Museum of Art researched and composed these menus designed to seduce the palate. There are complete menus for dinner, luncheon, and Sunday brunch, arranged by season. For example:
  Spinach Quiche Rosso Fiorentino
  Mediterranean Fish Soup with Rouille
  Romaine and Bibb Lettuce Salad
  French Bread
  Cheese Tray
  Cold Lemon Soufflé Vlaminck
106 pp., 10 illustrations (1 color); 8¾" x 11¼", clothbound.
10.00 (1.50)
Los Angeles County Museum of Art (member's discount 10%)

Entertaining
Is An Art

Private Collections: A Culinary Treasure

The Walters Art Gallery has had a long history of interest in food. It has sponsored a series of cooking demonstrations—including one by James Beard, who wrote the introduction to this book—to raise funds for the gallery. Members of the gallery have contributed more than 600 recipes for you to try. The book is lavishly illustrated with paintings and decorative arts from the collection that portray the enduring interest in the art of cooking throughout the ages. 256 pp., 58 illustrations (8 color); 8½" x 9", clothbound.
12.50 (1.25)
Walters Art Gallery, Baltimore (member's discount 10%)

Private
Collections:
A Culinary
Treasure

Cookbooks

Five cookbooks from the National Trust

Selected Recipes

The National Trust for Historic Preservation, Washington, D.C., administers properties that have been declared national landmarks. Five charming cookbooks containing traditional American recipes, many of which were actually used by the famous families who lived in these stately houses, have been carefully compiled for modern usage.

The Cliveden Recipe Book: A selection of 19th-century recipes from Cliveden, Germantown, PA. 36 pp., dark blue illustrations on pale blue paper; 5½" x 8½", paperback.
1.25 (0.50)

Coffee at the Shadows: A collection of old recipes used by the former owner of Shadows-on-the-Teche, New Iberia, LA. 38 pp., dark green illustrations on pale green paper; 5½" x 8½", paperback.
2.00 (0.50)

Oatlands Cooks Today: A group of favorite recipes of the staff and property council at Oatlands, near Leesburg, VA. 58 pp., light brown illustrations on pale yellow paper; 5½" x 8½", paperback.
2.75 (0.50)

Woodrow Wilson House Cookbook: Consisting of recipes from the Wilson House collection, with additional information about the Wilsons and the house. Woodrow Wilson House, Washington, D.C. 50 pp., brown illustrations on cream paper, 5½" x 8½", paperback.
2.00 (0.50)

Decatur House Desserts: Recipes selected by members of the Decatur House Council, as appropriate to the entertaining tradition established at Decatur House, Washington, D.C. 32 pp., deep purple illustrations on pale pink paper, 5½" x 8½", paperback.
1.50 (0.50)

National Trust for Historic Preservation, Washington, D.C. (member's discount 10%)

Cookbooks

Time-Honored
Norwegian Recipes

Time-Honored Norwegian Recipes

Erna Xan and Sigrid Marstrander present their family legacies in the art of cooking and have adapted the recipes to the modern American kitchen. The adaptations often proved interesting. For instance, in the old books from which these recipes were gathered, there appeared odd measurements including *barneskje* (child's spoon) and *knap en liter* (not quite a liter). Salt was never mentioned, since it was assumed that everyone knew to include it. Among the interesting recipes you might like to try are: Eplesuppe (Apple Soup), Svinekam (Pork Tenderloin), Blomkaalgratin (Cauliflower Soufflé), and Kremmerhus (Cornucopias).
82 pp., black-and-white drawings, 5 color illustrations; 6″ x 9″, spiral bound.
2.75 (0.50)
Norwegian-American Museum, Decorah, Iowa (member's discount 10%)

Green Corn and Violets

Green Corn and Violets: Amerindian Recipes for Camp and Kitchen is an introduction to modern Americans to the culinary heritage of the native American. In many instances, some of the flavor of the original method and ingredients is given as well as a modern version. Many of the nuts and seeds as well as honey which are sold in health-food stores today were staples for the native American. The earliest form of bread in this country was made of ground seeds or nuts such as sunflower seeds, acorns, and hazelnuts, pounded into meal and mixed with water to form the dough. They were called Seed Cakes. Recipes are provided for Seed Cakes and Acorn Bread. Honey was used to season everything and delicious recipes are given for: Honey Strawberries; Raspberries and Honey; and Cranberry Cake. Also included among the 68 entries are fish, fowl, meat, and vegetable dishes. There are helpful hints for the camper on building a fire, the use of various woods, clay-pot cooking, and smoking meats. 53 pp.; illus.; 6″ x 9″. Spiral bound.
1.75 (0.50)
Illinois State Museum, Springfield (member's discount not available on this item)

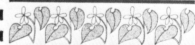

Green Corn and Violets

A Celebration of Art and Cookery

Peasants at a Roadside Inn, by Peter Brueghel, the Elder (Flemish, c. 1525–69) enhances the cover of this tempting cookbook from the North Carolina Museum of Art. Recipes collected from friends of the museum and for the dishes served at "Museum Fetes" are featured. There are chapters entitled "Menus" and "Private Collections." "Lagniappe" (an extra or unexpected gift) includes directions for pomanders, sachets, and herb bouquets. Interspersed are reproductions of works of art from the museum's collections. 230 pp.; 26 illus. (2 color); 8½″ x 9″; clothbound.
9.95 (1.00)
North Carolina Museum of Art, Raleigh (member's discount 10%)

A Celebration of Art and Cookery

Gallery Buffet
Soup Cookbook

Sauce for a Swan

More Treasured Recipes

Cookbooks

Gallery Buffet Soup Cookbook

"Soup's on!" Soup is universal. It is known on every continent, and its infinite variations reflect both the creative skills of the natives and the natural bounty of the locale. Soup ranges from the delicate texture of the appetizer, usually a clear broth or bouillon which prepares the palate for the culinary delights of the chef, to the hearty satisfying melange that serves as the main course. And, in between, lie scores of other gastronomical soup triumphs, from the rich bisque to the homely black bean. There are hearty, clear, vegetable, cream, chilled, and seafood soups, as well as exotic and foreign soups. Included in the latter are Cold Peach Soup with Fresh Blueberry Garnish, Cream of Pecan Soup, Waterzooi from Belgium, and Avgolemono from Greece. There are helpful hints for soupmaking and suggestions for garnishes. The cookbook is illustrated with color reproductions of works from the Dallas Museum of Fine Arts' pre-Columbian collection. 126 pp.; 12 color illus.; 5³/₄" x 8³/₄"; clothbound.
7.50 (1.00)
Dallas Museum of Fine Arts (member's discount 10%)

Sauce for a Swan: A Selection of Early English Recipes

Six very unusual recipes have been reproduced in print form from the collection of 16th-century English books in the Huntington Library. Among them is a fascinating method "To keepe the teeth both white and sound." 6 black and white prints, suitable for framing, in green folder. Each print measures 14" x 11".
5.00 (0.75)
Huntington Library, Art Gallery, and Botanical Gardens, San Marino, California (members receive a 10.00 annual credit toward purchases)

More Treasured Recipes

A fascinating collection of recipes from both America and Europe. The opening section is a selection of favorites of such celebrities as Bob Hope, Lawrence Welk, Barbara Walters, Princess Grace of Monaco, and Rose Kennedy. There are also special sections devoted to holiday cooking, quantity cooking, and a potpourri. 174 pp.; illus.; 6" x 8³/₄"; spiral bound.
3.95 (1.00)
In order to help you prepare the meals, there is a *mortar and pestle,* which has been reproduced from an original in the museum's collection. Wood. Mortar of either maple or walnut. 4⁵/₈" high. Pestle of oak. 6³/₄" long.
18.00 (handling and shipping charges included)
Dexter Area Museum, Michigan (member's discount 10%)

149

Cookbooks

The Taste of Country Cooking

Edna Lewis, a teaching assistant at the American Museum of Natural History, re-creates for our kitchens the country cooking of her youth on a farm in Freetown, Virginia. As each season reaps its own bounty, the menus are divided into Spring, Summer, Fall, and Winter. She also shares the ways her family prepared and enjoyed food. 256 pp.; 6½" x 8½".
10.00 cloth (0.75)
4.95 paper (0.75)
American Museum of Natural History, New York (member's discount 10%)

The Williamsburg Cookbook

A collection of 194 traditional and contemporary recipes initially compiled and adapted by Letha Booth and the staff of Colonial Williamsburg, with commentary by Joan Parry Dutton. Updated and enlarged. Eleven full-color illustrations by Taylor Biggs Lewis, Jr.; 40 line drawings by Vernon E. Wooten. 172 pp., 7" x 10".
3.50 paper (0.50)
8.95 cloth (0.50)
The Colonial Williamsburg Foundation (does not operate a membership program)

The Williamsburg Art of Cookery

Compiled by Helen Bullock, this volume enables today's cook to offer the same time-tested fare that pleased the taste of our colonial forebearers. Includes a table of favorite garden herbs. 18th-century typography is used. 276 pp., 5 line drawings; 4" x 6⅞".
4.00 cloth (0.50)
10.00 leatherbound (0.50)
The Colonial Williamsburg Foundation (does not operate a membership program)

Yesterday's Herbs for Today

You are invited to share a useful and entertaining book, carefully researched by Norma McAllister. The various herbs were grown on the grounds of the Dexter Area Museum and tended by its members. Read and enjoy the lore and history of herbs. Their delightful scents, luxurious growth, and zesty culinary and medicinal properties will enrich your life. 48 pp.; illus.; 8½" x 10"; paper.
2.75 (handling and shipping charges included)
Dexter Area Museum, Michigan (member's discount 10%)

Culinary Collection

The Member's Council of the Everson Museum of Art has collected over 700 recipes for your enjoyment. In addition to the individual recipes, complete menus for brunches, luncheons, teas, and dinners have been compiled according to the four seasons. Suggestions are made for a summer pool or garden party and for an autumn tailgate picnic before the game. And if you are looking for new sandwich ideas, there is even a section devoted to them. 256 pp., illustrated; 7" x 9", spiral bound.
4.00 (0.50)
Everson Museum of Art, Syracuse, New York (member's discount 10%)

Strawbery Banke Cook Book

A choice collection of favorite recipes contributed by the membership and staff of the Guild of Strawbery Banke®, Inc., an organization supporting the Strawbery Banke preservation project in Portsmouth, New Hampshire. All categories of food are included in the 400 recipes. A few examples are: Ha'penny Snacks, Strawbery Banke Lobster Pie, Banbury Tarts, and Squash Muffins "McIntyre." An extra-special section features recipes using one main ingredient—strawberries, of course! 156 pp., illustrated; 7" x 9", spiral bound.
7.95 (0.80)
The Guild of Strawbery Banke®, Inc., Portsmouth (member's discount 10%)

The Gunston Hall Cookbook

A selection of favorite recipes from the Regents of Gunston Hall. Illus.; 6½" x 9". Spiral bound.
3.95 (0.75)
Gunston Hall, Lorton, Virginia (member's discount 10%)

Ices Plain and Fancy

117 recipes from a delightful Victorian "book of ices" by Mrs. A. B. Marshall. Among the specialties: Apricot Cream Ice, Apple Ice Water, a Chateaubriand Bombe, Rum Sorbet, and Spinach Ice Cream. Many of them are a revelation to the modern palate. Engravings and contemporary photographs decorate the pages. Introduction and annotations by Barbara Ketcham Wheaton, preface by A. Hyatt Mayor. 122 pp., illustrated; 6¾" x 7⅝", clothbound.
5.95 (2.00) D0901
The Metropolitan Museum of Art, New York (member's discount 25%)

A Culinary Collection from
The Metropolitan Museum of Art

A selection of tempting recipes from the trustees and staff of the museum. 176 pp., illustrated; 7" x 9", spiral bound, boxed.
5.95 (2.00) D1310
The Metropolitan Museum of Art, New York (member's discount 25%)

The Collector's Cookbook

A group of 447 sumptuous recipes, from appetizers to finishing touches, compiled by the Friends of the Minneapolis Institute of Arts. 296 pp., illustrated; 6″ x 8³/₄″, paperback.
5.95 (0.50)
The Minneapolis Institute of Arts (member's discount 10%)

Artists' Cookbook

The Museum of Modern Art's *Artists' Cookbook* is a compilation of 155 recipes as prepared by 30 contemporary painters and sculptors. There are many taste-tempting treats from appetizers like Liverwurst in Beer (Robert Motherwell) to desserts like Timbale Elysée Lasserre (Salvador Dali) with perhaps Chinese Chicken fried with Tiger Lilies (Lowell Nesbitt) in between. Conversations with each artist are included as well as a photograph by Blaine Waller. The book was compiled by Madeleine Conway and Nancy Kirk. 165 pp.; 30 illus.; 6¹/₂″ x 9″. Spiral bound.
8.95 (0.50)
The Museum of Modern Art, New York (member's discount 25%)

Can You Stand 25 for Dinner?

A charming little cookbook designed to help any hostess be the "mostest" when faced with a crowd for dinner. Complete menus are featured, including:

A Fine Kettle of Fish
Restigouche Salmon
Cole Slaw
Bean Salad
Whole Wheat Bread
Chocolate Cream Puffs

Each menu is accompanied by a ready-made shopping list. 32 pp., illustrated; 5¹/₂″ x 8¹/₂″, paperback.
1.00 (0.50)
Art Gallery of Ontario, Toronto, Canada (member's discount 10%)

Art à la Carte

Unique among the museum cookbook offerings, this volume is devoted to vegetable cooking and dessert making. Many cooks find vegetables uninspiring and therefore never use much imagination in their preparation, but after you read the endless recipes that can be concocted in minutes, vegetables might become as important to your palates as they have been to the artists' palettes for centuries. You might try: Onions with Mushrooms and Sherry Cheese Sauce; Acorn Squash with Pineapple; or Balkan Vegetable Casserole. To complement the meal, choose one of the many desserts, both plain and fancy. The illustrations in the book are reproductions of art works by Montana artists. 94 pp., illustrated; 6³/₈″ x 9″, spiral bound.
4.95 (0.55)
Yellowstone Art Center, Billings, Montana (member's discount not available)

Books

Albright-Knox Art Gallery, Buffalo (member's discount 10%) (2.50 per book)

Albright-Knox Art Gallery: Painting and Sculpture from Antiquity to 1942.
528 pp.; 483 illus. (32 color); 9″ x 10″
35.00 cloth
18.95 paper

Contemporary Art, 1942–72: Collection of the Albright-Knox Art Gallery. Essays by Irving Sandler, Edward F. Fry, John Russell, R. W. D. Oxenaar, Lawrence Alloway, and others.
480 pp.; 535 illus. (82 color); 7¹/₂″ x 10¹/₂″
18.00 cloth
12.50 paper

Alfred Jensen: Paintings and Diagrams from the Years 1957–77. Essays by Linda L. Cathcart and Marcia Tucker.
97 pp.; 56 illus. (25 color); 10″ square
12.00 paper

Museum of American Folk Art, New York (member's discount 10%) (1.00)

The All-American Dog—
Man's Best Friend in Folk Art,
by Dr. Robert Bishop.
152 pp.; 128 illus. (24 color); 7″ x 10″
5.95 paper

American Cat-alogue—
The Cat in American Folk Art,
by Bruce Johnson.
132 pp.; 123 illus. (8 color); 6³/₄″ x 9″
4.95 paper

A Child's Comfort—Baby and Doll Quilts in American Folk Art. A catalogue to accompany an exhibition held at the Museum of American Folk Art in 1976. Directions for making four small quilts and instructions for preserving and mending quilts.
128 pp.; 87 illus. (48 color); 7″ x 9″
12.95 cloth
6.95 paper

Museum of the American Indian, New York (member's discount 15% on purchases of 5.00 or more) (0.35)

Beads and Beadwork of the American Indians, by William C. Orchard.
184 pp.; 41 illus. (16 color); 6³/₄″ x 10″
7.50 paper

Hopi Kachinas, by Edwin Earle and Edward Kennard.
50 pp. text; 28 plates; 8″ x 10″
12.50 cloth

The Technique of Porcupine Quill Decoration Among the Indians of North America, by William C. Orchard.
53 pp.; 36 illus.; 6¹/₂″ x 10″
3.50 paper

American Museum of Atomic Energy, Oak Ridge, Tennessee (does not operate a membership program) (0.50)

Oak Ridge, City that Changed the World. This book tells the story of Oak Ridge, its impact on history, its evolution from when it was known as the "Atomic City" to its present claim of "Energy Capitol of the World."
40 pp.; 96 illus.
2.00 paper

The American Museum of Natural History, New York (member's discount 10%) (1.00)

Ancient Mexico and Central America, by Gordon F. Ekholm. Photographs by Lee Boltin.
128 pp.; illus. (color); 7″ x 10″
5.00 paper

Costumes of the East, by Walter A. Fairservis, Jr. Garments worn by the peoples of the East, including Lapland, Middle East, China, and Siberia.
160 pp.; illus. (color); 8″ x 10″
15.00 cloth
5.95 paper

Naturalist's Color Guide, by Frank B. Smithe. Vinyl binder has 86 color chips with which to make precise identifications of the colors of birds and other animals. The book explains how the colors were chosen (mostly from Ridgeway) and gives correlations of bird plumage.
240 pp. book; vinyl binder with color chips; each measures 6″ x 9″
9.00 binder
5.00 book
12.00 the set

Arizona Historical Society, Tucson (member's discount 20%) (1.00 per book)

The Desert, by John C. Van Dyke. The 1903 classic poetic description of the Southwestern deserts, reproduced in facsimile with a new introduction by Lawrence Clark Powell.
10.00 cloth

Globe, Arizona, by Clara T. Woody and Milton L. Schwartz. A history of pioneer times in a mountain mining and ranching town.
15.00 cloth
9.50 paper

Temples in the Wilderness, by George B. Eckhart and James S. Griffith. The Spanish colonial churches of northern Sonora.
4.50 paper

The Asia Society Inc., New York (member's discount varies according to purchase) (1.95)

The Royal Hunter: Art of The Sasanian Empire, by Prudence Oliver Harper.
176 pp.; 173 illus. (10 color); 9¼" x 10¾"
19.95 cloth (member's price 15.00)
11.00 paper (member's price 8.50)

Southeast Asian Ceramics: Ninth Through Seventeenth Centuries, by Dean F. Frasche.
144 pp.; 109 illus. (10 color); 9" x 9½"
25.00 cloth (member's price 16.50)
7.50 paper (member's price 6.50)

The Baltimore Museum of Art (member's discount 10%) (1.25)

Picasso Drawings and Watercolors, 1899–1907, in the Collection of The Baltimore Museum of Art.
Commentary by Victor I. Carlson.
128 pp.; 46 illus. (5 color); 8" x 10"
25.00 linenbound
15.00 paper

Museum of Fine Arts, Boston (member's discount 10%) (1.00)

Greek Island Embroideries, by Susan MacMillan.
77 pp.; 50 illus. (8 color); 1 map; 8" x 9½"
3.95 paper

Alfred Stieglitz, Photographer.
146 pp.; 62 duotone facsimile illus.; 11" x 11¼"
15.00 cloth
7.00 paper

Andrew Wyeth.
224 pp.; 168 illus. (24 color); 10⅞" x 8½"
8.50 paper

The Brooklyn Museum (member's discount 15%) (1.50 for first book plus 0.50 for each additional book)

Stuart Davis: Art and Art Theory, by John R. Lane.
216 pp.; 181 illus. (16 color); 8½" x 11"
11.95 paper

Graphicstudio U.S.F. An Experiment in Art and Education, by Gene Baro.
208 pp.; 160 illus. (18 color); 6" x 12"
8.95 paper

King of the World: Ashur-nasir-pal II of Assyria, by Samuel M. Paley.
176 pp.; plus gatefold; 64 illus. (1 color); 9¼" x 12¼"
20.00 cloth

Buten Museum of Wedgwood, Merion, Pennsylvania (member's discount 10%) (0.50)

Wedgwood Guide to Marks and Dating, compiled by David Buten. Helpful guide to aid collectors in identifying and dating Wedgwood ceramics. Printed in pocket form.
3.50 paper

Carnegie Institute, Pittsburgh (member's discount 10%) (1.50)

Alechinsky: Paintings and Writings, by Eugene Ionesco and Pierre Alechinsky.
258 pp.; 256 illus. (16 color); 8⅝" x 12¼"
12.50 paper

Eight Hundred Years of Japanese Printmaking.
Introduction by Roger S. Keyes, foreward by Leon A. Arkus. A catalogue of more than 600 works from the James B. Austin Collection of Japanese woodblock prints. The catalogue is divided into 5 sections: Religious prints (12th–17th centuries); Primitive prints (mid-17th—mid-18th centuries); Ukiyo-e prints (mid-18th—mid-19th centuries); Foreigner and Meiji prints (mid-19th century–1912); and 20th century.
126 pp.; 145 illus. (8 color); 8¼" x 11½"
8.00 paper

Yörük, The Nomadic Weaving Tradition of the Middle East.
172 illus. (24 color); maps.
9.00 paper

The Art Institute of Chicago (member's discount 10%) (0.75)

Photographs from the Julien Levy Collection Starting with Atget. Essay and catalogue by David Travis. Among the photographers included: Cartier-Bresson, Cunningham, Evans, Moholy-Nagy, Man Ray, Sheeler, and Umbo.
96 pp.; 55 illus.
6.95 paper

Selected Works of 18th Century French Art in the Collections of the Art Institute of Chicago. Exhibition coordinator John Keefe.
219 pp.; 192 illus. (4 color)
12.50 paper

Stock Exchange Trading Room, by John Vinci. The reconstruction of one of the finest interiors of The Chicago School of Architecture, by Adler and Sullivan, at the Art Institute.
64 pp.; 40 illus. (4 color); 17 line drawings
4.95 paper

Chrysler Museum at Norfolk (member's discount 10%) (1.00)

Three Hundred Years of American Art in the Chrysler Museum.
270 pp.; 306 illus. (9 color); 8" x 10½"
10.00 paper

Books

Cincinnati Art Museum (membership discount not available) (0.75)

Change of Pace: Contemporary Furniture 1925–75. Foreword by Millard F. Rogers. Essay by Dr. Carol Macht.
24 pp.; 29 illus; 9″ x 10″
2.00 paper

Dine-Kitaj: A Two Man Exhibition. Essays by Jim Dine, R.B. Kitaj, and Richard Boyle.
40 pp.; 30 illus. (5 color); 9″ x 10″
2.00 paper

The Ladies God Bless'em: Cincinnati Women's Art Pottery of the Later 19th Century. Cincinnati was the home of the famous Rookwood Pottery works. Foreword by Millard F. Rogers. Introduction by Dr. Carol Macht.
70 pp.; 52 illus.; 9″ x 10″
3.00 paper

Museum of the City of New York (member's discount 20%) (0.75)

The City and the Theatre: The History of New York Playhouses—A 235-year journey from Bowling Green to Times Square, by Mary C. Henderson.
323 pp.; 150 photographs, drawings, maps
14.95 cloth

A Fabulous Dollhouse of the Twenties, by John Noble. The famous Stettheimer Dollhouse at the Museum of the City of New York.
48 pp.
1.75 paper

New York in the 30s, by Elizabeth McCausland. 97 photographs by Bernice Abbott from the collection of the Museum of the City of New York.
100 pp.
3.50 paper

Sterling and Francine Clark Art Institute, Williamstown, Massachusetts (does not operate a membership program) (0.50)

Dürer Through Other Eyes: His Graphic Works Mirrored in Copies and Forgeries of Three Centuries. Foreword by Julius S. Held. The catalogue for the exhibition was written by the students in a graduate seminar of the Williams College–Clark Art Institute Graduate Program in Art History.
99 pp.; 73 illus.; 7″ x 10¹/₂″
3.00 paper

List of Paintings in the Sterling and Francine Clark Art Institute. An illustrated checklist of the entire collection.
144 pp.; illus. (color cover); 7¹/₂″ x 9¹/₂″
5.00 paper

Claude Monet's Paintings of Rouen Cathedral, by George Heard Hamilton. A reprint of the 1959 Charlton Lectures at the University of Newcastle-on-Tyne.
28 pp.; 11 illus. (color cover); 6¹/₄″ x 10″
1.00 paper

The Colonial Williamsburg Foundation (does not operate a membership program) (0.50 per book)

Christmas Decorations from the Williamsburg's Folk Art Collection. This how-to craft book contains easy-to-follow instructions for making 90 decorations, many based on traditional folk crafts.
80 pp.; step-by-step drawings and photographs of the finished objects (28 color); 8¹/₄″ x 11″
6.95 cloth
3.50 paper

Gallery Guide to Abby Aldrich Rockefeller Folk Art Collection.
32 pp.; 30 illus. (28 color); 7″ x 10″
2.00 paper

The Harpsichord or Spinnet Miscellany, by Robert Bremmer. Preface by J. S. Darling. A facsimile reproduction of the original edition of about 1765, from a copy belonging to Colonial Williamsburg.
26 pp.; 12¹/₂″ x 9¹/₂″
5.95 cloth
2.95 paper

Colorado Springs Fine Arts Center (member's discount 10%) (1.00)

Hispanic Crafts of the Southwest. Edited by Dr. William Wroth. Articles covering the contemporary Hispanic crafts of the Southwest and their origins.

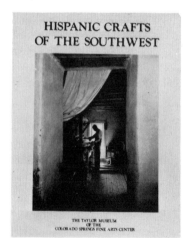

Weaving, Colcha embroidery, furniture, woodcarving, painting, jewelry, tinwork, and straw inlay are included.
130 pp.; 173 illus.
8.00 paper

Navaho Sandpaintings: The Huckel Collection, by Leland C. Wyman.
88 pp.; illus.
(color cover)
2.25 paper

The People of the Saints, by George Mills. The first study of the New Mexican *santos* to analyze in detail the Spanish American society that produced these images.
104 pp.; 32 color illus.
3.75 cloth

**Museum of Contemporary Crafts of the American
Crafts Council, New York** (member's discount varies
according to purchase) (handling and shipping charges
are included)

The Great American Foot. Exhibition devoted to the
foot—its function, fashion, and symbolism.
56 pp.; 100 illus.
4.60 paper (member's price 3.60)

Homage to the Bag. Functional and nonfunctional
contemporary, historic, and ethnic bags in all media.
24 pp.; 68 illus.
3.65 paper (member's price 3.40)

*Peter Voulkos,
A Dialogue with Clay.*
First book on this
important innovator,
prepared in conjunction
with a major retrospec-
tive of his work in 1978.
184 pp.; 80 illus.
(24 color); 9″ x 12″
27.50 cloth (member's
price 22.00)
(1.50)

**Country Music
Hall of Fame and
Museum, Nashville**
(does not operate a
membership program)
(1.00)

*Bill Monroe and His Blue Grass Boys: An Illustrated
Discography,* compiled, with an introduction and
commentaries, by Neil V. Rosenberg. Highlighted by
37 photographs, many of them old and rare, this
discography traces Monroe's recording career from
1940 through June 1974. Rosenberg, himself a
musician who has played with Monroe, adds
numerous historical details, as well as a biographical
sketch.
4.50 paper

My Husband Jimmie Rodgers, by Carrie Rodgers.
Long out of print, this warm and informative biography
of the father of country music has been sought after.
This edition is reprinted in its entirety, and is
enhanced by an introduction and chronology of
Rodgers's life by Nolan Porterfield.
5.95 paper

The 1921 Gibson Catalog, edited with a new
introduction by William Ivey. Pages of illustrations of
guitars, mandolins, harp-guitars, sheet music, and
accessories available from Gibson in 1921.
120 pp.; illus. (color cover)
4.50 paper

Craft and Folk Art Museum, Los Angeles (member's
discount 10%) (0.75)

Los Angeles Collects Folk Art. Preface by Edith Wyle.
Introduction by Lee Mullican.
62 pp.; 61 illus.; 8″ x 9″
4.00 paper

Nineteenth-Century American Coverlets. Introduction
by Sabra Petersmann.
23 pp.; 9 illus.; 5¼″ x 8¼″
1.25 paper

The Tool as Object. Introduction by Edward F. Tuttle.
39 pp.; 16 illus.; 7″ x 10½″
4.00 paper

Cranbrook Academy of Art, Bloomfield Hills, Michigan
(member's discount 10%) (0.75)

Historic Fiberworks/Cranbrook (CAAM vol 1, No. 4). An
exhibition catalogue of fiberworks from the collection
of the Cranbrook Academy of Art/Museum and
Institute of Science. Selections made by Gerhardt
Knodel, Head of the Fiber Department.
20 pp.; illus.
3.00 paper

Milles at Cranbrook. Picture study with notes of the
Swedish-American sculptor Carl Milles's work from
1931 to 1951.
53 full-page black and white photographs; spiral bound
4.50 cloth

The Saarinen Door. A photographic study of Eliel
Saarinen's work at Cranbrook.
64 pp.; 54 photographs
4.00 cloth

The Historical Society of Delaware, Wilmington
(member's discount 10%) (1.00)

The Delaware Continentals, 1776–83, by Christopher L.
Ward. The story of a regiment of the continental Army
distinguished for length of service, endurance of
hardship, and gallantry in action.
620 pp.; 6¼″ x 9½″
15.00 cloth

*Plantation Life at Rose Hill: The Diaries of Martha
Ogle Forman, 1814–45.* Edited by W. Emerson Wilson.
A thorough picture of life on a Maryland plantation by
the wife of Revolutionary War General Thomas Marsh
Forman.
451 pp.; 6¼″ x 9¼″
7.50 cloth

Denver Museum of Natural History (discount not
available with regular membership; higher category
member's discount 10%) (0.15)

Ancient Man in North America, by H. M. Wormington.
A complete archaeological survey of prehistoric man.
322 pp.; 72 illus.
5.00 paper

Prehistoric Indians of the Southwest, by H. M.
Wormington.
191 pp.; 58 illus.
3.50 paper

Books

Detroit Institute of Arts (member's discount 10%) (1.00)

Detroit Collects African Art. Foreword by Dr. Frederick Cummings. Essay by Michael Kan.
104 pp.; illustrated (color cover); 8½″ x 9″
6.00 paper

The Paper Cut-Outs of Henri Matisse—Complete Catalogue Entries for All Known Matisse Cut-Outs. Essay by Dr. John H. Neff.
272 pp.; 324 illus. (24 color); 8½″ x 11″
17.95 paper

Dexter Area Museum, Michigan (member's discount 10%) (handling and shipping charges included)

How to Make Dolls of Yesteryear. Compiled by members of the local historical society and illustrated by Mrs. Mary Rush. Contents: Clothespin doll, Yarn doll, Rag (stocking) doll, Dough doll, clothing construction, proportion guide, jointed wire body, Applehead doll, Cloth doll, Cornhusk doll, and wooden doll.
32 pp.; illus.; 8½″ x 10″
3.75 paper

M. H. de Young Memorial Museum, San Francisco (member's discount 20%) (1.00)

Four Centuries of French Drawings in the Fine Arts Museums of San Francisco, by Phyllis Hattis.
360 pp.; 500 illus. (8 color)
20.00 cloth
13.95 paper

Rodin's Sculpture: A Critical Study of The Spreckels Collection.
360 pp.; illus.
20.00 cloth
13.95 paper

The Triumph of Humanism: A Visual Survey of the Renaissance. Introduction by D. Graeme Keith.
96 pp.; 8 color illus.
6.95 paper

The Folger Shakespeare Library, Washington, D.C. (member's discount 15%) (1.00)

The Book of Common Prayer, 1559: The Elizabethan Prayer Book, edited by John E. Booty. The 1559 Book of Common Prayer has been the foundation of Anglican liturgy since the reign of Elizabeth I. A new edition that retains the style and cadence of the old and at the same time reproduces the text in modern spelling and punctuation.
437 pp.; index
15.00 cloth

Shakespeare on the American Stage: From the Hallams to Edwin Booth, by Charles H. Shattuck. An authoritative survey of Shakespeare's place in the formative years of the American theater.
184 pp.; more than 100 illus. (several color plates)
7.95 paper

The Widening Circle: The Story of the Folger Shakespeare Library and Its Collection, by Betty Ann Kane. A profusely illustrated and beautifully designed history of the Folger Library, its rare holdings, the building, and its scholarly and cultural activities.
76 pp.; illus.
3.95 paper

The Fort Worth Art Museum (member's discount 25%) (0.85)

Dan Flavin: Installations in Fluorescent Light and Drawing: Diagrams and Graphics from 1972 through 1975.
99 pp.; illus. (color); 10¾ x 8½″
10.00 paper

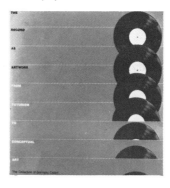

The Record as Artwork: From Futurism to Conceptual Art. The collection of Germano Celant. Both English and French text.
121 pp.; illus.; 6¾″ square
5.00 paper

Free Library of Philadelphia (member's discount 10%) (1.50)

Old Philadelphia in Early Photographs 1839–1914, by Robert F. Looney.
230 pp.; 215 illus.; 8⅞″ x 11¾″
6.00 paper

Thirty-two Picture Postcards of Old Philadelphia, by Robert F. Looney.
Postcards perforated so that you can take them out and mail. Each is an old photograph of Philadelphia from the period 1859–1928.
8¼″ x 11″
2.00 paper

Freer Gallery of Art, Washington, D.C. (does not operate a membership program) (1.25)

Art of the Arab World, by Esin Atil.
156 pp. text; 106 color illus.; 9³/₄″ x 10″
15.00 paper

The Freer Gallery of Art, I China.
184 pp.; 131 illus. (96 color); 10⁵/₈″ x 14⁵/₈″
15.00 cloth

The Freer Gallery of Art, II Japan.
184 pp.; 128 illus. (68 color); 10⁵/₈″ x 14⁵/₈″
15.00 cloth

Gibbes Art Gallery, Charleston (member's discount 10%) (1.00)

Contemporary Artists of South Carolina. Verbal portraits and photographic essays of a broad selection of modern painters, sculptors and printmakers of the state.
238 pp.; 340 illus. (40 color)
5.00

Plantations of the Carolina Low Country, by Samuel Gaillard Stoney. Edited by Albert Simons and Samuel Lapham, Jr. Introduction by John Mead Howells.
247 pp.; 78 pp. text, 3 maps, 147 photographs, 20 plans, 25 full-page drawings
27.50

South Carolina Architecture 1670–1970. Spans history that attests to the dramatic social, economic, cultural, and political changes within the state that influenced architectural design.
221 pp.; 110 illus.
5.00

The Solomon R. Guggenheim Museum, New York (member's discount 25%) (0.75 for the first book plus 0.25 for each additional book)

Klee at the Guggenheim Museum. Introduction by Thomas M. Messer. Essay by Dr. L. Svendsen.
84 pp.; 68 illus. (47 color)
6.95 paper

Wille de Kooning in East Hampton. Essay by Diane Waldman.
151 pp.; 98 illus. (27 color)
11.50 paper

Kenneth Noland: A Retrospective. Essay by Diane Waldman.
160 pp.; 100 illus. (72 color)
9.95 paper

Historic Deerfield, Inc., Massachusetts (member's discount 10%) (1.20)

The Heritage Foundation Collection of Silver with Biographical Sketches of New England Silversmiths 1625–1825, by Henry N. Flynt and Martha Gandy Fales.
A detailed description of the American silver in the Historic Deerfield collection.
Reproductions of over 800 marks of New England silversmiths.
391 pp.; illus.
30.00 cloth

Museum of Holography, New York (member's discount 10%) (1.50)

Harriet Casdin-Silver Holography. Catalogue of projected images by holographic artist.
illus.
1.50 paper

Holografi: Det 3-Dimensionella Mediet. Comprehensive catalogue of the Museum of Holography's exhibition of holograms in Stockholm, Sweden. Swedish and English text.
95 pp.
5.00 paper

Through the Looking Glass. Folio; catalogue of the opening show of the Museum of Holography. Basic explanation of holography.
illus.
5.00 paper

Illinois State Museum, Springfield (no member's discount on publications) (1.00)

Arts, Crafts, and Architecture in Early Illinois, by Betty Madden.
310 pp.; app. 600 illus. (36 color)
19.50 cloth
10.00 paper

Soft Drink Bottling— A History with Special Reference to Illinois, by John R. Paul and Paul W. Parmalee.
121 pp.; illus.; 8¹/₂″ x 11″
5.00 paper

Indiana University Art Museum, Bloomington (member's discount 10%) (0.75)

The American Scene 1820–1900.
144 pp.; 97 illus.; 8¹/₂″ x 10″
5.00 paper

The American Scene 1900–70.
120 pp.; 78 illus.; 8¹/₂″ x 10″
5.00 paper

German and Austrian Expressionism 1900–20.
166 pp.; 49 illus.; 8¹/₂″ x 10″
12.50 paper

Indianapolis Museum of Art (member's discount 10%) (0.75)

"Perceptions of the Spirit" in Twentieth-Century Art. Prepared for an exhibition in cooperation with the Graduate Theological Union, Berkeley.
177 pp.; 65 illus. (10 color).
6.00 paper (special member's price **5.00**)

Books

International Center of Photography, New York
(member's discount 15%) (1.00)

ICP Library of Photographers. 6 volumes available: *Werner Bishof, Robert Capa, Lewis W. Hine, David Seymour-Chim, Roman Vishniac,* and *Dan Weiner.*

Illus.; 7¼" x 8½"
3.00 each paper
15.00 the set paper

Spontaneity and Style: Munkacsi.
48 pp.; 33 illus.
8.00 paper

The Jewish Museum, New York (member's discount 15%) (0.75)

Fabric of Jewish Life. Textiles from the Jewish Museum Collection.
144 pp.; 250 illus. (25 color); 8" x 11"
12.95 paper

Kimbell Art Museum, Fort Worth, Texas
(does not operate a membership program) (1.00)

Kimbell Art Museum Catalogue.
335 pp.; 167 illus. (79 color); 11⅜" x 8½"
25.00 cloth

Light Is the Theme. Comments on architecture by Louis Kahn. Compiled by Nell E. Johnson.
80 pp.; 37 illus.; 9⅞" x 8"
5.00 paper

Lycoming County Historical Society and Museum, Pennsylvania (member's discount not available) (0.50)

Severin Roesen: A Chronology, by Lois Goldreich Marcus. A critical analysis of the work of the still-life painter Severin Roesen (born Germany, active in America), based on 21 signed and dated works executed between 1848 and 1872.
55 pp.; 39 illus. (color front and back cover); 8½" x 11"
5.00 paper (0.50)

Maine State Museum, Augusta (does not operate a membership program) (0.50 for first book plus 0.25 each additional book)

Archaeological Excavations at Pemaquid, Maine 1965–1974, by Helen Camp. Historical and archaeological findings of a 17th- and 18th-century colony.
89 pp.; illus.; 8½" x 11"
6.95 paper

The Historic Architecture of Maine, by Denys Peter Myers.
254 pp.; illus.; 6" x 9"
8.95 paper

Maine: A Guide "Downeast," edited by Dorris A. Isaacson. The first authoritative guide and source book on the Pine Tree State in print since 1937.
510 pp.; illus.; 5½" x 8¼".
6.50 cloth

Maxwell Museum of Anthropology, The University of New Mexico (member's discount 10% on publications) (0.65 per book)

Seven Families in Pueblo Pottery. Traces the development in style and technique in the pottery produced by seven Pueblo families. Key technical and historical terms are defined in a short glossary.
116 pp.; 165 illus. (7 color); 7" x 7"
4.95 paper

Southwestern Weaving, by Marion Rodee.
192 pp.; 324 illus. (24 color); 8" x 10"
15.00 cloth
6.95 paper

Weavers of the Jade Needle: Textiles of Highland Guatemala
20 pp.; 28 illus.; 8½" x 11"
1.95 paper

The Mercer Museum, Doylestown, Pennsylvania
(member's discount 10% on purchases over 10.00) (0.70)

Ancient Carpenter's Tools, by Henry C. Mercer. Explains and illustrates the implements of the carpenter, joiner, cabinetmaker, and lumberman, in use in the 18th century, with references to earlier tools.
339 pp.; 250 illus.
12.95 cloth

Felt-Silk-Straw Handmade Hats: Tools and Processes, by Mary Elizabeth McClellan. A detailed account of the nearly forgotten craft of hatmaking.
24 pp.; illus.
3.50 paper

The Metropolitan Museum of Art, New York (member's discount 25%) (2.00 per order)

Le Bestiaire, ou Cortége d'Orphée, by Guillaume Apollinaire. Translations by Lauren Shakely. Raoul Dufy created illustrations to complement the poet's light verses. A facsimile edition of a rare book.
88 pp.; 30 illus.; 10" x 13"
20.00 linen over boards, slipcased (D0214)

The Cloisters Apocalypse: A Fourteenth Century Manuscript in Facsimile. This facsimile volume reproduces all of the pages of an early manuscript illustrating the transcendent vision of St. John the Evangelist.
104 pp. (76 facsimile pages in color); 110 illus. (72 in color and gold); 9" x 12¹/₈"
18.75 cloth (D0330)

Eighteen Songs of a Nomad Flute, The Story of Lady Wen-chi. Introduction and text by Robert A. Rorex and Wen Fong. Eighteen paintings that comprise this masterpiece of southern Sung narrative painting are accompanied by a translation of the T'ang dynasty poem.
100 pp.; 36 full-color pages (18 double-page reproductions); 60 monochrome plates; 10³/₄" x 9³/₄"
9.95 linen over boards, slipcased (D0511)

Milwaukee Art Center (member's discount 10%) (1.50)

The Naïve Tradition/Haiti. Reproductions of works in the Flagg Tanning Corporation Collection at the Art Center.
120 pp.; 116 illus. (6 color); 8¹/₂" x 10"
7.00 paper

Personal Selections from the Collection of Mrs. Harry Lynde Bradley. Among the artists included are O'Keeffe, Chagall, Klee, Nolde, and Toulouse-Lautrec.
107 pp.; 102 color illus.; 8¹/₂" x 11"
25.00 cloth

The Minneapolis Institute of Arts (member's discount 10%) (0.75)

Charles Biederman: A Retrospective. Essay by Gregory Hedberg.
100 pp.; 226 illus. (66 color); 10¹/₂" x 12"
100.00 paper

I Wear The Morning Star. Exhibition of American Indian clothing.
94 pp.; 80 illus. (15 color); 8¹/₂" x 10"
7.50 paper

The Museum of Modern Art, New York (member's discount 25%) (0.50 for first book plus 0.20 for each additional book)

Cézanne: The Late Work. Edited by William Rubin.
416 pp.; 427 illus. (50 color); 9" x 11"
40.00 cloth
17.50 paper

Post-Impressionism, by John Rewald. A new, revised edition, which carries forward Mr. Rewald's account of the formation of modern art from 1886, the year of van Gogh's arrival in Paris, through Gauguin's return from Tahiti in 1893.
584 pp.; 500 illus. (50 color); 9" x 10"
40.00 cloth

Steichen: The Master Prints 1895–1914, by Dennis Longwell. Presentation of works from Steichen's early innovative period.
180 pp.; 73 illus. (6 color); 9" x 11"
35.00 cloth

Munson Williams Proctor Institute, Utica, New York (member's discount 10%) (0.60)

Charles Burchfield: Catalogue of Painting in Public and Private Collections. Introduction by Joseph S. Trovato.
367 pp.; 170 illus. (17 color); 8¹/₂" x 10"
15.00 cloth
12.00 paper

Mystic Seaport (member's discount 10%) (1.00)

Building The Herreshoff Dinghy, by Barry Thomas. A classic for small-boat builders.
6" x 9"
3.75 paper

J. E. Butterworth, 19th-century Marine Painter, by R. J. Schaefer. First complete illustrated biography of this English painter.
276 pp.; 121 illus. (24 color); 8¹/₂" x 11"
75.00 cloth

The Charles W. Morgan, by John F. Leavitt. The story of whaling and the history of this whaleship.
131 pp.; 43 illus.; 7" x 10"
9.95 cloth

National Air and Space Museum, Smithsonian Institution, Washington, D.C. (Smithsonian Associate member's discount 10%) (0.75)

Aircraft of the National Air and Space Museum, Smithsonian Institution, compiled by Claudia M. Oakes.
130 pp.; 237 illus., including 3 view drawings (12 color); 8¹/₂" x 11"
2.00 paper

Rockets, Missiles and Spacecraft of the National Air and Space Museum, Smithsonian Institution, by Lynne C. Murphy.
68 pp.; 108 illus. (16 color); 8¹/₂" x 11"
1.50 paper

Books

National Archives and Records Service, Washington, D.C. (member's discount 20%) (handling and shipping charges are included)

The Story of the Bill of Rights
24 pp.; 21 illus.
3.00 paper

Washington: The Design for the Federal City. This traces nearly 200 years of sporadic progress toward the accomplishment of the original dream.
80 pp.; 75 illus. (color cover)
3.00 paper

The Written Word Endures: Milestone Documents of American History.
112 pp.; 210 illus. (27 color)
12.50 cloth

National Trust for Historic Preservation, Washington, D.C. (member's discount 10%) (1.00)

America's Forgotten Architecture, by Tony P. Wrenn and Elizabeth D. Mulloy. Surveys in 475 photographs of what's worth saving and how to do it.
312 pp.; illus.
20.00 cloth
8.95 paper

Economic Benefits of Preserving Old Buildings, edited by the National Trust. Details the economic feasibility of reusing old buildings. Bankers, real estate agents, developers, and municipal officials explain the public and private benefits of preservation.
164 pp.; illus.
9.00 cloth
6.00 paper

What Style Is It?, by John Poppeliers, S. Allen Chambers, and Nancy Schwartz. An illustrated guide to American architectural styles from the 17th through the 20th century. Includes illustrated glossary and bibliography.
48 pp.; illus.
3.50 paper

The New York Public Library (member's discount 20%) (2.00)

A Midsummer Night's Dream. An heirloom edition of Shakespeare's play, illustrated by the renowned Arthur Rackham. Reproduced directly from the original manuscript, the only one in existence in the Library's collection. The entire text was handwritten by calligrapher Graily Hewitt.
14 two-color illus.;
16 full-color illus.; 9″ x 12″
32.50 cloth

North Carolina Museum of Art, Raleigh (member's discount 10%) (0.50)

A Selection from The Birds of America by John James Audubon. Commentary by Charlotte Hilton Green.
66 pp.; 26 illus.
(2 color); 8″ x 11″
4.00 paper

Old Sturbridge Village (member's discount 10%) (0.25 for the first book plus 0.05 for each additional book)

The ABCs of Canvas Embroidery, No. 1, by Muriel L. Baker. The history of canvas embroidery, its role in the history of needlework and its place in the modern home and church. Stitch charts and directions for making a large variety of stitches.
2.00 paper

The XYZs of Canvas Embroidery, by Muriel L. Baker. A companion to the above. 46 new stitches for filling and background. Directions for using different size stitches on a single canvas, joining and binding canvas, determining the proper thread thickness, etc.
2.50 paper

A Primer of New England Crewel Embroidery, by Catherine A. Hedlund. A history of the art from its English origins to the 20th century. Illustrated directions for stitches. 25 patterns that can be enlarged for working.
2.00 paper

Art Gallery of Ontario, Toronto, Canada (member's discount 10%) (0.75)

The Dutch Cityscape in the 17th Century and its Sources. Essays by Richard J. Wattenmaker, Dedalo Carasso, Bob Haak, and Boudewijn Bakker. Bilingual (Dutch and English).
272 pp.; 155 illus. (8 color)
18.50 cloth
10.00 paper

Lawren S. Harris: Urban Scenes and Wilderness Landscapes 1906–1930, by Jeremy Adamson. Traces the career of Harris, the unofficial leader of Canada's Group of Seven, from his student days to the beginnings of his abstract canvases.
232 pp.; 170 illus. (16 color)
22.50 cloth
15.00 paper

The Laurentians: Painters in a Landscape. Foreword by William J. Withrow. Preface, introduction, and biographies by Mela Constantinidi and Helen Duffy. Essay by Robert Ayre. Paintings, drawings, sketches, and prints by 15 artists with attachments to the Laurentian area, north of Montreal, during the past half century.
88 pp.; 68 illus. (12 color)
8.95 paper

Peabody Museum of Salem (member's discount 10%) (1.25)

The Collection of Japanese Sword Guards with Selected Pieces of Sword Furniture, by John Hamilton.
200 pp.; 118 illus. (8 color)
9.75 paper

A History of American Marine Painting, by John Wilmerding.
279 pp.; 186 illus. (18 color)
25.00 cloth

Pennsylvania Academy of Fine Arts, Philadelphia (member's discount 10%) (0.60)

Eight Contemporary American Painters, by Frank H. Goodyear, Jr.
62 pp.; 17 illus. (8 color); 8½″ x 11″
6.75 paper

The Pennsylvania Academy and Its Women 1850–1920, by Christine Jones Huber.
48 pp.; 18 illus. (1 color); 7½″ x 10″
1.75 paper

The Travel Sketches of Louis Kahn, by Vincent Scully, Frank H. Goodyear, Jr., and William Holman.
62 pp.; 34 illus. (4 color); 10″ x 8″
6.95 paper

Philadelphia Museum of Art (member's discount 10%) (1.00)

The Second Empire: Art in France under Napoleon III. Catalogue covers all aspects of the arts in France from 1852 to 1870. There are sections on architectural drawings, furnishings, metalwork, ceramics and glass, sculpture, painting, drawing, and photography. Contains historical and artistic introductions and chronology.
400 pp.; 402 illus. (12 color)
18.95 paper

The Thomas Eakins Collection, by Theodor Siegl. Introduction by Evan H. Turner. The paintings, drawings, sculpture, and photographs of Thomas Eakins are fully illustrated and discussed in this handbook to the largest collection of the artist's work. It presents significant new scholarship by the leading authority on this great American artist.
180 pp.; 160 illus. (color cover)
11.95 paper

The Phillips Collection, Washington, D.C. (does not operate a membership program) (0.75)

The Group of Seven: Canadian Landscape Painters, by Jeanne L. Pattison. Foreword by Laughlin Phillips.
40 pp.; 28 color illus.; 10″ x 11″
5.00 paper

Horace Pippin, by Romare Bearden. Foreword by Laughlin Phillips, Terry Dintenfass, and James F. Duff.
55 pp.; 46 color illus.; 11″ x 9″
6.00 paper

Portland Art Association, Oregon (member's discount 10%) (0.50)

Masterworks in Wood: The Woodcut Print. A history of the woodcut print from the 15th to the early 20th century.
142 pp.; 153 illus.; 8½″ x 11¾″
6.00 paper

The Mughal and Deccani Schools: Indian Miniature Painting. Material from the collection of Edwin Binney, 3rd.
241 illus. (20 color); 8½″ x 7¾″
10.00 paper

The Princess Captured by Spirit Bears. Adapted from a Haida myth by Rachael Griffin. Illustrated by Corinna and Virginia Campbell.
14 pp.; 11 color illus.; 8½″ x 7½″
2.50 paper

The Art Museum, Princeton University (member's discount 10%) (0.50)

Fragments of American Life, by John Ralph Willis. Exhibition of works by seven contemporary black artists.
76 pp.; 35 illus.
5.95 paper

Illuminated Greek Manuscripts from American Collections, edited by Gary Vikan. Exhibition in honor of Kurt Weitzmann.
232 pp.; 122 illus. (1 color)
8.95 paper

Jaina Figurines: A Study of Maya Iconography, by Mary Ellen Miller.
72 pp.; 28 illus.; maps
5.95 paper

Books

Museum of Art, Rhode Island School of Design, Providence (member's discount 30% on publications) (1.00 for first book plus 0.50 each additional book)

Classical Bronzes, by David Gordon Mitten. Survey of the museum's collection of household and ritual vessels, utensils, statuettes and jewelry.
210 pp.; 209 illus.; 9″ x 11″
15.00 paper

Classical Jewelry, by Tony Hackens. Jewelry ranging from 1300 B.C. to c. 500 A.D., treated from the standpoint of the jeweler's technique.
157 pp.; heavily illustrated; 9″ x 11″
10.00 paper

Classical Sculpture, by Brunilde Sismondo Ridgway.
225 pp.; 177 illus.; 9″ x 11″
10.00 cloth
8.00 paper

Institute for the Arts, Rice University (does not operate a membership program) (1.50)

Art Nouveau Belgium/France.
512 pp.; 754 illus.
(21 color); 8½″ x 9″
20.00 paper

Painting in the Age of Actuality: Marden, Novrose, Rothko, by Sheldon Nodelman.
96 pp.; 16 color illus.; 5½″ x 8½″
7.00 paper

The Historical Society of Rockland County, New York
(member's discount not available) (handling and shipping charges included)

The Artist and the Unicorn, by Brooks Wright. A biography of Arthur B. Davies.
144 pp.; illus.
17.95 cloth

Wine and Bitters, by Isabelle K. Savell. An account of the meetings of George Washington and Sir Guy Carleton and the first British naval salute to the new American nation at the end of the Revolution.
64 pp.
4.00 paper

Rosenbach Foundation, Philadelphia (member's discount varies according to purchase) (handling and shipping charges included)

Fantasy Sketches, by Maurice Sendak. A book of previously unpublished drawings by our most renowned children's book illustrator and author.
24 pp.; illus.
2.50 (member's discount 20%)

James Joyce's Ulysses. A Facsimile of the Manuscript. Critical introduction by Harry Levin. Bibliographical preface by Clive E. Driver. The 810 pages of Joyce's handwritten manuscript are reproduced in two volumes. Volume 3 is a reproduction, in reduced size, of a copy of the first edition (Paris, 1922) marked with the differences between this text, the manuscript, and the "Little Review" installments. 3 volumes. Edition limited to 1,750 sets.
150.00 (member's discount 10%)

Ten Little Rabbits. A Counting Book for Children with Mino the Magician, by Maurice Sendak.
26 pp.; color illustrations
2.00 (member's discount 20%)

Royal Ontario Museum, Canada (member's discount 10%) (10% of purchase)

Canadian Watercolours and Drawings in the Royal Ontario Museum, by Mary Allodi. More than 2,200 pictures are catalogued, dating from 1757 to 1930, including some 380 of the United States. More than 430 are illustrated, 30 in color. The subjects include exploration and military campaigns, immigration and settlement, urbanization and industry as seen by 270 artists.
12″ x 8½″
30.00 cloth, 2 volumes in slipcase

In the Presence of the Dragon Throne, by John E. Vollmer. A catalogue to accompany an exhibition of Ch'ing dynasty costume, which illustrates many of the sumptuous garments and explores their role in Chinese history and technology. It also explores the history of clothing technology in eastern Asia.
88 pp.; illus. (color); 9″ x 9″
3.50 paper

Studies in Textile History in Memory of Harold B. Burnham. Edited by Veronika Gervers. This important collection of 25 articles by world-renowned textile specialists presents an international perspective on problems in current textile research.
378 pp.; illus. (color);
8½" x 11"
25.00 cloth

The St. Louis Art Museum (member's discount 10%) (0.75)

The St. Louis Art Museum—Handbook of the Collections. Essay by Charles E. Buckley.
378 pp.; more than 850 illus. (many in color); 8½" x 9½"
12.50 paper

Fine Arts Gallery of San Diego (member's discount 10%) (1.00)

The Cross and the Sword/La Cruz Y La Espalda. An overview of the religious images produced in the Southwest during the Spanish Colonial and subsequent periods.
144 pp.; 165 illus.
5.95 paper

The Works of Tomioka Tessai. His art is a continuation of the free styles of the scholar literati painters of China and the Nanga artists of Japan, which he blended with the movement and brilliant color traditional to Japan.
140 pp.; 65 illus. (3 color)
3.95 paper

San Francisco Museum of Modern Art (member's discount 20%) (1.50)

Joseph Raffael: The California Years, 1969–1978, by Thomas H. Garver.
64 pp.; 32 color illus.; 12" x 9"
8.95 paper

Clyfford Still, by Henry Hopkins.
144 pp.; 34 color illus.
15.00 cloth

A View of California Architecture: 1960–1976, by David Gebhard and Susan King.
64 pp.; 82 illus. (7 color); 11" x 9"
7.50 paper

Shaker Museum, Old Chatham, New York (member's discount 10%) (0.50 per book)

The Shaker Adventure, by Marguerite Melcher. History of the Shakers.
illus.
7.50 cloth
4.75 paper

The Shaker Garden and Seed Industry, by Margaret F. Sommer.
illus.
5.50 cloth
2.00 paper

The Shaker Museum. A gallery-by-gallery description with articles on clockmaking, music, herbs, and cloaks.
48 pp.; illus.
1.00 paper

Shelburne Museum, Inc., Vermont (does not operate a membership program) (0.50 for first book plus 0.25 for each additional book)

Blacksmiths' and Farriers' Tools at Shelburne Museum, by H. R. Bradley Smith.
272 pp.; more than 500 illus.
7.50

Decoys at Shelburne Museum, by David S. Webster and William Kehoe.
144 pp.; 210 illus. (10 color)
7.50

Pieced Work and Appliqué Quilts at Shelburne Museum, by Lilian B. Carlisle.
96 pp.; 99 illus.
7.50

Sleepy Hollow Restorations, Tarrytown, New York (member's discount 10%) (0.50 per book)

Old Christmas, by Washington Irving. Illustrations by Randolph Caldecott. Facsimile edition of the First Edition published by Macmillan and Co. of London in 1875. New introduction by Andrew B. Myers. Printed on ivory stock; bound in dark green cloth, cover and spine die-stamped in (imitation) gold. Dust jacket.
208 pp.; 106 illus. (12 full-page duotones);
5⅛" x 7½"
10.00 cloth

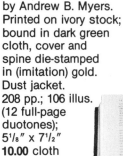
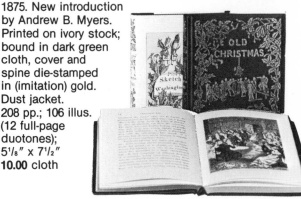

Rip Van Winkle and The Legend of Sleepy Hollow, by Washington Irving. Reproduction of two classic tales with the original 19th-century illustrations by F. O. C. Darley. Text from the author's Revised Edition of 1848. New introduction by Haskell Springer.
152 pp.; 12 color illus.; 10⅝" × 8⅜"
9.95 cloth

Books

South Street Seaport Museum, New York (member's discount 10%) (1.00)

Voyages, by Alfred Hill. Tales from the great age of sail as seen through the eyes of Captain Tristram Jordan and his son Frederic are told from personal diaries and logbooks.
illus.; 5¹/₂″ × 8¹/₂″
8.95

South Street— A Photographic Guide to New York City's Historic Seaport. Text by Ellen Fletcher Rosebrok. Photographs by Edmund V. Gillon, Jr.
illus.; 8³/₈″ x 9¹/₄″
4.00 paper

Historical Association of Southern Florida, Inc.
(member's discount not available) (0.75)
(All publications are reprints from original manuscripts with proper editing)

The Commodore's Story, by Ralph Middleton Munroe and Vincent Gilpin.
378 pp.; 56 illus.
5.00 paper

Official Directory of the City of Miami, 1904.
256 pp.
4.00 paper

They All Called It Tropical, by Charles M. Brookfield and Oliver Griswold.
77 pp.; 23 illus.; 1 map
1.95 paper

The Museums at Stony Brook, New York (member's discount 10%) (0.75)

William Sidney Mount: Painter of Rural America, by Alfred Frankenstein.
70 pp.; 61 illus. (7 color); 8″ x 10¹/₂″
3.50 paper

Ranald S. Mackenzie's Official Correspondence Relating to Texas, edited by Ernest Wallace. 2 volumes.
1871–73. 202 pp.; 5¹/₂″ x 8¹/₂″
6.50 cloth
1873–79. 241 pp.; 5¹/₂″ x 8¹/₂″
6.50 cloth

Paleoindian Lifeways, edited by Eileen Johnson.
197 pp.; 74 illus., charts, and maps; 5¹/₂″ x 8¹/₂″
5.00 paper

The Museum of Texas Tech University, Lubbock
(member's discount 10%) (1.50 for first book plus 0.50 for each additional book)

History and Prehistory of the Lubbock Lake Site, edited by Craig C. Black.
160 pp.; 35 illus. and maps; 5¹/₂″ x 8¹/₂″
5.00 paper

The Textile Museum, Washington, D.C. (member's discount 20%) (1.00)

From the Bosporus to Samarkand: Flat-woven Rugs, by Anthony N. Landreau and W. R. Pickering. Foreword by Charles Grant Ellis.
112 pp.; 113 illus. (9 color)
7.95 paper

The Principles of the Stitch, by Lilo Markrich. A guide to the history, development, and mastery of the embroider's art.
122 pp.; 141 illus. and diagrams (color)
17.95 cloth
7.95 paper

Warp-Patterned Weaves of the Andes, by Ann Pollard Rowe. Foreword by Junius B. Bird.
195 pp.
9.95 paper

UCLA Art Council, Los Angeles (member's discount varies according to purchase) (1.50)

Birds, Beasts, Blossoms and Bugs: The Nature of Japan, by Harold P. Stern. The book traces the development of this theme through an examination of some 140 objects from the 12th to 19th centuries. The wealth of material includes screens, kakemono, makemono, bronze, wood, lacquer, stone, papier-mâché, tsuba, inro, and netsuke.
196 pp.; 177 illus. (86 color)
12.50 paper (member's price 10.50)

Words and Images, by E. Maurice Bloch. The text discusses the involvement of the artist with the book, tracing its history from the 15th century to the present. Among the featured artists are Bontecou, Buckminster Fuller, Glarner, Johns, Rauschenberg, and Rivers.
100 pp.; 54 illus. (8 color)
12.80 paper (member's price 11.50)

Edwin A. Ulrich Museum of Art, Wichita State University (does not operate a membership program) (1.35)

Duane Hanson, by Martin H. Bush.
112 pp.; 59 illus. (24 color); 7″ x 10³/₄″
9.00 paper

Harry Sternberg: A Catalog Raisonné of His Graphic Work, by James C. Moore.
96 pp.; 231 illus.; 9″ x 9″
8.00 paper

Ernest Trova, by Martin H. Bush.
132 pp.; 123 illus. (2 color); 9″ x 9″
10.00 cloth
9.00 paper

Vancouver Museums and Planetarium Association, Canada (member's discount 10%) (1.00)

H. R. MacMillan Planetarium.
28 pp.; illus.; 8⅞″ x 8⅜″
1.50 paper

The Talking Jars. Introduction by C. Chan Gunn. Catalogue for an exhibition of oriental ceramic folkwares found in South East Asia.
74 pp.; illus.; 7″ x 9¼″
5.00 paper

Within the Potter's House. Introduction by Jean Fahrni. The development of pottery from early Stone Age earthenware to the fine porcelain of the 18th century.
70 pp.; illus.; 8½″ x 11″
6.00 paper

The Virginia Museum, Richmond (member's discount 10%) (0.50)

Faberge —A Catalogue of the Lillian Thomas Pratt Collection of Russian Jewels.
160 pp.; 328 color illus.; 9″ x 11″
17.50 cloth

Walters Art Gallery, Baltimore (member's discount 10%) (handling and shipping charges included)

Catalogue of the Painted Enamels of the Renaissance in the Walters Art Gallery, by Philippe Verdier.
423 pp.; 320 illus. (8 color); 8″ x 10⅝″
30.00 cloth

The History of Bookbinding 525–1950 A.D., compiled by Dorothy E. Miner.
275 pp.; 106 illus.; 8¾″ x 11¼″
15.00 paper

2000 Years of Calligraphy, compiled by Dorothy E. Miner, Victor Carlson, and P. W. Filby. This volume illustrates the art of writing in regions using the Latin alphabet from Roman times through the 20th century.
201 pp.; 218 illus.; 8½″ x 11″
21.50 cloth

Whitney Museum of American Art (discount not available with regular membership; higher category member's discount 25%) (0.75 for first book plus 0.25 for each additional book)

Jasper Johns, by Michael Crichton.
276 pp.; 277 illus. (61 color)
12.50 paper

Synchromism and American Color Abstraction 1910–25, by Gail Levin.
144 pp.; 216 illus. (50 color)
11.95 paper

Turn-of-the-Century America: Paintings, Graphics, Photographs, 1890–1910, by Patricia Hills.
194 pp.; 215 illus. (7 color)
10.00 paper

Winterthur Museum, Delaware (member's discount 10%) (0.75)

American Furniture: The Federal Period, 1788–1825, by Charles F. Montgomery.
498 pp.; 605 illus. (7 color)
12.98 cloth

The Treasure House of Early American Rooms, by John A. H. Sweeney.
188 pp.; 211 illus. (8 color)
5.98 cloth

A Winterthur Guide to Chinese Export Porcelain, by Arlene M. Palmer.
144 pp.; 134 illus. (16 color)
6.95 cloth
3.95 paper

Yale Center for British Art, New Haven (does not operate a membership program) (0.50)

Rowlandson Drawings from the Paul Mellon Collection, by John Riely. Rowlandson, best known today as a caricaturist, is represented for his achievement as a draftsman.
111 pp.; 36 illus. (6 color)
5.00 paper

Selected Paintings, Drawings and Books. Foreword by Paul Mellon. Preface by Edmund P. Pillsbury. A selection from the Paul Mellon Collection at the Yale Center for British Art.
111 pp.; 99 illus. (17 color)
8.00 paper

Yale Center for British Art. An account of the architecture of the Center, its design, the circumstances of the building, and its significance as the final building of Louis I. Kahn.
72 pp. of text; 47 photographs, architectural diagrams, and drawings
15.00 cloth

Yale University Art Gallery, New Haven (member's discount 10%) (0.75)

Early Italian Paintings in the Yale University Art Gallery, by Charles Seymour, Jr.
312 pp.; 186 illus.
14.50 cloth

European Drawings and Watercolors in the Yale University Art Gallery, by E. Haverkamp-Begemann and Anne-Marie S. Logan.
vol 1. 391 pp.; vol 2, 256 pp.; 321 illus.
35.00 2-volume set, cloth

The Works of Colonel John Trumbull, Artist of the American Revolution, by Theodore Sizer and Caroline Rollins.
181 pp.; 276 illus.
22.50 cloth

Miscellany

Wrapping Paper

Four subjects from the *Index of American Design.*
Each package contains two sheets of paper (36″ x
24½″) and two matching gift enclosures.
Top left: Early American Chintz, rendering by Julius
Mihalik. Full color on white paper.
Top right: Apotheosis of Franklin, rendering by A.
Zimet. Red on white paper.
Bottom left: Appliqué Coverlet, rendering by Dorothea
Bates. Full color on white paper.
Bottom right: Friendship Quilt, 1830, by Mary Ann
Burton. Full color on white paper.
0.75 per package (1.00)
National Gallery of Art, Washington, D.C. (does not
operate a membership program)

Wrapping Paper, National Gallery of Art

Wrapping Paper

The Los Angeles County Museum of Art has
transformed two elegant textile fragments from its
collection into beautiful wrapping paper. Each sheet
measures 28″ x 19½″. There are two sheets of one
design per package. (Please specify design when
ordering.)
Left: Textile fragment, Persia, late 17th century.
Brocaded compound twill, silk, and silver on a white
silk core. An arabesque of flowering vines plus a
variety of blossoms, birds, and parakeets decorate this
Safavid silk textile. The Safavid dynasty, founded in
Persia in 1502, was a period of great luxury and
elegance when the arts flourished under royal
patronage. Shades of orange, blue, green, brown, and
beige.
Right: Textile fragment, France, 1790. Resist-block
print on linen. Reminiscent of an oriental stencil motif,
these stylized white flowers on a blue ground create a
striking pattern.
1.25 per package of two sheets of one design (1.50)
Los Angeles County Museum of Art (member's
discount 10%)

Wrapping Paper,
Los Angeles County
Museum of Art

Dragon Motif Wrapping Paper

Made from the bark of the Daphine bush, or paper
tree, as the Nepalese call it, this paper is crafted by
hand according to an ancient process in the
Himalayan kingdom of Nepal. The woodblock print is
adapted from a tomb tablet, Chinese, Shangtung
Province, Han Dynasty (206 B.C.– A.D. 220), depicting a
Taoist dragon, the symbol of the life force. The
original, in the collection of the Museum of Art,
Carnegie Institute, was made of clay with impressed
and incised designs which have traces of red and
white pigments. Red dragons and black border on
natural. Each sheet measures: 32″ x 22″.
1.00 for 2 sheets (0.50)
Carnegie Institute, Pittsburgh (member's discount
10%)

Dragon Motif
Wrapping Paper

Wrapping Paper, Walters Art Gallery

Money Clip

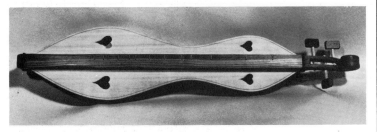

Appalachian Dulcimer

Mustache Guard

Miscellany

Wrapping Paper

Two unusual designs to enhance any package are selected from the collection of manuscripts and rare books at the Walters Art Gallery.
Top: A decorated initial from an illuminated manuscript, *Antiphonary,* Florence, about 1375. Red and blue on white paper.
Bottom: Calligraphic designs from an 18th-century printed book, *Nova Escola* . . . by Manoel de Andrade de Figueyredo, Lisbon. Red on light blue paper. Sheet size: 24″ x 36″. Each packet contains 4 sheets and 12 gift enclosures.
2.00 per packet (1.25 for 1–4 packets; 2.00 for 5 or more)
Walters Art Gallery, Baltimore (member's discount not available on this item)

Money Clip

Hold on to your money with a sturdy clip decorated with a treble clef. Sterling silver. 1″ x 2⅛″.
22.50 (2.25)
Lincoln Center for the Performing Arts, New York (does not publish a member's discount)

Appalachian Dulcimer

This unique and beautiful stringed instrument was made first by the Scotch-Irish settlers in the Appalachian mountains. Because of its ancestry, it is often referred to as the stringed bagpipe. The notes produced by the dulcimer resemble those of the bagpipe but are quieter and more fragile. It is played with a quill. The traditional double-belly Thomas style is made with three strings and equipped with wood friction tuning pegs. The backs and sides may be made with a variety of woods, usually American hardwoods such as walnut, and the top is spruce for improved sound quality. 34″ long, 7″ wide, and 1½″ deep.
85.00 (3.00 UPS delivery)
Country Music Hall of Fame and Museum, Nashville (does not operate a membership program)

Mustache Guard

A unique item for the man with a mustache who does not have everything—at least not yet. The original guard was designed and made in Nyack, New York, in 1901 and now has been reproduced exclusively for The Historical Society of Rockland County. It slips over a cup to protect the mustache. Steel. 2″ wide, 2½″ long.
1.00 (0.25)
The Historical Society of Rockland County, New York (member's discount not available)

Miscellany

Wrought Iron Hanger

On the premises of the Shaker Museum, Old Chatham, is a complete blacksmith's shop with two triphammers displaying the forger's and founder's art. This hanger has been handcrafted at the shop. A series of these would be perfect in the kitchen for hanging pots and pans, and other utensils. Iron. Black. 3½" high, 7" long.
4.50 (0.75)
Shaker Museum, Old Chatham, New York (member's discount 10%)

Triple Hanger and Pegboard

Pegboards were found in abundance in Shaker buildings as part of a very simple and utilitarian furnishing. They are perfect for hanging hats, coats, and sweaters, and with the hanger a space saving device for any closet. Assorted hardwoods. Natural, unfinished. Hanger and pegboards in various lengths are ordered separately.

Triple Hanger. 20" long.	**6.00**
Board with 2 pegs	**4.00**
Board with 4 pegs	**8.00**
Board with 6 pegs (illustrated) 53" long	**12.00**
Board with 8 pegs	**16.00**

(1.75 for each item)
Shaker Museum, Old Chatham, New York (member's discount 10%)

Corn Dryer

Originally used in country kitchens to dry corn, this reproduction could be used in a modern kitchen for hanging utensils or displaying colorful Indian corn. Painted steel. Black. 19" x 5".
14.00 (2.00)
Guild Hall, East Hampton, New York (member's discount 10%)

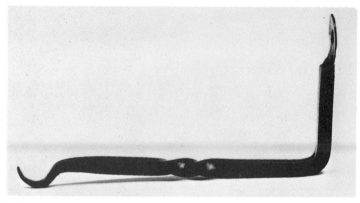

Wrought Iron Hanger

Triple Hanger and Pegboard

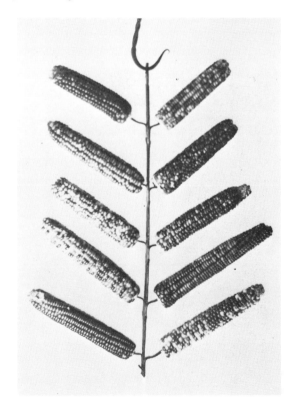

Corn Dryer

Pipe Tamper

Miscellany

Pipe Tamper

A handy gadget for the pipe smoker. It helps the user pack the tobacco evenly and firmly for a smoother draw. A portrait of George Washington enhances this reproduction of an early American pipe tamper, c. 1800, from the collection of the Essex Institute. Gold-colored metal. 2½" x 1".
1.00 (0.50)
Essex Institute, Salem, Massachusetts (member's discount not available)

Sock Stretcher

Our ancestors actually used this to dry their socks. While its practicality today could be questioned, this reproduction, based on an original in the Guild Hall, makes an attractive decorative wall hanging. Surely a conversation piece. Wood. 22" x 5".
12.00 (2.00)
Guild Hall, East Hampton, New York (member's discount 10%)

Sock Stretcher

Broom

Handmade of cornstraw at Old Sturbridge Village, this broom is typical of the kind used in America from 1790 to 1840. 3′ long.
7.25 (1.75)
Old Sturbridge Village (member's discount 10%)

Weather Vane

Weather Vane

A handsome and useful finishing touch to the roof of any house or barn is a handwrought iron weather vane, made by the blacksmiths at the Conner Prairie Settlement. The design is based on an original, made in America in the early 19th century. The smiths at the settlement employ traditional tools and techniques, thus preserving the heritage of the crafts. The oil-blackened finish comes direct from the forge. Includes pole. 33" x 21".
45.00 (5.00)
Conner Prairie Pioneer Settlement, Noblesville, Indiana (member's discount 15%)

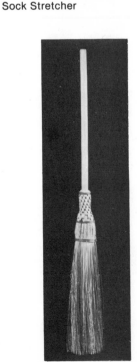

Broom

Miscellany

Fire-iron Set

Carefully crafted, using traditional tools and techniques, this reproduction of an early 19th-century American fire-iron set is made by the blacksmiths at the Conner Prairie Settlement. It is handwrought of iron and forge-welded, an almost-lost smithing art. The oil-blackened finish comes direct from the forge. Set includes stand, shovel, and poker. 30″ high.
80.00 the set (8.00)
Conner Prairie Pioneer Settlement, Noblesville, Indiana (member's discount 15%)

Thimble

Delicate handcrafted vines and strawberries encircle this thimble. An elegant way to make sure your hands survive your sewing ventures. Sterling silver. Sizes: 8, 9, 10, 11, 12. (Please specify size when ordering.)
28.00 (1.00)
The Guild of Strawbery Banke®, Inc., Portsmouth (member's discount 10%)

Sewing Box

An unusual find for sewing enthusiasts! A reproduction, in walnut, from the collection of McCall's at Old City Park. The bottom drawer holds needles, tape measure, and other sewing necessities. The top lifts off (by the pincushion) to reveal wooden dowels for holding spools of thread. The thread can be pulled through the holes in the front of the box. This avoids snarling and keeps the thread ready for use. 7″ x 7″ x 5³/₈″.
24.95 (2.50)
McCall's at Old City Park, Dallas (member's discount not available)

Shaker Carrier

The functional simplicity of design and the high quality of craftsmanship for which the Shakers are known is apparent in this reproduction of a Shaker carrier. Originally they were produced for sale to the World's people (non–Shakers). This one is made from a pattern that was used to make the original Shaker oval box. Pine and maple. Medium stain. 9¹/₂″ x 14¹/₂″ x 10¹/₄″.
45.00 (2.25)
Shaker Museum, Old Chatham, New York (member's discount 10%)

Fire-iron Set

Thimble

Sewing Box

Shaker Carrier

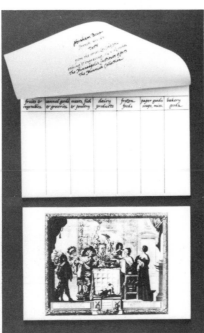

Miscellany

Market Basket

Market Basket

The Shakers were noted for their fine workmanship. A market basket, similar to those used by the Shakers, has been handcrafted specifically for the Shaker Museum. Wood splint. Natural. 16″ x 18¹/₂″ x 14″.
15.00 (2.25)
Shaker Museum, Old Chatham, New York (member's discount 10%)

Daily Reminder

Don't forget an important event when it's so simple to remember by using a note holder. The original of this one hung in the kitchen at Washington Irving's Home, Sunnyside. Painted tin. 16″ x 4¹/₄″.
17.50 (1.75)
Sleepy Hollow Restorations, Inc., Tarrytown, New York (member's discount 10%)

Grocery List

Brighten up the dull routine of shopping by writing your list on this conveniently subdivided shopping pad. The cover reproduction is *Taste* from the series *Les Cinq Sens,* etching and engraving by Abraham Bosse (French, 1602–76). Beige cover. Black-and-white pages. 50 sheets. 5¹/₂″ x 8¹/₂″.
1.00 (0.50)
The Minneapolis Institute of Arts (member's discount 10%)

Jewish Marriage Contract (Ketubah)

An original silkscreen by Jack Beal, with calligraphy by Mark Loeb, commissioned for The Jewish Museum. The edition is 100 and the signatures are in the plate. There are blank spaces to be filled in with the names of the bride and groom, date of the wedding, and other details. Silkscreened in 7 colors. 40¹/₂″ x 29″.
50.00 (6.00)
The Jewish Museum, New York (member's discount 15%)

Grocery List

Daily
Reminder

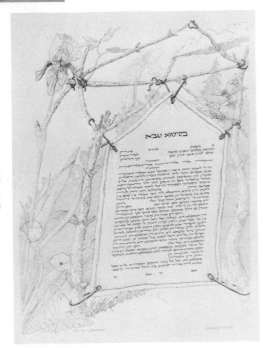

Jewish
Marriage
Contract
(Ketubah)

Miscellany

Sand Paintings

Sand Paintings

Sand paintings, used by the Navaho Indians in healing ceremonies, have been reproduced for the Museum of the American Indian. No two are alike since they are handmade. Sand applied by a special process to compressed board. Earth colors: brown, tan, white, green, yellow, and rust. 24″ square.
300.00 each (5.00)
Museum of the American Indian, New York (member's discount 15%)

Folk Art Postcards

The Museum of American Folk Art, New York, has published three sets of postcards based on popular themes in American Folk Art.
Decoys. 8 full-color photographs of ducks, geese, and shore birds taken in their natural surroundings. Some of the decoys have been created by such well-known carvers as A. Elmer Crowell, the Ward Brothers, and Charles "Shang" Wheeler. 5½″ x 8″.
2.40 (1.00)
Quilts. 12 full-color reproductions of quilts in traditional or original patterns with intricate piecework, appliqué, or a combination of these quilt-making techniques. 6″ x 7½″.
3.60 (1.00)
Folk Art. 12 full-color reproductions of primitive paintings of children, animals, and landscapes. Included in the set are Edward Hicks' *Peaceable Kingdom,* the flag gate, and chalkware cat. 6″ x 7½″.
3.60 (1.00)
Museum of American Folk Art, New York (member's discount 10%)

Folk Art Postcards

Flower Press

Enjoy flowers all year round. You can preserve a variety of blooms with this charming press, which has been produced for the Dexter Area Museum. Natural pine, lightly varnished and hand stenciled, with cardboard and blotters. 7″ square.
7.95 (handling and shipping charges included)
Dexter Area Museum, Michigan (member's discount 10%)

Flower Press

Owl-Ouette

A Planting Guide to Los Angeles Butterflies

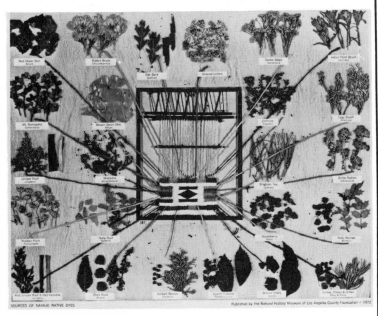

Sources of Navajo Native Dyes

Miscellany

Owl-Ouette

Protect your birds from injury or death. The owl silhouette, when placed on the inside of a window, will prevent birds from flying into the window. This device has been tested through several migratory seasons. Made exclusively for The Cleveland Museum of Natural History. Brown. Paper decal. 12″ x 20″.
1.50 (0.50)
The Cleveland Museum of Natural History (member's discount 10%)

A Planting Guide to Los Angeles Butterflies

Identification of caterpillars and the butterflies they become is only one of the functions this chart serves. It also aids you in planning a garden with the proper plants to attract them. Full-color offset. 21″ x 17″.
1.25 (1.25)
Los Angeles County Museum of Natural History (member's discount 10%)

Sources of Navajo Native Dyes

The rubber plant, mistletoe, holly berries, red and brown onions, and walnut shells are among the variety of familiar plant life which are sources of dyes used for the brilliant and subtle coloring of the wool in such fine rugs as Wide Ruins, Chinle and other Navajo rugs. This chart provides a source for the better understanding and appreciation of the weaving arts of this American Indian tribe. Full-color offset. 19″ x 23″.
3.50 (1.25)
Los Angeles County Museum of Natural History (member's discount 10%)

Miscellany

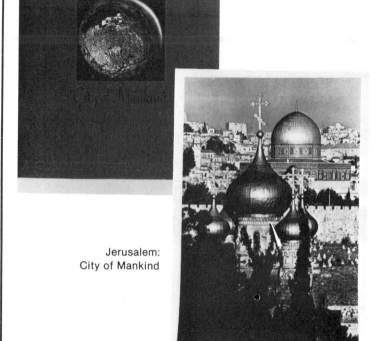

Jerusalem:
City of Mankind

Jerusalem: City of Mankind

The Jerusalem Commemorative Portfolio consists of twelve works of the highest photographic quality by outstanding international photographers commissioned for the exhibition *Jerusalem: City of Mankind* and shown at The First International Triennale of Photography, Jerusalem, 1973. Color prints were made by dye transfer process from original transparencies; black and white enlargements from original negatives. All prints were produced under the personal supervision of the participating photographers. The edition, signed and numbered, is limited to 100. The portfolio is boxed in a handsome lucite slipcase and bound in red linen with gold lettering. A symbolic color photograph of Jerusalem by Marvin Newman is mounted on the cover. Each signed and numbered print comes matted and enclosed in its own folio. An illuminated introduction, written by Teddy Kollek, Mayor of the City of Jerusalem, completes the presentation. Portfolio size: 17½″ x 14½″. Works included:
Via Dolorosa on Friday (color), Micha Bar-Am
Moonrise over the Knesset (color), Werner Braun
At the Western Wall (black and white), Robert Burroughs
View from the Israel Museum Sculpture Garden (black and white), Cornell Capa
Reading from Sephardic Torah Scrolls (black and white), Leonard Freed
In the Arab Quarter, Old City (color), Ernst Haas
Easter, Holy Fire (color), Charles Harbutt
Wallscape (black and white), Ron Havilio
Midday Prayers, Al Agsa Grounds (black and white), Bhupendra Karia
Ecumenical Landscape (illustrated here, color), Marc Riboud
Billy Rose Garden, Israel Museum (color), Marc Riboud
Benedictine Nun, Mount of Olives (color), Ted Spiegel
1,500.00 (handling and shipping charges to be arranged)
International Center of Photography, New York
(member's discount not available on this item)

Franklin Memorial Coin

This coin depicts the bust of Benjamin Franklin on one side and The Franklin Institute on the other. Brass with copper finish. 2½″ diameter.
1.50 (0.25)
The Franklin Institute Science Museum, Philadelphia
(member's discount 10%)

Franklin Memorial Coin

Milestones of Flight

Key Ring

Program Light Magnifier

Miscellany

Milestones of Flight

The *Milestones of Flight* commemorative cover series produced by the National Air and Space Museum of the Smithsonian Institution honors significant achievements in the history of flight. These are specially cacheted covers, each canceled on the anniversary date of the event being commemorated at the location where it occurred. The series began on October 14, 1972, and since then, there have been 61 issues, most of which are still available. Please write for particulars regarding the back issues. Because of the limited quantity of each issue, there is a limit of five per customer.

1.35 each cover numbers 7 through 34 (supply a #10 stamped self-addressed envelope)
1.25 each cover numbers 35 through 64 (supply a #10 stamped self-addressed envelope)
14.00 per year for subscription to series (2.00)
Cover album: deep blue leatherette with gold-embossed museum logo; plastic sleeves to protect and hold 100 issues; metal holding rod. 11″ x 8″ x 2″
12.00 (handling and shipping charges included)
National Air and Space Museum, Smithsonian Institution, Washington, D.C. (Smithsonian Associate member's discount not available on these items)

Key Ring

A bookworm. What better motif to represent The New York Public Library? This design was especially created for the library by the Kruger Gallery. It will delight young and old. Pewter. Bookworm: 1¹/₈″ x ³/₄″ dangles from a key ring. Also available as pendant on silk cord.
9.00 key ring (2.00)
8.00 pendant on cord (2.00)
The New York Public Library (member's discount 20%)

Program Light Magnifier

When the lights go out, you will still be able to read your program with this handy light magnifier, especially packaged for Lincoln Center. Plastic. Pen light battery. Black or cream leatherette pouch with gold lettering. (Please specify color choice when ordering.) 6″ long.
6.50 (1.20)
Lincoln Center for the Performing Arts, New York (does not publish a member's discount)

Miscellany

Mining Lamps

It is always hard to find the perfect gift for the person who has everything, but chances are that someone does not own a mining lamp made in the early 19th century.

Cap lights were worn by the miners on their heads as they entered the mine. They operate on a gas formed by carbide and water, which ignites when the hand passes quickly over the flint. Each one is an original, made in the early 19th century and supplied exclusively to the Arizona Historical Society, which has many of this type in its permanent collection. Brass. Varying sizes, but approximately 5" high.
24.00 (2.00)

Candle lights were stuck into the timber inside the mines to light the way. This is a reproduction of such a light, originally made around 1800, in the collection of the Arizona Historical Society. Adjustable to candle width. Steel. Black. 10" long.
17.50 (2.00)
Arizona Historical Society, Tucson (member's discount 10%)

Mining Lamps

Sundial

The use of sundials (solar time pieces) to determine time dates back to the Egyptians and Babylonians. It was further used, in various forms, by the Greeks, Romans, Chinese, and the peoples of Peru and Mexico. In Colonial America when mechanical clocks were ordered from abroad, miniature sundials (about the size of this one) were often sent with the shipment so the clock would be set according to the sun. Complete instructions for using the sundial accompany each piece. Gray metal. 4" diameter.
2.49 (0.75)
The Franklin Institute Science Museum, Philadelphia (member's discount 10%)

Sundial

Star Chart

A unique chart with rotating disc enabling the user to locate constellations, major stars, and the planets according to season and time of day. Sunrise, sunset, and meteor showers may also be located with this device. Heavy paper board. 10½" x 10½".
1.95 (0.50)
Oregon Museum of Science and Industry, Portland (member's discount 10%)

Star Chart

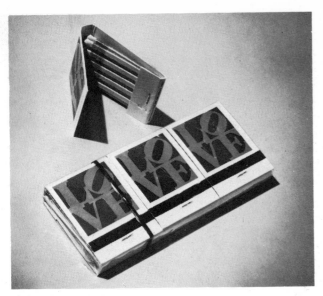
Love Matchbooks

Matchbooks

Rim Lock

Miscellany

Love Matchbooks

Robert Indiana's famous image *Love,* which he created in various media, and which has been transformed into several other media, including a U.S. postage stamp, now adorns these striking matchbook covers. Red, green, and blue. Package of 6 matchbooks.
6.00 24 packages (1.00)
Indianapolis Museum of Art (member's discount 10%)

Matchbooks

Close cover before striking to reveal *Mouth #11,* by Tom Wesselmann (American, b. 1931). The original painting hangs in the Dallas Museum of Fine Arts.
2.50 box of 25 matchbooks (1.35)
Dallas Museum of Fine Arts (member's discount 10%)

Rim Lock

The Williamsburg Rim Lock, so called because the entire lock is exposed, is made of heavy brass, hand fitted and polished by expert craftsmen. It is a reproduction of a lock used in 18th-century Williamsburg. Available with solid brass drop handles, it includes a complete lock assembly with one large colonial brass or stainless-steel key.
The locks are made in three different sizes to fit the scale of individual doors with right-hand or left-hand openings. The side of the door on which the keeper is placed determines whether the lock is right or left hand. Orders should specify lock size, right or left hand, thickness of door, and preference for either brass or stainless-steel key.
225.00 #1 large (illustrated), 5³/₄″ x 10″ x 1³/₈″
180.00 #2 medium, 4¹/₂″ x 8″ x 1″
147.00 #3 small, 4″ x 6³/₄″ x ⁷/₈″
(handling and shipping charges are included in the above prices)
The Colonial Williamsburg Foundation (does not operate a membership program)

Museum Index

Albright-Knox Art Gallery
Address for orders:
Albright-Knox Art Gallery
1285 Elmwood Avenue
Buffalo, NY 14222
Checks and money orders made payable to:
The Gallery Shop
Regular membership: 20.00 per year
Members receive a 10% discount on purchases

Alexandria Bicentennial Museum Shop
Address for orders:
Alexandria Bicentennial Museum Shop
201 South Washington
Alexandria, VA 22314
Checks and money orders made payable to:
Alexandria Bicentennial Corporation
Does not operate a membership program

Museum of American Folk Art
Address for orders:
Museum of American Folk Art
49 West 53d Street
New York, NY 10019
Checks and money orders made payable to:
Museum of American Folk Art
Regular membership: 20.00 per year
Members receive a 10% discount on purchases

Museum of the American Indian
Address for orders:
The Museum Shop
Museum of the American Indian
Broadway at 155th Street
New York, NY 10032
Checks and money orders made payable to:
The Museum Shop
Regular membership: 20.00 per year
Members receive a 15% discount on purchases of
$5.00 and over

American Museum of Atomic Energy, Oak Ridge, Tennessee
Address for orders:
The Discovery Shop
American Museum of Atomic Energy
P.O. Box 117
Oak Ridge, TN 37830
Checks and money orders made payable to:
Oak Ridge Associated Universities
Does not operate a membership program

The American Museum of Natural History, New York
Address for orders:
Museum Shop
The American Museum of Natural History
79th Street and Central Park West
New York, NY 10024
Checks and money orders made payable to:
Museum Shop, A.M.N.H.
Regular membership: 10.00 per year
Members receive a 10% discount on purchases

Arizona Historical Society, Tucson
Address for orders:
Arizona Historical Society
Territorial Mercantile Co.
949 E. 2d Street
Tucson, AZ 85719
Checks and money orders made payable to:
Arizona Historical Society—Territorial Mercantile Co.
Regular membership: 9.50 per year
Member's discount varies according to purchase

The Asia Society, Inc.
Address for orders:
The Asia Society, Inc.
112 East 64th Street
New York, NY 10021
Checks and money orders made payable to:
The Asia Society, Inc.
Regular membership: 50.00 per year
Member's discount varies according to purchase

The Baltimore Museum of Art
Address for orders:
The Museum Shop
The Baltimore Museum of Art
Art Museum Drive
Baltimore, MD 21218
Checks and money orders made payable to:
The Baltimore Museum of Art
Regular membership: 15.00 per year
Members receive a 10% discount on purchases over
2.00

Museum of Fine Arts, Boston
Address for orders:
Museum Shop
Museum of Fine Arts
479 Huntington Avenue
Boston, MA 02115
Checks and money orders made payable to:
Museum Shop—Museum of Fine Arts
Regular membership: 20.00 per year
Members receive a 10% discount on purchases of 2.00
and over

The Brooklyn Museum
Address for orders:
The Brooklyn Museum Gallery Shop
Eastern Parkway
Brooklyn, NY 11238
Checks and money orders made payable to:
The Brooklyn Museum Gallery Shop
Regular membership: 20.00 per year
Members receive a 15% discount on purchases

Buten Museum of Wedgwood
Address for orders:
Buten Museum of Wedgwood
246 North Bowman Avenue
Merion, PA 19066
Checks and money orders made payable to:
Buten Museum of Wedgwood
Regular membership: 20.00 per year
Member's discount varies according to purchase

Carnegie Institute
Address for orders:
Museum Shops
Carnegie Institute
4400 Forbes Avenue
Pittsburgh, PA 15213
Checks and money orders made payable to:
Museum Shops—Carnegie Institute
Regular membership: 17.50 per year
Members receive a 10% discount on purchases

Art Institute of Chicago
Address for orders:
The Museum Store
Art Institute of Chicago
Michigan Avenue at Adams
Chicago, IL 60603
Checks and money orders made payable to:
The Museum Store
Regular membership: 20.00 per year
Members receive a 10% discount on purchases

Chrysler Museum at Norfolk
Address for orders:
Chrysler Museum at Norfolk
Olney Road and Mowbray Arch
Norfolk, VA 23510
Checks and money orders made payable to:
Chrysler Museum
Regular membership: 15.00 per year
Members receive a 10% discount on purchases

Cincinnati Art Museum
Address for orders:
Cincinnati Art Museum Shop
Eden Park
Cincinnati, OH 45202
Checks and money orders made payable to:
Cincinnati Art Museum Shop
Regular membership: 25.00 per year
Membership discount not available on purchases

Museum of the City of New York
Address for orders:
Museum of the City of New York
Fifth Avenue at 103d Street
New York, NY 10029
Checks and money orders made payable to:
Museum of the City of New York
Regular membership: 15.00 per year
Members receive a 20% discount on purchases

Sterling and Francine Clark Art Institute, Williamstown, Massachusetts
Address for orders:
Sterling and Francine Clark Art Institute
Williamstown, MA 01267
Checks and money orders made payable to:
Sterling and Francine Clark Art Institute
Does not operate a membership program

The Cleveland Museum of Natural History
Address for orders:
Ark in the Park Shop
The Cleveland Museum of Natural History
Wade Oval, University Circle
Cleveland, OH 44106
Checks and money orders made payable to:
The Cleveland Museum of Natural History
Regular membership: 15.00 per year
Members receive a 10% discount on purchases

The Colonial Williamsburg Foundation
Address for orders:
Craft House
Williamsburg, VA 23185
Checks and money orders made payable to:
The Colonial Williamsburg Foundation
Does not operate a membership program

Colorado Springs Fine Arts Center
Address for orders:
Colorado Springs Fine Arts Center, Sales Shop
30 West Dale Street
Colorado Springs, CO 80903
Checks and money orders made payable to:
Colorado Springs Fine Arts Center
Regular membership: 15.00 per year
Members receive a 10% discount on purchases

Conner Prairie Pioneer Settlement
Address for orders:
Conner Trading Post
30 Conner Lane
Noblesville, IN 46060
Checks and money orders made payable to:
Conner Trading Post
Regular membership: 10.00 per year
Members receive a 15% discount on purchases

Museum of Contemporary Crafts of the American Crafts Council, New York
Address for orders:
American Crafts Council
Publication Sales
44 West 53d Street
New York, NY 10019
Checks and money orders made payable to:
American Crafts Council
Regular membership: 18.00 per year
Member's discount varies according to purchase

The Corcoran Gallery of Art, Washington, D.C.
Address for orders:
The Corcoran Shop
The Corcoran Gallery of Art
17th Street and New York Avenue, N.W.
Washington, DC 20006
Checks and money orders made payable to:
The Corcoran Shop
Regular membership: 25.00 per year
Members receive a 10% discount on purchases

Country Music Hall of Fame and Museum
Address for orders:
Country Music Hall of Fame and Museum
4 Music Square East
Nashville, TN 37203
Checks and money orders made payable to:
Country Music Hall of Fame and Museum
Does not operate a membership program

Craft and Folk Art Museum, Los Angeles
Address for orders:
Craft and Folk Art Museum
5814 Wilshire Boulevard
Los Angeles, CA 90036
Checks and money orders made payable to:
Craft and Folk Art Museum
Regular membership: 25.00 per year
Members receive a 10% discount on purchases

Museum Index

Cranbrook Academy of Art, Bloomfield Hills, Michigan
Address for orders:
Museum Bookstore
Cranbrook Academy of Art
500 Lone Pine Road
Bloomfield Hills, MI 48013
Checks and money orders made payable to:
Cranbrook Academy of Art Bookstore
Regular membership: 15.00 per year
Members receive a 10% discount on purchases

Dallas Museum of Fine Arts
Address for orders:
The Museum Shop
Dallas Museum of Fine Arts
Fair Park
Dallas, TX 75226
Checks and money orders made payable to:
"Gallery Buffet Soup Cookbook" (when ordering cookbooks)
Dallas Museum of Fine Arts (when ordering all other merchandise)
Regular membership: 25.00 per year
Members receive a 10% discount on purchases

Delaware Art Museum
Address for orders:
Delaware Art Museum Store
2301 Kentmere Parkway
Wilmington, DE 19806
Checks and money orders made payable to:
Delaware Art Museum
Regular membership: 15.00 per year
Members receive a 10% discount on purchases

The Historical Society of Delaware, Wilmington
Address for orders:
The Historical Society of Delaware Store
505 Market Street Mall
Wilmington, DE 19801
Checks and money orders made payable to:
The Historical Society of Delaware
Regular membership: 15.00 per year
Members receive a 10% discount on purchases

Denver Art Museum
Address for orders:
Volunteer Office
Denver Art Museum
100 West 14th Avenue Parkway
Denver, CO 80204
Checks and money orders made payable to:
Denver Art Museum
Regular membership: 25.00 per year
Members receive a 10% discount on purchases

Denver Museum of Natural History
Address for orders:
Gift Shop
Denver Museum of Natural History
City Park
Denver, CO 80205
Checks and money orders made payable to:
Denver Museum of Natural History
Regular membership: 15.00 per year Discount not available with regular membership; higher category members receive a 10% discount on purchases

Detroit Historical Museum
Address for orders:
Old Detroit Shop
Detroit Historical Museum
5401 Woodward Avenue
Detroit, MI 48202
Checks and money orders made payable to:
Detroit Historical Society Sales Booth
Regular membership: 15.00 per year
Members receive a 15% discount on purchases of 5.00 and over

Detroit Institute of Arts
Address for orders:
Museum Shops
Founders Society, Detroit Institute of Arts
5200 Woodward Avenue
Detroit, MI 48202
Checks and money orders made payable to:
Founders Society
Regular membership: 25.00 per year
Members receive a 10% discount on purchases

Dexter Area Museum, Michigan
Address for orders:
Dexter Area Museum Gift Shop
7482 Chamberlain Road
Dexter, MI 48130
Checks and money orders made payable to:
Dexter Museum Gift Shop
Regular membership: 3.00 per year
Members receive a 10% discount on purchases

M. H. de Young Memorial Museum
Address for orders:
The Museum Society Bookshop
M. H. de Young Memorial Museum
Golden Gate Park
San Francisco, CA 94118
Checks and money orders made payable to:
Museum Society Bookshop
Regular membership: 20.00 per year
Members receive a 20% discount on purchases

Drake House Museum, Plainfield, New Jersey
Address for orders:
Drake House Museum Store
602 West Front Street
Plainfield, NJ 07060
Checks and money orders made payable to:
Drake House Bicentennial Fund
Regular membership: 7.50 per year
Member's discount not available on purchases

Essex Institute, Salem, Massachusetts
Address for orders:
Essex Institute Gift Shop
132 Essex Street
Salem, MA 01970
Checks and money orders made payable to:
Essex Institute Gift Shop
Regular membership: 15.00 per year
Member's discount not available on purchases

Everson Museum of Art
Address for orders:
Everson Museum of Art—Sales Gallery
401 Harrison Street
Syracuse, NY 13035
Checks and money orders made payable to:
Everson Museum of Art
Regular membership: 15.00 per year
Members receive a 10% discount on purchases

The Folger Shakespeare Library
Address for orders:
The Folger Shakespeare Library
Sales Department
201 East Capitol Street, S.E.
Washington, DC 20003
Checks and money orders made payable to:
The Folger Shakespeare Library
Regular membership: 50.00 per year
Members receive a 15% discount on purchases

Follett House Museum, Sandusky, Ohio
Address for orders:
Follett House Museum
c/o Sandusky Library Association
Corner Columbus Avenue and West Adams Street
Sandusky, OH 44870
Checks and money orders made payable to:
Follett House
Does not operate a membership program

The Fort Worth Art Museum
Address for orders:
Museum Book Store
The Fort Worth Art Museum
1309 Montgomery
Fort Worth, TX 76107
Checks and money orders made payable to:
The Fort Worth Art Museum
Regular membership: 25.00 per year
Member's discount varies according to purchase

The Franklin Institute Science Museum, Philadelphia
Address for orders:
The Franklin Institute
Benjamin Franklin Parkway at 20th Street
Philadelphia, PA 19103
Checks and money orders made payable to:
The Franklin Institute
Regular membership: Information furnished upon request
Members receive a 10% discount on purchases

Free Library of Philadelphia
Address for orders:
Friends of the Free Library Gift Shop
Logan Square
Philadelphia, PA 19103
Checks and money orders made payable to:
Friends of the Free Library
Regular membership: 15.00 per year
Members receive a 10% discount on purchases

Freer Gallery of Art
Address for orders:
Freer Gallery of Art
12th and Jefferson Drive, S.W.
Washington, DC 20560
Checks and money orders made payable to:
Freer Gallery of Art
Does not operate a membership program

Gibbes Art Gallery
Address for orders:
The Turtle
Gibbes Art Gallery
135 Meeting Street
Charleston, SC 29401
Checks and money orders made payable to:
The Turtle
Regular membership: 15.00 per year
Members receive a 10% discount on purchases

Grand Rapids Art Museum
Address for orders:
The Gallery Shop
Grand Rapids Art Museum
230 E. Fulton
Grand Rapids, MI 49503
Checks and money orders made payable to:
The Gallery Shop
Regular membership: 15.00 per year
Members receive a 10% discount on purchases

The Solomon R. Guggenheim Museum
Address for orders:
Bookstore—Solomon R. Guggenheim Museum
1071 Fifth Avenue
New York, NY 10028
Checks and money orders made payable to:
Solomon R. Guggenheim Foundation
Regular membership: 25.00 per year
Members receive a 25% discount on purchases

Guild Hall, East Hampton, New York
Address for orders:
Guild Hall Museum Shop
158 Main Street
East Hampton, NY 11937
Checks and money orders made payable to:
Guild Hall Museum Shop
Regular membership: 35.00 per year
Members receive a 10% discount on purchases

The Guild of Strawbery Banke®, Inc.
Address for orders:
The Guild of Strawbery Banke®, Inc.
93 State Street
Portsmouth, NH 03801
Checks and money orders made payable to:
The Guild of Strawbery Banke®, Inc.
Regular membership: 5.00 per year
Members receive a 10% discount on purchases over 5.00

Gunston Hall, Lorton, Virginia
Address for orders:
Gunston Hall Gift Shop
Lorton, VA 22079
Checks and money orders made payable to:
Board of Regents, Gunston Hall
Regular membership: 15.00 per year
Members receive a 10% discount on purchases

Hagley Museum
Address for orders:
Hagley Museum Store
Barley Mill Road
Greenville, Wilmington, DE 19807
Checks and money orders made payable to:
Hagley Museum Store
Regular membership: 15.00 per year
Members receive a 10% discount on purchases

Art Gallery of Hamilton, Ontario, Canada
Address for orders:
Gallery Shop
Art Gallery of Hamilton
123 King Street, West
Hamilton, Ontario
Canada L8P 4S8
Checks and money orders made payable to:
Gallery Shop Collector's Jewellery
Regular membership: 15.00 per year
Members receive a 10% discount on purchases

Museum Index

Historic Bethlehem Inc.
Address for orders:
Goundie House Museum Shop
501 Main Street
Bethlehem, PA 18018
Checks and money orders made payable to:
Historic Bethlehem Inc.
Regular membership: 10.00 per year
Members receive a 10% discount on purchases

Historic Deerfield, Inc., Massachusetts
Address for orders:
Hall Tavern Gift Shop
Main Street
Deerfield, MA 01342
Checks and money orders made payable to:
Historic Deerfield, Inc.
Regular membership: 25.00 per year
Members receive a 10% discount on purchases

Museum of Holography, New York
Address for orders:
Museum of Holography Bookstore
11 Mercer Street
New York, NY 10013
Checks and money orders made payable to:
Museum of Holography Bookstore
Regular membership: 25.00 per year
Members receive a 10% discount on purchases

Honolulu Academy of Arts
Address for orders:
Academy Shop
Honolulu Academy of Arts
900 S. Beretania Street
Honolulu, HI 96814
Checks and money orders made payable to:
Academy Shop
Regular membership: 12.00 per year
Members receive a 10% discount on purchases

Huntington Library, Art Gallery, and Botanical Gardens, San Marino, California
Address for orders:
Huntington Library, Art Gallery, and Botanical Gardens
1151 Oxford Road
San Marino, CA 91108
Checks and money orders made payable to:
Huntington Library
Regular membership: 25.00 per year
Members receive a 10.00 annual credit toward purchases

Huntsville Museum of Art
Address for orders:
Huntsville Museum Sales Gallery
700 Monroe Street
Huntsville, AL 35801
Checks and money orders made payable to:
Huntsville Museum Sales Gallery
Regular membership: 10.00 per year
Members receive a 10% discount on certain purchases

Hyde Collection
Address for orders:
Hyde Collection Museum Shop
161 Warren Street
Glens Falls, NY 12801
Checks and money orders made payable to:
Hyde Collection Museum Shop
Regular membership: 10.00 per year
Members receive a 10% discount on purchases over 3.00

Illinois State Museum, Springfield
Address for orders:
Illinois State Museum Society
Spring and Edward Streets
Springfield, IL 62706
Checks and money orders made payable to:
Illinois State Museum Society
Regular membership: 10.00 per year
Members receive a 10% discount on purchases except publications

Indiana University Art Museum, Bloomington
Address for orders:
Friends of Art Bookstall
Indiana University Art Museum
Bloomington, IN 47401
Checks and money orders made payable to:
Friends of Art Bookstall
Regular membership: 25.00 per year
Members receive a 10% discount on purchases

Indianapolis Museum of Art
Address for orders:
Alliance Museum Shop
Indianapolis Museum of Art
1200 West 38th Street
Indianapolis, IN 46208
Checks and money orders made payable to:
Alliance Museum Shop
Regular membership: 25.00 per year
Members receive a 10% discount on certain purchases

International Center of Photography, New York
Address for orders:
International Center of Photography
Museum Shop
1130 Fifth Avenue
New York, NY 10028
Checks and money orders made payable to: ICP
Regular membership: 25.00 per year
Members receive a 15% discount on certain purchases

The Jewish Museum, New York
Address for orders:
The Jewish Museum Shop
1109 Fifth Avenue
New York, NY 10028
Checks and money orders made payable to:
The Jewish Museum
Regular membership: 20.00 per year
Members receive a 15% discount on purchases

Joslyn Art Museum
Address for orders:
Joslyn Art Museum Shop
2200 Dodge Street
Omaha, NE 68102
Checks and money orders made payable to:
Joslyn Art Museum Shop
Regular membership: 10.00 per year
Members receive a 10% discount on purchases

Kimbell Art Museum, Fort Worth, Texas
Address for orders:
Kimbell Art Museum Bookstore
P.O. Box 9440
Fort Worth, TX 76107
Checks and money orders made payable to:
Kimbell Art Museum
Does not operate a membership program

Lawrence Hall of Science,
University of California
Address for orders:
Discovery Corner
Lawrence Hall of Science
University of California
Berkeley, CA 94720
Checks and money orders made payable to:
Regents of the University of California
Regular membership: 12.50 per year
Members receive a 10% discount on purchases
over 3.00

Lincoln Center for the Performing Arts, Inc., New York
Address for orders:
Lincoln Center Gift Shop
140A West 65th Street
New York, NY 10023
Checks and money orders made payable to:
Lincoln Center Gift Shop
Regular membership: Information furnished upon
request
Does not publish a member's discount

Loch Haven Art Center, Orlando, Florida
Address for orders:
Loch Haven Art Center Shop
2416 North Mills Avenue
Orlando, FL 32803
Checks and money orders made payable to:
Loch Haven Art Center Shop
Regular membership: 15.00 per year
Members receive a 10% discount on purchases

Long Beach Museum of Art
Address for orders:
Long Beach Museum of Art Bookshop and Gallery
2300 East Ocean Boulevard
Long Beach, CA 90803
Checks and money orders made payable to:
Long Beach Museum of Art Bookshop and Gallery
Regular membership: 25.00 per year
Members receive a 10% discount on purchases

Los Angeles County Museum of Art
Address for orders:
Museum Shop
Los Angeles County Museum of Art
5905 Wilshire Boulevard
Los Angeles, CA 90036
Checks and money orders made payable to:
Los Angeles County Museum of Art
Regular membership: 30.00 per year
Members receive a 10% discount on purchases

Los Angeles County Museum of Natural History
Address for orders:
Museum Shops
Los Angeles County Museum of Natural History
900 Exposition Boulevard
Los Angeles, CA 90007
Checks and money orders made payable to:
Book Shop—Los Angeles County Museum of Natural
History (dyes and planting charts only)
Ethnic Arts Shop—Los Angeles County Museum of
Natural History (all other merchandise)
Regular membership: 15.00 per year
Members receive a 10% discount on purchases

Lycoming County Historical Society and Museum,
Pennsylvania
Address for orders:
Lycoming County Historical Society and Museum
858 West Fourth Street
Williamsport, PA 17701
Checks and money orders made payable to:
Lycoming County Historical Society
Regular membership: 5.00 per year
Member's discount not available on purchases

Maine State Museum, Augusta
Address for orders:
Maine State Museum Gift Shop
State House
Augusta, ME 04333
Checks and money orders made payable to:
Maine State Museum
Does not operate a membership program

Maxwell Museum of Anthropology
Address for orders:
Maxwell Museum Gift Shop
Maxwell Museum of Anthropology
University of New Mexico
Albuquerque, NM 87131
Checks and money orders made payable to:
Maxwell Museum Gift Shop
Regular membership: 10.00 per year
Members receive a 10% discount on purchases
of museum publications

McCall's at Old City Park
Address for orders:
McCall's at Old City Park
1717 Gano
Dallas, TX 75215
Checks and money orders made payable to:
Dallas County Heritage Society Concessions
Regular membership: 15.00 per year
Member's discount not available on purchases

Memorial Art Gallery of the University of Rochester,
New York
Address for orders:
Gallery Shop
Memorial Art Gallery of the University of Rochester
490 University Avenue
Rochester, NY 14607
Checks and money orders made payable to:
Memorial Art Gallery
Regular membership: 25.00 per year
Members receive a 10% discount on purchases

Museum Index

The Mercer Museum
Address for orders:
The Mercer Museum Shop
Pine and Ashland Streets
Doylestown, PA 18901
Checks and money orders made payable to:
The Bucks County Historical Society
Regular membership: 15.00 per year
Members receive a 10% discount on
purchases over 10.00

The Metropolitan Museum of Art
Address for orders:
The Metropolitan Museum of Art
Box 255 Gracie Station
New York, NY 10028
Checks and money orders made payable to:
The Metropolitan Museum of Art
Regular membership: Information furnished
upon request
Member's discount varies according to purchase

Milwaukee Art Center
Address for orders:
Milwaukee Art Center—Gallery Shop
750 N. Lincoln Memorial Drive
Milwaukee, WI 53202
Checks and money orders made payable to:
Milwaukee Art Center
Regular membership: 20.00 per year
Members receive a 10% discount on purchases

The Minneapolis Institute of Arts
Address for orders:
Minneapolis Institute of Arts—Mail Sales
2400 3d Avenue South
Minneapolis, MN 55404
Checks and money orders made payable to:
Minneapolis Institute of Arts
Regular membership: 15.00 per year
Members receive a 10% discount on purchases

The Museum of Modern Art, New York
Address for orders:
The Museum of Modern Art
Customer Sales Service
11 West 53d Street
New York, NY 10019
Checks and money orders made payable to:
The Museum of Modern Art
Regular membership: 25.00 per year
Members receive a 25% discount on certain
purchases

Monterey Peninsula Museum of Art
Address for orders:
Monterey Peninsula Museum Shop
559 Pacific Street
Monterey, CA 93940
Checks and money orders made payable to:
M.P.M.A. Shop
Regular membership: 10.00 per year
Members receive a 10% discount on purchases

Munson Williams Proctor Institute, Utica, New York
Address for orders:
Munson Williams Proctor Institute Art Shop
310 Genesee Street
Utica, NY 13502
Checks and money orders made payable to:
Munson Williams Proctor Institute
Regular membership: 7.50 per year
Members receive a 10% discount on purchases

Mystic Seaport
Address for orders:
Mystic Seaport Museum Store, Inc.
POB ME-2
Mystic, CT 06355
Checks and money orders made payable to:
Mystic Seaport Museum Store, Inc.
Regular membership: 25.00 per year
Members receive a 10% discount on purchases

National Air and Space Museum, Smithsonian Institution
Address for orders:
Spacearium Shop
National Air and Space Museum,
Smithsonian Institution
Washington, DC 20560
Checks and money orders made payable to:
Smithsonian Institution
Does not operate a membership program; however,
Smithsonian Associate members receive a 10%
discount on certain purchases

National Archives and Records Service, Washington, D.C.
Address for orders:
National Archives and Records Service (GSA)
8th and Pennsylvania Avenue, N.W.
Washington, DC 20408
Checks and money orders made payable to:
National Archives Trust Fund
Regular membership: 15.00 per year
Members receive a 20% discount on purchases

National Gallery of Art, Washington, D.C.
Address for orders:
Publications Service
National Gallery of Art
6th and Constitution Avenue, N.W.
Washington, DC 20565
Checks and money orders made payable to:
Publications Service, National Gallery of Art
Does not operate a membership program

National Trust for Historic Preservation, Washington, D.C.
Address for orders:
Preservation Bookshop
National Trust for Historic Preservation
740 Jackson Place, N.W.
Washington, DC 10006
Checks and money orders made payable to:
National Trust for Historic Preservation
Regular membership: 15.00 per year
Members receive a 10% discount on purchases

Newark Museum
Address for orders:
Newark Museum
49 Washington Street
Newark, NJ 07101
Checks and money orders made payable to:
Newark Museum
Regular membership: 10.00 per year
Members receive a 10% discount on purchases

The New York Botanical Garden
Address for orders:
Shop in the Garden
The New York Botanical Garden
Bronx, NY 10458
Checks and money orders made payable to:
The New York Botanical Garden
Regular membership: Information furnished upon
request
Members receive a 10% discount on purchases

The New York Public Library
Address for orders:
The Sales Shop, Room 50A
The New York Public Library
Fifth Avenue at 42d Street
New York, NY 10018
Checks and money orders made payable to:
The New York Public Library
Regular membership: 25.00 per year
Members receive a 20% discount on purchases

North Carolina Museum of Art
Address for orders:
The Museum Store
North Carolina Museum of Art
107 East Morgan Street
Raleigh, NC 27611
Checks and money orders made payable to:
North Carolina Museum of Art
Regular membership: 15.00 per year
Members receive a 10% discount on purchases

Norwegian-American Museum
Address for orders:
VESTERHEIM Museum Shop
Norwegian-American Museum
502 West Water Street
Decorah, IA 52101
Checks and money orders made payable to:
Norwegian-American Museum
Regular membership: 5.00 per year
Members receive a 10% discount on purchases

The Old State House (The Bostonian Society)
Address for orders:
The Old State House (The Bostonian Society)
206 Washington Street
Boston, MA 02109
Checks and money orders made payable to:
The Bostonian Society
Regular membership: 10.00 per year
Member's discount not available on purchases

Old Sturbridge Village
Address for orders:
Museum Gift Shop
Old Sturbridge Village
Sturbridge, MA 01566
Checks and money orders made payable to:
Old Sturbridge, Inc.
Regular membership: 15.00 per year
Members receive a 10% discount on purchases

Art Gallery of Ontario
Address for orders:
Gallery Shop
Art Gallery of Ontario
Grange Park
Toronto, Ontario
Canada M5T 1G4
Checks and money orders made payable to:
Gallery Shop
Regular membership: 15.00 per year
Members receive a 10% discount on purchases

Oregon Historical Society, Portland
Address for orders:
Oregon Historical Society Bookstore
1230 S.W. Park Avenue
Portland, OR 97205
Checks and money orders made payable to:
Oregon Historical Society Bookstore
Regular membership: 10.00 per year
Members receive a 10% discount on purchases

Oregon Museum of Science and Industry, Portland
Address for orders:
OMSI
4015 S.W. Canyon Road
Portland, OR 97221
Checks and money orders made payable to:
OMSI
Regular membership: 10.00 per year
Members receive a 10% discount on purchases

George C. Page Museum of La Brea Discoveries, Los Angeles
Address for orders:
George C. Page Museum Shop
5801 Wilshire Boulevard
Los Angeles, CA 90036
Checks and money orders made payable to:
Los Angeles County Museum of Natural History
Regular membership: 15.00 per year
Members receive a 10% discount on purchases

Peabody Museum of Salem
Address for orders:
Peabody Museum of Salem
East India Square
Salem, MA 01970
Checks and money orders made payable to:
Peabody Museum of Salem
Regular membership: 20.00 per year
Members receive a 10% discount on purchases

Pennsylvania Academy of Fine Arts
Address for orders:
Pennsylvania Academy of Fine Arts
Broad and Cherry Streets
Philadelphia, PA 19102
Checks and money orders made payable to:
P.A.F.A.
Regular membership: 15.00 per year
Members receive a 10% discount on purchases

Philadelphia Maritime Museum
Address for orders:
Philadelphia Maritime Museum
321 Chestnut Street
Philadelphia, PA 19106
Checks and money orders made payable to:
Philadelphia Maritime Museum
Regular membership: 10.00 per year
Members receive a 10% discount on purchases

Museum Index

Philadelphia Museum of Art
Address for orders:
Museum Shop
Philadelphia Museum of Art
P.O. Box 7858
Philadelphia, PA 19101
Checks and money orders made payable to:
Museum Shop—PMA
Regular membership: 20.00 per year
Members receive a 10% discount on purchases

The Phillips Collection, Washington, D.C.
Address for orders:
The Phillips Collection
1600–1612 21st Street, N.W.
Washington, DC 20009
Checks and money orders made payable to:
The Phillips Collection
Does not operate a membership program

Portland Art Association, Oregon
Address for orders:
Museum Shop
Portland Art Association
1219 Southwest Park
Portland, OR 97205
Checks and money orders made payable to:
Museum Shop
Regular membership: 15.00 per year
Members receive a 10% discount on purchases

Portland Museum of Art, Maine
Address for orders:
Portland Museum of Art
111 High Street
Portland, ME 04101
Checks and money orders made payable to:
Portland Museum of Art
Regular membership: 15.00 per year
Members receive a 10% discount on purchases

The Art Museum, Princeton University
Address for orders:
The Art Museum
Princeton University
Princeton, NJ 08540
Checks and money orders made payable to:
The Art Museum, Princeton University
Regular membership: 20.00 per year
Members receive a 10% discount on purchases

**Museum of Art,
Rhode Island School of Design**
Address for orders:
Museum Shop
Museum of Art
Rhode Island School of Design
224 Benefit Street
Providence, RI 02903
Checks and money orders made payable to:
Museum of Art, Rhode Island School of Design
Regular membership: 15.00 per year
Member's discount varies according to purchase

Institute for the Arts, Rice University
Address for orders:
Institute for the Arts
P.O. Box 1892
Houston, TX 77001
Checks and money orders made payable to:
Institute for the Arts
Does not operate a membership program

The Historical Society of Rockland County, New York
Address for orders:
The Historical Society of Rockland County
P.O. Box 495
New City, NY 10956
Checks and money orders made payable to:
The Historical Society of Rockland County
Regular membership: 7.50 per year
Member's discount not available on purchases

Rosenbach Foundation, Philadelphia
Address for orders:
Rosenbach Foundation
2010 Delancey Place
Philadelphia, PA 19103
Checks and money orders made payable to:
Rosenbach Foundation
Regular membership: 15.00 per year
Member's discount varies according to purchase

Royal Ontario Museum, Canada
Address for orders:
Publication Services
Royal Ontario Museum
100 Queen's Park
Toronto, Ontario
Canada M5S 2C6
Checks and money orders made payable to:
Royal Ontario Museum
Regular membership: 25.00 per year
Members receive a 10% discount on purchases

The St. Louis Art Museum
Address for orders:
The St. Louis Art Museum
Forest Park
St. Louis, MO 63110
Checks and money orders made payable to:
Museum Shop
Regular membership: 20.00 per year
Members receive a 10% discount on purchases

**St. Louis Museum of Science
and Natural History**
Address for orders:
St. Louis Museum of Science
and Natural History
Shop for Science
Oak Knoll Park
St. Louis, MO 63105
Checks and money orders made payable to:
Shop for Science
Regular membership: 15.00 per year
Members receive a 10% discount on purchases

Museum of Fine Arts, St. Petersburg
Address for orders:
Gourmet Gallery Cookbook
Museum of Fine Arts
255 Beach Drive North
St. Petersburg, FL 33707
Checks and money orders made payable to:
Gourmet Gallery Cookbook
Regular membership: 15.00 per year
Members receive a 10% discount on purchases

Fine Arts Gallery of San Diego
Address for orders:
Fine Arts Gallery of San Diego
The Gallery Store
P.O. Box 2107
San Diego, CA 92112
Checks and money orders made payable to:
Fine Arts Gallery of San Diego
Regular membership: 15.00 per year
Members receive a 10% discount on purchases

San Francisco Museum of Modern Art
Address for orders:
The Museum Bookshop
San Francisco Museum of Modern Art
Van Ness Avenue at McAllister Street
San Francisco, CA 94102
Checks and money orders made payable to:
San Francisco Museum of Modern Art
Regular membership: 25.00 per year
Members receive a 20% discount on purchases

Shaker Museum, Old Chatham, New York
Address for orders:
The Shaker Museum Shop
Shaker Museum Road
Old Chatham, NY 12136
Checks and money orders made payable to:
The Shaker Museum
Regular membership: 10.00 per year
Members receive a 10% discount on purchases

Shelburne Museum, Inc.
Address for orders:
Shelburne Museum, Inc.
Shelburne, VT 05482
Checks and money orders made payable to:
Shelburne Museum
Does not operate a membership program

Norton Simon Museum of Art at Pasadena
Address for orders:
Norton Simon Museum Bookshop
Colorado at Orange Grove
Pasadena, CA 91105
Checks and money orders made payable to:
Norton Simon Museum Bookshop
Regular membership: 25.00 per year
Members receive a 20% discount on purchases

Sleepy Hollow Restorations, Tarrytown, New York
Address for orders:
Sleepy Hollow Restorations
150 White Plains Road
Tarrytown, NY 10591
Checks and money orders made payable to:
Sleepy Hollow Restorations
Regular membership: 12.50 per year
Members receive a 10% discount on purchases

Smithsonian Institution
Address for orders:
Smithsonian Institution
P.O. Box 2456
Washington, DC 20013
Checks and money orders made payable to:
Smithsonian Institution
Regular membership: 12.00 per year
Members receive a 10% discount on purchases

South Dakota Memorial Art Center
Address for orders:
South Dakota Memorial Art Center Shop
Medary Avenue at Harvey Dunn Street
Brookings, SD 57007
Checks and money orders made payable to:
South Dakota Memorial Art Center
Does not operate a membership program

South Street Seaport Museum, New York
Address for orders:
South Street Seaport Museum
Mail Order
16 Fulton Street
New York, NY 10038
Checks and money orders made payable to:
South Street Seaport Museum
Regular membership: 10.00 per year
Members receive a 10% discount on purchases

Historical Association of Southern Florida, Inc.
Address for orders:
Historical Association of Southern Florida, Inc.
3280 South Miami Avenue
Miami, FL 33129
Checks and money orders made payable to:
Historical Association of Southern Florida, Inc.
Regular membership: 15.00 per year
Member's discount not available on purchases

The J. B. Speed Art Museum
Address for orders:
J. B. Speed Art Museum Shop
2035 South 3d Street
Louisville, KY 40208
Checks and money orders made payable to:
J. B. Speed Museum Shop
Regular membership: 15.00 per year
Members receive a 10% discount on purchases

The Museums at Stony Brook, New York
Address for orders:
Dark Horse Museum Store
The Museums at Stony Brook
Stony Brook, NY 11790
Checks and money orders made payable to:
The Museums at Stony Brook
Regular membership: 15.00 per year
Members receive a 10% discount on purchases

The Museum of Texas Tech University
Address for orders:
The Museum Shop
The Museum of Texas Tech University
West Texas Museum Association
P.O. Box 4499
Lubbock, TX 79409
Checks and money orders made payable to:
The Museum Shop
Regular membership: 15.00 per year payable to the
West Texas Museum Association
Members receive a 10% discount on purchases

The Textile Museum, Washington, D.C.
Address for orders:
Textile Museum Shop
2320 "S" Street, N.W.
Washington, DC 20008
Checks and money orders made payable to:
The Textile Museum
Regular membership: 20.00 per year
Members receive a 20% discount on purchases

Museum Index

The Toledo Museum of Art
Address for orders:
The Toledo Museum of Art
Bookstore
Monroe at Scottwood
Toledo, OH 43697
Checks and money orders made payable to:
The Toledo Museum of Art
Regular membership: 20.00 per year
Members receive a 10% discount on purchases

UCLA Art Council
Address for orders:
UCLA Art Council Gallery Shop
405 Hilgard Avenue
Los Angeles, CA 90024
Checks and money orders made payable to:
UCLA Art Council Gallery Shop
Regular membership: 12.50 per year
Member's discount varies according to purchase

Edwin A. Ulrich Museum of Art,
Wichita State University
Address for orders:
Edwin A. Ulrich Museum of Art
Wichita State University
Wichita, KS 67208
Checks and money orders made payable to:
Edwin A. Ulrich Museum of Art
Does not operate a membership program

University Museum, Philadelphia
Address for orders:
University Museum Shop
University Museum
University of Pennsylvania
33d and Spruce Streets
Philadelphia, PA 19104
Checks and money orders made payable to:
University Museum Shop
Regular membership: 20.00 per year
Members receive a 10% discount on purchases

Vancouver Museums and Planetarium Association,
Canada
Address for orders:
Vancouver Museums and Planetarium Association
Gift Shop
1100 Chestnut Street
Vancouver, British Columbia
Canada V6J 3J9
Checks and money orders made payable to:
V.M.P.A. Gift Shop
Regular membership: 10.00 per year
Members receive a 10% discount on purchases

The Virginia Museum
Address for orders:
The Council Sales Shop of
The Virginia Museum
Boulevard and Grove Avenue
Richmond, VA 23221
Checks and money orders made payable to:
The Virginia Museum
Regular membership: 15.00 per year
Members receive a 10% discount on purchases

Walker Art Center
Address for orders:
Walker Art Center
Center Book Shop
Vineland Place
Minneapolis, MN 55403
Checks and money orders made payable to:
Walker Art Center
Regular membership: 20.00 per year
Members receive a 10% discount on certain
purchases

Walters Art Gallery
Address for orders:
Walters Art Gallery Museum Store
600 North Charles Street
Baltimore, MD 21201
Checks and money orders made payable to:
Walters Art Gallery
Regular membership: 15.00 per year
Members receive a 10% discount on certain
purchases

Whitney Museum of American Art
Address for orders:
Whitney Museum of American Art
945 Madison Avenue
New York, NY 10021
Checks and money orders made payable to:
Whitney Museum of American Art
Regular membership: 25.00 per year
Discount not available with regular membership;
higher category members receive a 25% discount
on purchases

Winterthur Museum
Address for orders:
Winterthur Bookstore
Winterthur Museum
Winterthur, DE 19735
Checks and money orders made payable to:
Winterthur Museum
Regular membership: 25.00 per year
Members receive a 10% discount on purchases of
5.00 and over

The State Historical Society of Wisconsin
Address for orders:
The State Historical Society of Wisconsin
816 State Street
Madison, WI 53706
Checks and money orders made payable to:
Patterns of History
Regular membership: 10.00 per year
Members receive a 10% discount on purchases

Worcester Art Museum
Address for orders:
Museum Shop
Worcester Art Museum
55 Salisbury Street
Worcester, MA 01608
Checks and money orders made payable to:
Worcester Art Museum
Regular membership: 16.00 per year
Members receive a 10% discount on purchases

Yale Center for British Art, New Haven
Address for orders:
Yale Center for British Art Sales Desk
1080 Chapel Street
Box 2120 Yale Station
New Haven, CT 06520
Checks and money orders made payable to:
Yale Center for British Art
Does not operate a membership program

Yale University Art Gallery
Address for orders:
Yale University Art Gallery
Sales and Information Desk
2006 Yale Station
New Haven, CT 06520
Checks and money orders made payable to:
Yale University
Regular membership: 20.00 per year
Members receive a 10% discount on purchases

Yellowstone Art Center
Address for orders:
Yellowstone Art Center
401 North 27th Street
Billings, MT 59101
Checks and money orders made payable to:
Yellowstone Art Center
Regular membership: 10.00 per year
Member's discount not available on purchases

John Young Museum
Address for orders:
John Young Museum Gift Shop
810 East Rollins Avenue
Orlando, FL 32803
Checks and money orders made payable to:
John Young Museum
Regular membership: 15.00 per year
Members receive a 10% discount on purchases

Museum Publications Index

This index indicates if (and how often) a museum issues a mail-order catalogue, and whether lists of greeting and note cards, post cards, and other publications are available on request.

Museum entries are found on the following pages:	Mail order catalogue (issues per year)	Greeting and note cards	Post cards	Publications
Albright-Knox Art Gallery, 45, 56, 62, 72, 113, 125, 138, 152, 178	1	X	X	X
Alexandria Bicentennial Museum Shop, 11, 26, 36, 100, 178	—	—	—	—
Museum of American Folk Art, New York, 152, 172, 178	—	—	X	—
Museum of the American Indian, New York, 125, 152, 172, 178	—	X	—	X
American Museum of Atomic Energy, Oak Ridge, 152, 178	1	—	X	—
The American Museum of Natural History, New York, 66, 68, 87, 111, 134, 150, 152, 178	—	—	X	X
Arizona Historical Society, 125, 138, 152, 176, 178	—	X	X	X
The Asia Society, New York, 47, 133, 153, 178	—	—	—	X
The Baltimore Museum of Art, 28, 31, 32, 46, 76, 77, 101, 126, 144, 153, 178	1	—	X	X
Museum of Fine Arts, Boston, 23, 24, 25, 41, 81, 93, 107, 138, 146, 153, 178	2	X	X	X
The Brooklyn Museum, 17, 22, 25, 29, 31, 34, 37, 40, 45, 47, 84, 85, 88, 89, 92, 93, 95, 96, 103, 110, 126, 153, 178	1	X	X	X
Buten Museum of Wedgewood, 28, 86, 153, 178	1	—	—	X
Carnegie Institute, 19, 20, 37, 39, 50, 97, 101, 108, 110, 111, 126, 153, 166, 179	—	X	X	X
Art Institute of Chicago, 139, 153, 179	—	—	X	X
Chrysler Museum at Norfolk, 24, 153, 179	—	X	X	X
Cincinnati Art Museum, 58, 119, 154, 179	—	X	X	X
Museum of the City of New York, 48, 74, 106, 126, 154, 179	1	—	—	—
Sterling and Francine Clark Art Institute, 53, 57, 127, 154, 179	—	X	X	X
The Cleveland Museum of Natural History, 81, 105, 173, 179	1	—	X	—
The Colonial Williamsburg Foundation, 11, 12, 17, 25, 81, 82, 150, 154, 177, 179	1	—	—	X
Colorado Springs Fine Arts Center, 121, 134, 154, 179	—	X	X	X
Conner Prairie Pioneer Settlement, 32, 169, 170, 179	—	—	—	—
Museum of Contemporary Crafts of the American Crafts Council, New York, 52, 143, 155, 179	—	—	—	X
The Corcoran Gallery of Art, 47, 84, 104, 127, 179	—	X	X	X

Museum entries are found on the following pages:	Mail order catalogue (issues per year)	Greeting and note cards	Post cards	Publi-cations
Country Music Hall of Fame and Museum, 155, 167, 179	—	—	—	X
Craft and Folk Art Museum, Los Angeles, 155, 179	—	—	—	X
Cranbrook Academy of Art, 155, 180	—	—	—	X
Dallas Museum of Fine Arts, 60, 149, 177, 180	—	X	—	X
Delaware Art Museum, 117, 180	—	X	X	X
The Historical Society of Delaware, 54, 102, 155, 180	—	—	X	X
Denver Art Museum, 145, 180	—	—	X	X
Denver Museum of Natural History, 51, 60, 112, 155, 180	—	—	—	—
Detroit Historical Museum, 37, 51, 180	—	—	—	—
Detroit Institute of Arts, 68, 107, 127, 156, 180	—	X	X	X
Dexter Area Museum, 149, 150, 156, 172, 180	—	—	—	—
M. H. de Young Memorial Museum, 49, 118, 123, 156, 180	—	—	—	X
Drake House Museum, 118, 180	—	—	X	X
Essex Institute, 14, 80, 91, 169, 180	1	X	X	X
Everson Museum of Art, 150, 180	—	—	—	—
The Folger Shakespeare Library, 36, 41, 80, 105, 108, 122, 156, 181	1	X	X	X
Follett House Museum, 21, 181	—	—	—	—
The Fort Worth Art Museum, 54, 156, 181	—	—	—	—
The Franklin Institute Science Museum, 27, 36, 113, 174, 176, 181	1	—	—	—
Free Library of Philadelphia, 128, 156, 181	1	X	—	X
Freer Gallery of Art, 33, 40, 60, 70, 83, 88, 91, 92, 103, 114, 157, 181	1	X	X	X
Gibbes Art Gallery, 54, 157, 181	—	—	—	X
Grand Rapids Art Museum, 103, 117, 181	—	—	—	—
The Solomon R. Guggenheim Museum, 44, 128, 157, 181	—	X	X	X
Guild Hall, East Hampton, 45, 168, 169, 181	—	—	—	—
The Guild of Strawbery Banke®, Inc., 29, 106, 118, 150, 170, 181	—	—	—	—
Gunston Hall, 13, 19, 29, 78, 96, 109, 118, 150, 181	—	X	X	X
Hagley Museum, 38, 39, 181	—	—	—	—
Art Gallery of Hamilton, 91, 181	—	—	—	—
Historic Bethlehem, Inc., 74, 182	—	X	—	X
Historic Deerfield, Inc., 100, 114, 124, 134, 157, 182	—	—	—	X
Museum of Holography, 89, 135, 136, 157, 182	3	—	—	X
Honolulu Academy of Arts, 34, 182	—	—	X	X
Huntington Library, Art Gallery, and Botanical Gardens, 50, 128, 135, 149, 182	1	X	X	X
Huntsville Museum of Art, 83, 111, 182	—	—	—	—
Hyde Collection, 57, 129, 182	1	X	X	X
Illinois State Museum, 50, 148, 157, 182	—	X	X	X
Indiana University Art Museum, 46, 157, 182	—	X	X	X
Indianapolis Museum of Art, 20, 83, 104, 117, 139, 157, 177, 182	1	X	X	X
International Center of Photography, New York, 51, 136, 158, 174, 182	1	—	—	—
The Jewish Museum, New York, 63, 64, 77, 84, 85, 86, 95, 124, 158, 171, 182	1	—	—	—
Joslyn Art Museum, 145, 182	—	—	—	—
Kimbell Art Museum, 57, 158, 183	—	—	—	—
Lawrence Hall of Science, University of California, 38, 50, 82, 183	1	—	—	—
Lincoln Center for the Performing Arts, Inc., 35, 48, 68, 75, 76, 77, 94, 104, 112, 167, 175, 183	1	—	—	—
Loch Haven Art Center, 113, 183	—	—	—	—

Museum entries are found on the following pages:	Mail order catalogue (issues per year)	Greeting and note cards	Post cards	Publi-cations
Long Beach Museum of Art, 75, 183	—	—	—	X
Los Angeles County Museum of Art, 109, 146, 166, 183	1	X	X	X
Los Angeles County Museum of Natural History, 106, 115, 173, 183	—	—	—	—
Lycoming County Historical Society and Museum, 129, 158, 183	—	X	X	X
Maine State Museum, 61, 158, 183	—	—	—	X
Maxwell Museum of Anthropology, 158, 183	—	—	—	X
McCall's at Old City Park, 15, 16, 73, 74, 102, 170, 183	—	—	—	X
Memorial Art Gallery of the University of Rochester, 80, 183	—	X	X	X
The Mercer Museum, 23, 27, 38, 65, 66, 116, 158, 184	1	—	—	X
The Metropolitan Museum of Art, 14, 17, 18, 19, 20, 22, 23, 25, 27, 34, 39, 40, 42, 62, 66, 67, 71, 74, 92, 94, 109, 116, 123, 137, 139, 140, 144, 150, 159, 184	4	X	X	X
Milwaukee Art Center, 56, 159, 184	—	X	X	X
The Minneapolis Institute of Arts, 45, 49, 60, 79, 95, 140, 151, 159, 171, 184	1	X	X	X
The Museum of Modern Art, New York, 35, 140, 141, 151, 159, 184	1	X	X	X
Monterey Peninsula Museum of Art, 78, 120, 184	—	—	—	—
Munson Williams Proctor Institute, 56, 159, 184	—	—	—	—
Mystic Seaport, 13, 24, 26, 28, 32, 58, 84, 96, 101, 159, 184	1	X	—	—
National Air and Space Museum, Smithsonian Institution, 52, 59, 159, 175, 184	—	—	—	X
National Archives and Records Service, Washington, D.C., 53, 58, 160, 184	2	—	X	X
National Gallery of Art, Washington, D.C., 53, 166, 184	1	—	—	—
National Trust for Historic Preservation, Washington, D.C., 42, 97, 107, 110, 129, 147, 160, 184	1	—	—	X
Newark Museum, 90, 107, 185	—	X	X	X
The New York Botanical Garden, 20, 103, 185	1	—	—	X
The New York Public Library, 37, 46, 51, 55, 85, 89, 102, 160, 175, 185	—	—	—	X
North Carolina Museum of Art, 129, 148, 160, 185	—	X	X	X
Norwegian-American Museum, 121, 130, 148, 185	—	X	—	X
The Old State House (The Bostonian Society), 120, 185	—	—	—	—
Old Sturbridge Village, 21, 24, 28, 31, 62, 160, 169, 185	—	X	—	X
Art Gallery of Ontario, 151, 160, 185	2	X	X	X
Oregon Historical Society, 61, 185	—	—	X	X
Oregon Museum of Science and Industry, 176, 185	1	—	—	—
George C. Page Museum of La Brea Discovery, 81, 93, 115, 185	—	—	—	X
Peabody Museum of Salem, 19, 36, 59, 66, 69, 85, 90, 130, 161, 185	1	—	—	X
Pennsylvania Academy of Fine Arts, 119, 161, 185	—	—	—	X
Philadelphia Maritime Museum, 27, 58, 185	—	—	X	—
Philadelphia Museum of Art, 18, 26, 30, 43, 73, 79, 80, 85, 87, 93, 97, 100, 101, 104, 115, 117, 119, 120, 122, 123, 130, 141, 142, 161, 186	1	X	X	X
The Phillips Collection, 57, 130, 161, 186	—	X	X	X
Portland Art Association, Oregon, 49, 86, 143, 161, 186	—	—	X	X
Portland Museum of Art, Maine, 29, 49, 131, 186	—	X	X	X
The Art Museum, Princeton University, 69, 131, 161, 186	—	X	X	X
Museum of Art, Rhode Island School of Design, 94, 95, 106, 162, 186	—	X	X	X
Institute for the Arts, Rice University, 162, 186	—	—	—	—
The Historical Society of Rockland County, 162, 167, 186	—	—	—	—
Rosenbach Foundation, 71, 162, 186	—	—	X	X
Royal Ontario Museum, 162, 186	—	—	—	X

Museum entries are found on the following pages:	Mail order catalogue (issues per year)	Greeting and note cards.	Post cards	Publi- cations
The St. Louis Art Museum, 105, 114, 143, 163, 186	—	—	X	X
St. Louis Museum of Science and Natural History, 60, 64, 186	—	—	—	—
Museum of Fine Arts, St. Petersburg, 146, 186	—	—	—	—
Fine Arts Gallery of San Diego, 46, 163, 187	—	X	X	X
San Francisco Museum of Modern Art, 163, 187	—	—	X	X
Shaker Museum, Old Chatham, 15, 47, 67, 75, 163, 168, 170, 171, 187	—	X	X	X
Shelburne Museum, Inc., 64, 92, 105, 163, 187	—	—	—	X
Norton Simon Museum of Art at Pasadena, 131, 187	—	X	X	X
Sleepy Hollow Restorations, 13, 55, 56, 61, 163, 171, 187	2	—	—	X
Smithsonian Institution, 21, 23, 37, 63, 69, 71, 77, 110, 122, 142, 187	2	X	—	—
South Dakota Memorial Art Center, 30, 187	—	X	X	X
South Street Seaport Museum, 51, 65, 164, 187	—	—	—	X
Historical Association of Southern Florida, Inc., 164, 187	—	X	X	X
The J. B. Speed Art Museum, 131, 187	—	—	X	X
The Museums at Stony Brook, 112, 132, 164, 187	—	—	—	—
The Museum of Texas Tech University, 164, 187	—	—	—	X
The Textile Museum, Washington, D.C., 98, 99, 108, 164, 187	—	X	X	X
The Toledo Museum of Art, 59, 132, 188	—	X	X	X
UCLA Art Council, 49, 164, 188	—	—	—	—
Edwin A. Ulrich Museum of Art, Wichita State University, 48, 164, 188	—	—	—	X
University Museum, Philadelphia, 67, 68, 69, 70, 188	1	—	—	—
Vancouver Museums and Planetarium Association, 165, 188	—	—	—	—
The Virginia Museum, 83, 88, 165, 188	—	—	X	—
Walker Art Center, 46, 48, 188	—	—	X	X
Walters Art Gallery, 71, 78, 116, 132, 146, 165, 167, 188	1	X	X	X
Whitney Museum of American Art, 46, 48, 111, 165, 188	—	X	X	X
Winterthur Museum, 165, 188	—	—	—	X
The State Historical Society of Wisconsin, 102, 188	—	X	X	X
Worcester Art Museum, 30, 79, 106, 108, 132, 145, 188	1	—	X	X
Yale Center for British Art, 165, 189	1	X	X	X
Yale University Art Gallery, 69, 90, 105, 165, 189	—	X	X	X
Yellowstone Art Center, 151, 189	—	—	—	—
John Young Museum, 64, 87, 189	—	—	—	X